MW01009440

BATTLE LINE

BATTLE LINE
THE UNITED STATES NAVY
1919–1939

Thomas C. Hone and Trent Hone

Naval Institute Press
Annapolis, Maryland

Naval Institute Press
291 Wood Road
Annapolis, MD 21402

ISBN 13: 978-1-59114-378-9

Library of Congress Cataloging-in-Publication Data
Hone, Thomas.
    Battle line : the U. S. Navy between the wars, 1919–1939/Thomas C. Hone
and Trent Hone.
        p. cm.
    Includes bibliographical references and index.
    ISBN 1-59114-378-0 (alk. paper)
  1. United States. Navy—History—20th century.   I. Hone, Trent. II. Title.
  VA58.H53 2005
  359.0097'09042—dc22

                                                200503115

Printed in the United States of America on acid-free paper

12 11 10 09 08   9 8 7 6 5 4 3 2

Frontispiece: The light cruiser *Memphis* (CL-13) was launched on 17 April 1924 and
commissioned at the Philadelphia Navy yard on 4 February 1925.—*Navy Department,
National Archives*

CONTENTS

ACKNOWLEDGMENTS

This book has been a joint effort of father and son. The former has drafted most of the book, but the latter has been responsible for all the research and writing involved in producing chapter 5, "The Tactics of a Battle Line Engagement," and for suggestions that have strengthened the entire text.

Many individuals assisted us as we prepared this book. First among them is Frank Uhlig Jr., former editor of both the *Naval War College Review* and the *Proceedings* of the United States Naval Institute. William R. Braisted, emeritus professor of history at the University of Texas at Austin, provided ideas, his own research, and encouragement. His work also provided a model of careful research and thoughtful analysis. Paul Stillwell, former director of the oral history program of the U.S. Naval Institute, suggested valuable sources and inspired us with his own publishing efforts.

Special thanks and praise go to friend and colleague Norman Friedman, whose books on the Navy's technical and scientific development are fascinating and well researched. Since the modern Navy was created in the 1880s, it has been a highly technical enterprise, and its success in war has depended on groups of trained specialists able to bend technology to the Navy's service. Norman Friedman has done more than any other writer to bring the history of their efforts to light and to give the development of technology its proper place in the modern Navy's story.

Mark D. Mandeles deserves a note of thanks for sharing his thoughts on the development of Marine Corps doctrine before World War II. It was a paper of his that persuaded us to include a chapter on the Marines.

Archivists, especially those at the Navy's Classified Operational Archives at the Naval Historical Center, also deserve our thanks. Chief among them is Bernard F. Cavalcante. In the past few years, Kenneth Johnson has also provided extraordinary help. Charles Haberlein, who supervises the Naval Historical Center's collection of photographs, and Edward Finney, his assistant, have also assisted us on numerous occasions. Mr. Finney was instrumental, for example, in helping to identify the photos of the 6-inch gun crew on cruiser

Memphis (CL-13). Mark Wertheimer of the center's professional staff answered questions about fire control equipment. The center's senior historian, Edward J. Marolda, invited the older of us to present a draft of a research paper to a conference on the topic of "Franklin D. Roosevelt and the U.S. Navy." Two former directors of the Naval Historical Center, Dean C. Allard and Ronald H. Spector, were also generous with their suggestions and time.

At the National Archives, we have been supported by Richard Peuser and by Timothy Nenninger, chief of the Modern Military Records branch. Paul White, formerly of the archives staff, helped locate Navy Department photographs. Christopher Wright, editor of *Warship International*, generously shared his knowledge of the records of the Bureau of Ordnance and the Bureau of Construction and Repair.

Thanks go also to former Navy colleagues, including the late Captain Charles D. Allen, cruiser and destroyer captain, and the late Captain William Kirkconnell, carrier air group commander. Rear Admiral John Chase and Captain William Taylor answered questions regarding command and combat.

Commander Robert Nazak started the older of us on the path to becoming a Defense Department executive.

Commander Allen put the elder of us in touch with Captain Wayne P. Hughes Jr., who taught and still teaches at the U.S. Naval Postgraduate School. It was the encouragement of Captain Hughes that led to the chapter in this book on the tactics of the battle line.

We also wish to thank the faculty and staff of the Naval War College at Newport, Rhode Island, particularly Professor William Turcotte, Captain Robert Watts, Evelyn Cherpak, and Mary Estabrooks. Professor Donald Chisholm, a specialist on military administration currently teaching at the War College, read parts of the manuscript.

Military and civilian colleagues in the Naval Air Systems Command (formerly the Bureau of Aeronautics), especially Vice Admirals Joseph Dyer and William S. Bowes, former commanders, contributed their knowledge of Navy Department administration. Captain Peter Swartz, an assistant to General Colin Powell when the general was chairman of the Joint Chiefs of Staff, shared his research on Navy deployments.

Mary K. Jackson of Charleston, West Virginia, reviewed portions of the manuscript and introduced the elder of us to Joseph Geiger and Debra Basham, who opened the records of the West Virginia Archives and History

Cultural Center. Ephriam D. Dickson III, executive director of the Battleship *Texas* Foundation, gave us a very useful tour of the ship when we visited there in 1998. Josh Graml and his colleagues at the Mariners' Museum in Newport News, Virginia, also helped find useful material for this book. The Earhart Foundation of Ann Arbor, Michigan, financed the purchase of photographs and ships' plans from the National Archives.

The following individuals corresponded with the older of us regarding the Navy of the 1920s and '30s: Vice Admiral Edwin B. Hooper, Theodore C. Mason, C. W. Marino, Rear Admiral Edgar Keats, William H. Honan, and retired Marine Corps Lieutenant Colonel Roy M. Stanley. Retired Navy Captains Pliny G. Holt and H. B. Seim took time to describe, respectively, aircraft operations and antiaircraft drill on light cruisers of the Omaha type. Captain A. L. Raithel Jr. gave us his copy of *Navy Wings Between Wars,* parts 5, 6, and 7. The Naval Cryptologic Veterans Association provided memoirs and other material from its members.

Finally, the authors want to acknowledge a debt to the late Vice Admiral Lloyd Mustin and his wife, who entertained the older of us in their home and talked at length about the prewar and wartime Navy. The admiral had clear, sharply defined memories of the pre-World War II Navy. Those memories have been captured by the Naval Institute in the admiral's oral history and this and many other oral histories have recently been published. He and other veterans have opened a window on a vanished past that *Battle Line* strives to keep open for its readers.

A NOTE ON TERMS

In this book, the authors respect the tradition that holds that a ship's name is a proper noun, like a person's name. So you will read "battleship *Nevada*" instead of "the battleship *Nevada*," just as we say "Babe Ruth" when we refer to the baseball player instead of "the Babe Ruth." This practice extends to airships *Akron* (ZRS-4) and *Macon* (ZRS-5), whose military function, like that of a 1920s cruiser, was scouting. This book also refers to ships as "she." That is how it was done before World War II, and *Battle Line* adheres to the practice of that time.

Before World War II (and even today), the Navy used (as it uses still) special symbols and hull numbers to designate ships. Hull numbers increase as older ships of a given type are succeeded by newer ones. Newer ships generally have (and had before World War II) higher hull numbers. So BB-42 was battleship *Idaho*, the forty-second of her type. CV-2 was aircraft carrier *Lexington*, the second of her kind. CA-30 was heavy cruiser *Houston*. CL-4 was light cruiser *Omaha*, and DD-348 was destroyer *Farragut*. SS-170 was submarine *Cachalot*, and CM-4 was *Oglala*, a minelayer. Navy auxiliaries had letter designations that began with "A." Hence destroyer tender *Whitney* was AD-4, and repair ship *Vestal* was AR-4, while tanker *Neches* was AO-5.

Aircraft had their own designations, such as "VB" for bomber and "VF" for fighter, *plus* another letter to designate the manufacturer. For example, "F" stood for Grumman; "C" stood for Curtiss Aircraft. So F2F-1 (the "V" was left off by the mid-1930s) designated the first version of a second model in a series of fighters built by Grumman. SBC-3 stood for the third scout bomber of its type manufactured by Curtiss. Only just before the war do you see aircraft with names such as "Wildcat" (F4F-2) and "Catalina" (PBY-2, a seaplane patrol bomber manufactured by Consolidated Aircraft).

As a bureaucracy accountable to the Congress and a very traditional organization, the Navy developed a complicated nomenclature and an even more complex filing system by the 1920s. The authors try, in the pages that follow, to keep the reader from being perplexed by either.

INTRODUCTION

This book has its roots in a child's fascination with the photograph of battleships *Tennessee* (BB-43) and *Nevada* (BB-36). That photograph was in an encyclopedia that Tom and Lois Hone purchased in 1940, before either of their children (one of whom is Thomas, coauthor of this book) were born. They wanted an encyclopedia because, like decent parents everywhere, they believed in the worth of education and wanted to provide the tools for learning in their home. Little could they know that, many decades later, just one photograph in that multivolume encyclopedia would play out as this book. The authors only wish they had lived to see it.

Battle Line is meant to be a "portrait"—and not a detailed history—of the Navy between World War I and World War II. A model for a thorough, scholarly history of the Navy up to the Washington Naval Conference of 1921–22 is William R. Braisted's *The United States Navy in the Pacific, 1909–1922* (Austin: University of Texas Press, 1971). Where possible, this work duplicates Professor Braisted's meticulous research methods. However, *Battle Line* is aimed less at scholars and more at general readers who enjoy the modern Navy and its history; therefore, some topics are not covered or are covered only briefly. These include the various naval arms limitation conferences, the efforts of organizations such as the Navy League to influence naval policy, and various organizational issues within the Navy's bureaus.

Aside from a collection of spectacular photographs, what makes this Navy attractive? Some of the attraction has to do with the love of great machines. Many of the people interested in the Navy are fascinated by ships, aircraft, or submarines. Machines come alive for them, and they focus their attention on this Navy because it possessed the machines—especially battleships—that have so great a hold on their hearts. But there's more involved here than that. The Navy, after all, is essentially a group of people who are organized in a certain complex and hierarchical way to prepare for and then execute acts of war. Why should their daily routines, exercises, planning, decision-making processes, and values interest us just as much as or even more than the machines they commanded?

Some of the answer is in a little book called *Naval Leadership* that was given to Naval Academy midshipmen in the late 1920s to prepare them to become capable officers. Like all such books, *Naval Leadership* contains its share of platitudes. But it also contains observations like the following:

> In a sense our pay is not pay at all. The Navy is a profession, it is true. But perhaps it would be more accurate, if less popular, to call it a vocation. In a way it is not unlike Holy Orders. We do not sell our services to the government. We are not hired. Rather does the government educate and train us and then guarantee us our expenses and our jobs for life, for which we, in turn, agree to do whatever and as much as we are told, when we are told, as we are told, and to *like it*.[1]

A modern American institution built upon this sort of philosophy cannot help but be strikingly unusual and profoundly engaging.

Finally, this Navy of the 1920s and 1930s was an incredible amalgam of the old and the new, of the traditional and the unorthodox, and the future and the past. The chapters to come will show that the Navy—like so many of this nation's enduring institutions—was caught trying to straddle a fence in the years between the world wars. On one side of that fence was an inherited culture of armed seamanship, with its mostly illiterate or semiliterate but skilled sailors led by a small elite of "officers and gentlemen." On the other side was the rising tide of the young men of a democracy—both enlisted and officer. These young men treasured intelligence and ingenuity over seniority. They were utilitarian in their thinking. "What worked?" That's what they wanted to know, and, once they knew it, they wanted to get on with it. This confrontation was—and remains—the fundamental conflict of modern life.

The lives of all those reading this book have been shaped by this conflict. What *Battle Line* does is talk about how the effort to combine the authority of tradition with the energy of modern life produced our Navy. Claude Swanson, Secretary of the Navy in the first two administrations of Franklin D. Roosevelt, set the tone for the chapters that follow when he said, "I have found so much joy in the sea and so much beauty in the Navy . . ."[2]

BATTLE LINE

1
THE THREE NAVIES
AN UNBALANCED FLEET

As a force, the U.S. Navy was, by the late 1930s, an amalgam of three different navies. The first, built before, during, and right after World War I, was composed mostly of battleships, destroyers, and submarines. The second, whose shape was molded by the Treaty for the Limitation of Armament (hereafter the Washington Naval Treaty) of 1922, was composed almost entirely of heavy cruisers, two battle cruisers converted to aircraft carriers, and one aircraft carrier designed and built as such. The third, influenced by both the London Naval Treaty of 1930 and the Great Depression of the 1930s, consisted mostly of light cruisers, destroyers, two battleships, three aircraft carriers, and submarines.

In short, the U.S. Navy in 1939 was not one fleet but several, and the several different fleets did not fit together well. In 1939, the Navy had twelve first-line battleships, all heavily armored but with a speed in formation of less than twenty knots. At the same time, the Navy's four best carriers (*Lexington, Saratoga, Enterprise,* and *Yorktown*) easily steamed at speeds above thirty knots, and they were escorted and shielded by heavy and light cruisers and the newer destroyers. This division of capability also extended to the submarine force. The older, smaller S-class submarines were not effective commerce raiders or fleet scouts. They lacked sustained speed, range, and a heavy torpedo armament. The newer undersea raiders had names—*Snapper* and *Shark*, for example—and they had the size, speed, endurance, and armament to scout for the fleet and, on their own, to seek out and destroy enemy ships.

This awkward aggregation of ships, forced together by the constraints of the budget and arms-limitation treaties, constantly placed the Navy's civilian and military leaders in a difficult position. What was the Navy's real heart, its *essence*? The seamanship and gunnery of the heavy surface combat ships? The mobility and dashing of its carrier air forces? The stealth of its submarines? Or perhaps the combination of naval power with the amphibious concepts of the Marine Corps? Complicating the search for the Navy's essential heart was the rate of technological change in a variety of areas, from carrier aircraft to antiaircraft gunnery.

The two decades between World War I and World War II were tumultuous ones for the U.S. Navy, and for other navies, too. Naval technology had taken great strides during World War I. The challenge facing naval officers and enlisted personnel in the postwar years was to sort out the key technical innovations and new technologies, integrate them into operations, and anticipate future developments.

After World War I, naval leaders around the world were like gamblers entering a casino. The political and social reaction to the losses and suffering of World War I led to a generation-long effort to restrain arms competition, and the agreements that resulted from this effort limited the resources that navies' leaders could bring to the gaming tables. Yet the postwar arms limitation agreements did not eliminate the possibility of war, and therefore the requirement persisted that nations make optimal use of their resources to sustain and develop powerful fleets. Every navy—even the wealthier ones—had to take major risks. Given the long lives of large ships such as battleships and aircraft carriers, heads of naval departments had to choose wisely. Poor decisions could lead to crushing defeats. In World War I, it was said that the commander of Great Britain's Grand Fleet, Admiral John Jellicoe, was the only military leader who could "lose the war in an afternoon." After World War I, his successors in the Royal Navy had been joined by their counterparts in Japan and the United States as admirals who could hazard their countries' fortunes in one battle or campaign—on a few throws of the dice in the casino of international conflict.

The pressure on naval leaders and planners, on the designers of ships, submarines, and aircraft, and on financial officers was hard and unrelenting. Navies cost huge sums to build, maintain, and man. Where was the right balance between maintaining such forces and investing in the forces that would replace them? After all, the tensions among states had not been eliminated by the world war. The government of Japan wanted further concessions from China. The imperial powers of the Pacific most opposed to Japan—Great Britain and the United States—had their own political, economic, and social interests in China (to say nothing of their colonies in Southeast Asia), so the stage was set for conflict.

Friction in the Pacific was unavoidable. Would it lead to war? If so, when? It's no accident that one of the more provocative and well-researched "what if" books was published in 1925: English correspondent Hector C. Bywater's *The Great Pacific War: A History of the American-Japanese Campaign of 1931–33.* Its publication should remind us that the 1920s were definitely not a period when the U.S. Navy was able to rest on its achievements in the world war, which included the transportation of the American Expeditionary Force to France, the Navy's antisubmarine campaign, and its development of a serious naval air arm. The 1920s were a period of great experimentation. It had to be.

In 1919, civilian populations in Europe and the United States wanted to slash spending on navies and armies. They wanted what people in the early 1990s called a "peace dividend." Naval officers, especially those who had watched carefully the improvements in technologies such as aviation, electronics, and submarines, craved more funds to take advantage of these new—and potentially war-winning—means of waging war at sea.[1]

In 1939, the "old" Navy consisted of what had been produced before or as a consequence of the congressional naval authorizations of August 1916. In an effort to stop German attacks on neutral shipping, Congress had authorized the Navy to build ten battleships, six battle cruisers, ten scout cruisers, fifty destroyers, nine large submarines and fifty-eight coast defense submarines, and sixteen auxiliaries. In one stroke, the U.S. Navy became—at least on paper—a navy second to none (that is, more or less equal in fighting strength to Britain's Royal Navy).

As it happened, the emergency shipbuilding requirements of World War I forced the Navy to defer much of this building program. Work on the battleships and battle cruisers was put off in order to build merchant ships, convoy escorts (destroyers and submarine chasers), and submarines. Instead of 50 destroyers, for instance, 271 were authorized between 1916 and 1918, and 265 of them were completed. Instead of 58 smaller, short-range submarines, 84 were acquired (27 R-class, 51 S-class, and even 6 H-class that had originally been built for czarist Russia by the Electric Boat Company). The ten scout (or light) cruisers of the Omaha class were also completed, though none was commissioned before 1923.

Should all the authorized battleships and battle cruisers be built? That question could not be answered until some sorting out of wartime experience had been done. For example, advocates of the submarine and the military airplane (whether it flew from land bases or was launched at sea) argued privately and in public that the battleship was already obsolete. Advocates of disarmament took the position that resuming an expensive naval building program would only heighten tensions between the United States, on the one side, and Britain and Japan, on the other. New technology combined with an intense antagonism to war threatened the Navy's 1916 plan to build a force strong enough to stand up to even Britain's mighty Royal Navy.

Complicating every decision about the nature of the American naval force was the need to defend the Philippines against Japan. Navy planners assumed that, in the event of war, Japanese naval forces would carry elements of its army to the Philippines in an effort to defeat the American forces based there. Could the U.S. Navy reach the Philippines in time to relieve the besieged American garrison on the Bataan Peninsula? The Army planned to hold Manila Bay. The defenses there were formidable. How long would it take the Navy to reach them? And what sort of force was needed?

To enable its forces to fulfill this rescue mission, Navy designers gave their newest ships great steaming range *and* impressive combat power by combining several cutting-edge technologies, including advanced (for their time) steam turbines and oil fuel (which replaced coal). The result was warships such as battleship *Nevada*, commissioned in March 1916. *Nevada* had a steaming range of fifteen thousand nautical miles at a speed of ten knots. At a speed of eighteen knots (her best), she could steam about six thousand nautical miles. With her main armament of ten 14-inch guns, she was as powerful as any battleship in the world. Her armor protection was better than that of any other battleship.

But what about the ships of the 1916 authorization? Four battleships with eight 16-inch guns each had been launched by 1921. Six others, each a third larger than any predecessor, plus six very large and very fast battle cruisers, were on hold, pending decisions regarding American strategy by the administration of President Woodrow Wilson. And what about the Navy's aviation? The Navy's aviation arm had grown spectacularly in World War I. By the time the armistice was declared in 1918, the Navy had almost seven thousand officers and thirty-three thousand enlisted sailors flying and servicing over twenty-one hundred aircraft. Rapid demobilization in the first half of 1919 cut those numbers significantly, but the importance of aviation to the Navy was already clear to its most forward-thinking officers.

Secretary of the Navy Josephus Daniels was advised by a senior committee of admirals, the General Board. The board held a series of secret hearings in the spring of 1919 to try to find the best naval aviation policy. At the end of June, the board told Daniels that "fleet aviation must be developed to the fullest extent." The members recommended that he ask Congress for permission to construct one aircraft carrier for each division of four battleships. They also argued that gunfire spotting planes should be placed on all battleships and cruisers, that Daniels should persuade Congress to finance the construction of numbers of large seaplanes for scouting, and that the Navy should begin a program of experimenting with long-range rigid airships.

Daniels, however, could find support for only a miniature version of this ambitious program. In July, Congress authorized the conversion of the modern collier *Jupiter* to an experimental aircraft carrier (later named *Langley*). The Navy was also granted authority to purchase a merchant ship for conversion to a seaplane tender and to acquire two dirigibles. Could aviation supplant the expensive battleships and battle cruisers of the 1919 program? The General Board had told Daniels that the 1916 program had to be resumed. They proposed to *add* extra monies for naval aviation. Members of Congress were not so disposed.

One reason was because Army aviators thought that battleships were obsolete. They believed that heavy bombs dropped from a high altitude in mass attacks by land-based, multiengine bombers would smash any fleet. Their leader, the dashing Brigadier General William "Billy" Mitchell, challenged the Navy to a "shoot out" at sea. Part of America's World War I reparations was a small collection of warships that had been part of the German High Seas Fleet. The Navy Department planned to shell and bomb these ships in 1921 in order to learn more about how to defend ships from attack. General Mitchell, however, upstaged his Navy counterparts in January of that year in testimony to the Appropriations Committee of the House of Representatives. "Give us warships to attack and come and watch it," he challenged.

The Army and the Navy thereupon began a catfight that lasted for a generation. On July 21, 1921, Mitchell's aviators sank the ex-German battleship *Ostfriesland* with bombs dropped from aircraft alone. A month later, however, the Joint Board of the Army and Navy, chaired by General John J. Pershing, decided that the battleship still had a role to play and rejected General Mitchell's claims that the bomber had rendered the battleships of all navies relics. Mitchell and his disciples, convinced that their weapon—the heavy, high flying bomber—had revolutionized warfare, were dismayed and angry.[2]

However, what really mattered that summer was the decision by the administration of President Warren G. Harding to seek serious naval disarmament. It was this decision, and not Mitchell's bombers, that halted work on the "old" Navy.

In November 1921, the representatives of Great Britain, the United States, Japan, France, and Italy met in Washington, D.C., to attempt to reach an agreement limiting naval construction and the advance of naval technology.

In February 1922, they signed an agreement that did both. The specifics of the agreement, the Washington Naval Treaty, are in appendix A. Briefly, the treaty (a) limited the size, firepower, and number of battleships, (b) put off new battleship construction for the next ten years, (c) constrained the size and number of aircraft carriers, (d) and limited the size of new cruisers and the tonnage of cruisers the signatories were permitted. Advocates of disarmament cheered. Senior officers in the navies concerned suddenly found their options and their futures narrowly constrained.

The Washington Naval Treaty put an end to the further development of the "old" Navy. This wasn't necessarily such a bad thing, despite claims to the contrary from those casting a wary eye on Japan's attitude toward China. The U.S. Navy was given equality in battleship strength with Britain's Royal Navy, and an advantage of five to three in numbers of battleships over the Imperial Navy of Japan. That meant the U.S. Navy could retain eighteen battleships, including three of the Maryland class of the four then under construction, each with eight 16-inch guns. The treaty compelled the Navy to cease construction of the seven other battleships and four of the six battle cruisers then authorized or under construction. Two of the battle cruisers could be converted to large aircraft carriers. Older, "second line" battleships had to be cut up for scrap.

The result was dramatic from a fiscal point of view. In 1919, the Navy spent over $43 million to operate and maintain its battleship force. The comparable figure for 1925 was $30.4 million. For 1926, it was $28.8 million. Money saved by not supporting marginal battleships could be spent on something else, or not spent at all. Similarly, a reduction in the size of the battleship force allowed the Navy to retain in active service only the best of its eleven-hundred-ton and twelve-hundred-ton four-stack destroyers instead of the whole cluster of 265 flush-deck speedsters. A smaller main fleet needed fewer destroyers to escort it. The others could be put into mothballs.

The treaty permitted the Navy to complete its ten Omaha-class scout cruisers, but the agreement also set a high upper bound on future cruiser designs: ten thousand tons standard displacement and guns no larger than 8-inch. There was, as a result, a rush by the major navies to build large "treaty" cruisers to replace or complement ships worn out by wartime service or handicapped by outmoded technology. Congress authorized the construction of eight of these "light" cruisers in December 1924 as replacements for the older coal-burning armored cruisers such as *Pittsburgh* (CA-4, later ACR-4) and *Seattle* (CA-11, later ACR-11). The moves by the major navies to build the new, large, and expensive cruisers led their governments to convene another arms limitation conference in Geneva in 1927, but all that did was reveal a lack of agreement among the major navies regarding size and armament limits for destroyers and submarines. It did not impose any new limits on warship construction.

In the meantime, the Harding and then Coolidge administrations had gained congressional authorization for a sizeable number of the ten-thousand-ton treaty cruisers: all eight (hull numbers 24 through 31) in December 1924. Construction of these beautiful and graceful but lightly armored ships was held up while the major naval states were trying to set limits on their numbers in Geneva. When that failed, the ships were built, the first (*Salt Lake City*, CA-25) commissioning in December 1929. All eight were in service by April 1931. Nine more "heavy" cruisers, as they came to be called, were authorized in 1929, once it was clear that limits on the type would not be reached by modifying the Washington Naval Treaty. Two of the ships authorized in 1929, *Portland* (CA-33) and *Indianapolis* (CA-35), were modified versions of the earlier *Northampton* (CA-26) and *Houston* (CA-30). Six of the remaining seven were built to a new design, one that embodied defensive armor that allowed them to fight it out at long range with ships of their own general size and strength.

The Republican administrations also completed the expensive and time-consuming conversions of the battle cruisers *Lexington* (CV-2) and *Saratoga* (CV-3). Congress authorized the reconstruction of both ships in July 1922, but *Lexington* was not placed in commission until December 1927, one month after her sister ship *Saratoga*. Both carriers were huge but fast ships, each with an overall length of 888 feet and displacing officially thirty-three thousand tons: they were well protected against shell fire and torpedo attack, and heavily armed with 8-inch and 5-inch guns. But they were also accidental carriers, creatures of arms limitation. The Navy wanted to make the best use of the remaining carrier tonnage permitted it by the Washington Naval Treaty.

The result was *Ranger* (CV-4), authorized in February 1929 and commissioned in June 1934. *Ranger*, at an official displacement of fourteen thousand tons, was considerably smaller than the two converted battle cruisers, but she was considered a far superior design when the contract to build her was signed with Newport News Shipbuilding and Dry Dock Company in November 1930. The hangar deck of *Lexington*, for example, was 393 feet by 68 feet. *Ranger's* was

510 feet by 56 feet. *Lexington's* flight deck was longer and wider—866 feet by 105 feet vs. *Ranger's* 709 feet by 86 feet—and her protection against shell fire and torpedoes was much greater. But what the so-called "fleet problems" of the 1920s had shown was that the need for lots of aircraft with the fleet was the key factor in deciding how many and what kinds of carriers to build. Put another way, three smaller carriers gave the fleet more air striking power in 1930 than two large ones.

The fleet problems were the Navy's largest and most sophisticated exercises of the interwar period. The culmination of the annual training schedule, they were designed to provide a realistic simulation of wartime conditions and test the fleet's readiness for war, tactical doctrine, and strategic assumptions with a thoroughness that smaller exercises could not achieve. Fleet problems were held every year between 1923 and 1940. During each problem, all available ships were divided into two opposing "fleets." Each fleet was assigned a color (white, black, blue, brown, gray), and its commander was given a strategic task. These tasks were generally designed to simulate the problems that would arise during a war in the Pacific against the most likely enemy, Japan.

Besides carriers, other ship types were not ignored. The production of several hundred four-stack destroyers had eliminated the need for further warships of that type, but Navy submarine officers carefully studied surrendered German U-boats at the end of World War I and then pressed to have several new types of their own built. One was the large (almost three thousand tons) so-called cruiser submarine, armed with two 6-inch guns in open deck mounts and equipped for commerce raiding. The idea was that such large, high-endurance submarines could cruise the Pacific shipping lanes near Japan, stopping unescorted merchant ships, removing their crews, and sinking the ships with their powerful deck guns. Two (*Narwhal* and *Nautilus*) were authorized in 1925. The previous year, Congress had authorized the Navy to build a similar large submarine (*Argonaut*) as a minelayer. The Navy also requested submarines larger than the existing S type as long-range scouts for the fleet. Congress obliged with three boats, all authorized in 1929.

By the late 1920s, there was talk of the "balanced" fleet—a force that met the treaty limits and that contained enough ships of the different types to stand up against potential enemies. But the basic pressures that had led the United States to convene the Washington conference in the fall of 1921 were again pushing navies to plan and authorize new ships. The result was yet another naval limitation conference, this time set in London in the winter of

1930 after preliminary discussions between President Herbert Hoover and British Prime Minister Ramsey MacDonald on the latter's visit to the United States in October 1929.

The product of the conference was an agreement that supplemented the Washington Naval Treaty. This London Naval Treaty limited the size of new submarines to two thousand tons, set a ceiling on the displacement (1,850 tons) and gun size (5.1 inch maximum) of destroyers, extended the "holiday" on battleship construction to 1936, and pushed "treaty" force ratios among the United States, Great Britain, and Japan to heavy cruisers, light cruisers, and destroyers. The limits set by the Washington Naval Treaty on aircraft carrier tonnage were affirmed, as was the limit (thirty-five thousand tons standard displacement) on the size of new battleships. The specific provisions of the treaty are in appendix A.

The first consequence of the treaty that mattered to the Navy was the end of the race to build heavy cruisers. Second, future cruiser construction would emphasize what were called "light" cruisers, ships of up to ten thousand tons standard displacement but armed with 6-inch guns instead of with 8-inch guns like the "heavy" cruisers. Third, the major navies were not allowed any additional tonnage for aircraft carriers. U.S. Navy planners were therefore forced to consider converting passenger liners and merchant ships in the event of war. Fourth, there would be no new battleships until after 1936 unless the "treaty system" collapsed altogether. The fleet might be "balanced," but it would still rest on an awkward combination of relatively slow battleships and a small number of very fast aircraft carriers escorted by swift cruisers. Fifth, "big" submarines and destroyers were prohibited. Sixth, two new types of ship were allowed. The first was defined as a "surface combatant" displacing under two thousand tons, with no "more than four guns above 3-inch," without torpedoes, and designed to steam at a speed no greater than twenty knots. The second was a cruiser with "a landing-on platform or deck for aircraft." The U.S. Navy was allowed to allot 25 percent of its "total tonnage in the cruiser category" to what was called the "flying-deck cruiser" type. The Navy built two ships of the first sort, the "gunboats" *Erie* (PG-50) and *Charleston* (PG-51), each with four 6-inch guns. The second type, the flying deck cruiser, was intensively studied but never built.[3]

It has been said that President Franklin Roosevelt considered the Navy his personal toy and that, like his famous cousin, Theodore Roosevelt, he enjoyed reviewing it, commanding it, and being heavily involved in its administration. Unlike Theodore Roosevelt, however, Franklin had to deal with two major constraints on his favorite military service. The first was the continuation of the treaty system. The second was the Great Depression. When Franklin Roosevelt took the oath of office in 1933, the Navy was at a low point, and his first actions promised to reduce the Navy's strength and readiness even further. By the end of 1939, that situation had been reversed. It was an extraordinary turnaround.

Despite steadily reduced funding in the 1920s, some elements within the Navy Department were quite progressive. One was aviation; another was the submarine force. Their development will be treated in more detail in separate chapters. By comparison, the 1930s look quiet and conservative. The fleet's striking power remained in its battleship force—its "battle line." The carrier force, constrained by treaty, could not field enough aircraft to wipe an enemy battleship force from the surface of the sea. Submarines were also constrained by treaty, though the legal constraint on displacement was not the problem. Instead, the international prohibition against unrestricted submarine warfare meant that submarine captains trained to scout for their own battleships and aircraft carriers and to attack enemy heavy ships. The chance that the stealthy subs might be unleashed against Japan's merchant marine in a campaign of unrestricted submarine warfare was not—and could not be—acknowledged.

But the 1930s did bring some significant changes, though they tended to be invisible except to Navy personnel. One change was an emphasis on signals intelligence in combat operations at sea. The Navy had developed its own medium-frequency direction-finding stations along the Atlantic Coast for tracking German submarines in World War I but had relied on the Royal Navy for intelligence derived from code-breaking. In 1921, the Office of Naval Intelligence, with the knowledge of the New York City police, stole a copy of the Japanese navy's 1918 communications code dictionary by breaking into the office of the Japanese consul general. It took five years to translate it. In the meantime, enlisted radiomen in the Philippines taught themselves how to transcribe coded radio messages in Japanese katakana telegraphy, which was not the same as Morse code. This meant that radio intercept specialists could type out messages in the Japanese naval code and turn them over to officers and civilians who'd been trained to decipher them.

Because all navies were forced to use either high-frequency radio or undersea telegraph cables for long-range communication, it was almost impossible for any navy to keep others from listening in. All a navy could do about this problem was to construct complicated codes—codes that other navies could not solve. Once the Navy's communications intelligence specialists found that they could reliably intercept and decipher Japanese naval messages, the Navy began building intercept stations in China (Shanghai and later Peking), Oahu, Guam, and Manila. By the late 1930s, these stations were complemented by a set of high-frequency direction finding (HFDF) antennas aimed at the Japanese fleet. These very clever eavesdroppers picked up strategic intelligence on Japanese fleet procedures and operational intelligence on Japanese fleet movements.

In the 1930s, these specialists started to serve with fleet units at sea, and what they learned was used *tactically*. In May 1934, for example, in Fleet Problem XV, the radio intercept unit on board battleship *Mississippi* located the main "enemy" formation through high-frequency direction finding. In the 1936 fleet problem, both "sides" located "enemy" submarines by intercepting radio messages broadcast by the submarines as they cruised on the surface. In Fleet Problem XX in 1939, carrier *Ranger*'s communications intelligence detachment gained a fix on her opponent, carrier *Enterprise*, and *Ranger*'s attack air squadrons surprised *Enterprise* before the latter could launch her own strike.

This was a potentially decisive hole card for the Navy. Because it was so important an innovation, and also so easily disrupted if an enemy were aware of how it could be used in operations, signals intelligence—both what was called "traffic analysis" and code-breaking—was a cleverly guarded secret. In 1934, Admiral Joseph M. Reeves took command of the fleet. Reeves was an aviation pioneer, a critic of the fleet's organization, and an advocate of using signals intelligence in planning and conducting operations. At his instigation, fleet officers began encoding the bulk of their radio messages, making the lives of junior officers on the smaller ships (such as destroyers) miserable from the extra work but making *routine* a practice that would pay great dividends once war came. During Fleet Problem XVII in 1936, fleet officers kept newsreel cameramen and photographers off many of the participating ships so that they would not see or photograph the small but odd shaped high-frequency direction-finding antennas that would have told the intelligence officers of foreign navies that the U.S. Navy was tracking them through their communications.[4]

Another hidden innovation was the development of mechanisms to direct the fire of naval guns. In the 1920s, for example, special optical range finders on the larger ships were used to estimate the height of approaching bombers.

Analog computers then calculated how much time it would take for 5-inch antiaircraft shells to reach the altitude of the planes. The data from these computers were next used to set the fuses in the shells. This was a relatively slow process. As aircraft flew faster, there was not time to go through these steps and still fire shells accurately. The solution was to combine the range finder with the computer and then use the output of the computer to aim and fire the guns. In practice, that meant placing a whole nest of guns under the control of one "director." The Navy's Bureau of Ordnance cooperated with the Massachusetts Institute of Technology to move this new technology from the engineering bench to the factory and then to the fleet.

A more obvious area of progress was in the field of aviation. The heavy investment in rigid, aircraft-carrying airships produced two ingenious giants, *Akron* and *Macon*. Because they were filled with helium, both airships were "lighter than air," and because they did not need to expend fuel to remain airborne the way "heavier than air" planes did meant that they had very great range. They were therefore meant to be the fleet's very-long-range scouts. Each could carry five small planes to extend the airship's line of sight. Technological marvels in their time, they had one great weakness: they could neither fly above powerful storms nor survive an encounter with them. *Akron* was driven into the Atlantic on a stormy night in April 1933. She took seventy-three of the seventy-six men aboard down with her, including the redoubtable Chief of the Bureau of Aeronautics, Rear Admiral William A. Moffett. *Macon*, her sister ship, perished in another storm off the California coast in February 1935.

Seaplane patrol bombers and high-frequency direction-finding stations took up the role each was intended to play. Early large seaplanes, such as the PN type initially built at the Naval Aircraft Factory in Philadelphia, showed that such aircraft could travel relatively great distances without suffering major mechanical malfunctions. As the power and reliability of aircraft engines improved, the early PN models were superseded by improved versions and by the Martin Company's streamlined P2M and P3M types. What made them potential weapons, however, was the development of an effective bombsight by inventor Carl Norden.

The attack potential of these aircraft took on greater importance with the signing of the London Naval Treaty in 1930. The treaty extended the limits on the tonnage of aircraft carriers for the major navies. The U.S. Navy faced, as a result, an acute problem. Every trans-Pacific war campaigned on paper at the

Naval War College showed that the Navy would need the equivalent of at least three times the number of carriers allowed it by the Washington treaty. The naval architects in the Bureau of Construction and Repair therefore examined various ways of quickly augmenting the size of the carrier force, including the conversion of existing passenger liners. But the conversions took too long. In any war with Japan, the Navy would have to reach the Philippines before the defenses of Manila Bay surrendered.

However, the London Naval Treaty did *not* limit the number of large seaplanes a navy could have, and suddenly large seaplanes looked like possible replacements for airships *and* a very useful complement to the aircraft carriers. The contract for the first "Catalina" flying boat, which made such a name for itself in World War II, was signed in October 1933, and the first operational models flew in 1936. In 1934, Rear Admiral Ernest J. King (who later served as fleet commander and Chief of Naval Operations in World War II) testified to the General Board that "patrol planes are [a] powerful striking force." His successor as Chief of the Bureau of Aeronautics told the board in the fall of 1937 that seaplanes then being designed would carry a heavy bomb load (eight thousand pounds) and fly on missions lasting as long as three days.

As it happened, the large seaplanes were a disappointment as high-level bombers. Without fighter escort, they could not withstand attacks by first-line Japanese land-based and carrier-based fighters in World War II, and land-based U.S. Army and Navy bombers during the war were better suited for long-range, high-level missions. But seaplanes like the *Catalina* did perform a very valuable service in war as in peace, and that was by doing the long-range reconnaissance so essential to a naval war in the Pacific. The use of the seaplanes as scouts, operating from forward-based tenders, released scarce carrier attack aircraft for strike missions. Catalinas also served effectively as rescue aircraft.

The most visible components of the post–London treaty U.S. Navy, however, were its ships. *Indianapolis*, the first of the new heavy cruisers authorized in 1929, appeared in November 1932. *Portland*, her sister ship, was commissioned in February 1933. The others followed: *New Orleans* (CA-32) and *San Francisco* (CA-38) in February 1934, three more that same year, and one each in 1936, 1937, and 1939. Six of the ten-thousand-ton cruisers authorized in 1929 were built armed with 6-inch instead of 8-inch guns, and they began joining the fleet in the late 1930s: one in 1937, three in 1938, and two in 1939.

The onset of the Great Depression almost derailed this program of ship construction. As unemployment grew and the nation's wealth declined in 1930, 1931, and 1932, tax revenues fell dramatically. The economic orthodoxy of the time called for a reduction in military spending in particular and government spending in general to avoid throwing the federal government deep into debt. Because of this view, neither President Hoover nor a majority of the Congress accepted the argument that increased Navy shipbuilding would aid the task of public relief. In the presidential election of 1932, neither Herbert Hoover, the incumbent, nor his challenger, Franklin Roosevelt, advocated deficit government spending on military items as a key element in bolstering the level of private employment. In the immediate aftermath of his victory and then his inauguration, Roosevelt did not *publicly* change his view that the military services would have to endure further reductions in their funding.

Privately, however, his view was different, and it coincided with that of Republican Carl Vinson, chairman of the House Naval Affairs Committee. The worsening economic situation in the spring of 1933 also persuaded a majority of both houses of Congress that a change in policy was necessary, and they went along with the administration's proposal to fund warship authorizations from National Industrial Recovery Act funds. The result was a series of ship construction appropriations in June 1933: for two new carriers (*Yorktown* and *Enterprise*), one heavy cruiser (*Vincennes*), three light cruisers (*Nashville*, *Philadelphia*, and *Savannah*), eighteen new destroyers, and four new submarines.

But pay for personnel was not increased. Congress, with the agreement of the president, imposed a 15 percent reduction in pay on sailors and their officers. Congress also discontinued the reenlistment bonus and refused to grant increases for personnel based on length of service. In his annual report for 1933, the Secretary of the Navy noted, "This is a hardship to all and is particularly oppressive in the lowest pay grades of both officers and men." In the 1920s, Navy pay had not kept up with the rate of inflation. In the early years of the Depression, in the words of the secretary, "Navy personnel now feel doubly hard the cuts they have received . . . the officer personnel of the Navy is now paid 4 percent less than it was under the 1908 schedule." Yet over 93 percent of sailors reenlisted that year.

The Navy had fallen on hard times. Of 460 ships and self-propelled craft in commission or serving in various naval bases, 155 were fighting ships in full commission. That is, they had about 85 percent of their authorized complements.

That wasn't enough to fully man the 5-inch antiaircraft and broadside guns of all the newer battleships. Another fifteen fighting ships were in "reduced commission," and thirty destroyers and submarines were in something called the "rotating reserve." The latter, based on a plan developed by the Chief of Naval Operations, was a way of moving ships from active operations to reserve status and then, after a time, back to active operations again. There were also 134 "self-propelled craft assigned to shore activities." The Chief of Naval Operations, Admiral William V. Pratt, was desperate. The Secretary of the Navy observed that "our weakened position does not serve the cause of peace."

All this changed in 1934. Legislation in 1933 allowing public relief funds to be spent on Navy shipbuilding provided only a temporary solution to the Navy's shortage of modern ships. Chief of Naval Operations Pratt had pressed for a long-term, planned building program, one that would allow for an orderly and steady increase of the fleet to the limits set by international agreement. In December 1933, the Bureau of the Budget accepted this idea, and Navy officials soon began assisting Representative Vinson in drafting legislation that would give the Navy a blanket one-time authorization to build to treaty limits.

Despite opposition from those opposed to military expenditures, Vinson's bill, cosponsored by Senator Park Trammell, the chairman of the Senate Naval Affairs Committee, was approved at the end of March 1934 as the Naval Parity Act. It authorized the construction of over one hundred warships and one thousand aircraft over the next five years. It did not free the administration from the obligation to request funds every year for this long-term program, but it did eliminate the need to annually request a new ship and aircraft construction authorization bill.

The Navy immediately began planning to build two new battleships, one carrier, thirty submarines, and sixty-five destroyers. Although Congress only appropriated enough funds for twenty-two submarines and fifty-seven destroyers, the actual increase was dramatic enough. Because of the Naval Parity Act, the Navy would at last have a balanced force of new surface ships and submarines. As if in celebration, President Roosevelt ordered the Navy to stage a fleet review in New York at the end of May 1934, at the conclusion of Fleet Problem XV, which had been staged in the Caribbean. The fleet formed an impressive parade as it passed the presidential party at sea, and then the ships docked and anchored in New York to show the city's population what their tax money was paying for.

The Navy's troubles were still not over, however. As Admiral Pratt's successor, Admiral William H. Standley, noted in a classified memo, "The first seven of our fifteen battleships will be overage by 31 December, 1936." The older submarines and destroyers would also soon be at the end of their lives. As Standley observed, "The S-class submarine is nearing the age where the cost of repair and maintenance is incommensurate with the value of the vessel but this class must be retained until replaced by new tonnage." Eighty-one of the older, four-stacker destroyers were already marked for scrapping, and still more would have to go if the restrictions of the 1930 London Naval Treaty were extended beyond 1936. Moreover, the Navy was still short of auxiliaries. Not authorized but needed were seaplane tenders, repair ships, and high-speed tankers.[5]

The government of the United States had sent an important message to the Japanese government in 1934: the U.S. Navy would be built to its treaty limits. In response, the Japanese government suggested a new "treaty regime" and threatened to withdraw from the treaty system altogether if it could not build up its naval forces to match those of the United States and Britain. The key year was 1936. The treaty system would collapse if the major naval powers could not agree during that year either to extend the 1922 and 1930 agreements or to work out new limits.

Delegates met in London in December 1935 to negotiate a new agreement. The Japanese delegation announced that their government was no longer bound by the naval limitation agreements. The delegations from the United States and Great Britain nevertheless drafted an agreement that their governments later ratified. It stipulated that the next round of cruiser construction would be limited to ships carrying guns no larger than 6.1-inches and displacing no more than eight thousand tons. It also reaffirmed the limit of thirty-five thousand tons for new battleships and limited their guns to 14-inches *except* when a party to the new treaty believed it had to go to 16-inch guns (and a displacement of forty-five thousand tons) because of the likelihood that a navy not party to the treaty would do so. Finally, it limited new aircraft carriers to twenty-three thousand tons displacement. These provisions applied to the new U.S. Navy battleships, to the carrier *Hornet* (CV-8), and to the new cruisers of the Atlanta class.

The British historian Stephen Roskill's verdict on this last gasp of the treaty system is hard to dispute: "It is difficult for the historian who has waded through the mountain of paper accumulated in the course of the negotiations . . . not to come to the conclusion that the whole proceedings were a colossal waste of time and effort." The American historian George Baer was just as direct in his assessment: "The Second London Naval Conference . . . came to nothing. After it, the treaty structure collapsed and a naval arms race began."[6]

The result was another spurt of growth for the U.S. Navy. In May 1938, Congress passed the Naval Expansion Act, which authorized the Navy to build 20 percent more warships than the numbers allowed by the Naval Parity Act of 1934 and to possess "not less than 3,000 useful airplanes." The appropriation act for 1938, passed in 1937, had provided funds for eight destroyers and four submarines. That for 1939, implementing the additional authorized tonnage, added two battleships, two cruisers, eight destroyers, and six submarines. After passage of the Naval Expansion Act, Congress added two more battleships, one aircraft carrier, and two cruisers. In 1939, in the act for fiscal year 1940, Congress appropriated funds for two more battleships, two cruisers, eight destroyers, and eight submarines. Congress also provided for new auxiliaries, including three "fast" (eighteen-knot) tankers.[7]

By the end of 1939, the "treaty fleet" was in the process of transformation. The fast battleships scheduled to replace the existing battle line were under construction or on order. When they joined the fleet, the existing cruiser-carrier task forces would have battleship escort, though the notion of the battle line still guided much tactical thinking. Very effective destroyer and submarine designs had been developed, and the lack of modern auxiliaries was finally being addressed. The elimination of treaty constraints in most categories meant that ships could grow to fit the military missions assigned to them. The fleet's aircraft force, including both carrier aircraft and seaplanes, was large and increasingly modern. The balanced fleet was in hand or in the building yards and aircraft factories. Unfortunately, presidential and congressional support for adequate numbers of personnel lagged behind support for new ships and aircraft. As the Secretary of the Navy noted in his annual report for fiscal year 1939, "The annual appropriation provided funds for a total enlisted strength insufficient to fill the various [ships'] complements." Only submarines were at full strength.[8]

In 1939, there were still two fleets within the fleet: the battle line, with its screening light cruisers and destroyers, and the very mobile carrier force, accompanied and shielded by the 8-inch gunned Washington Naval Treaty cruisers. There was no amphibious force to speak of, and the huge fleet of auxiliaries (from destroyer tenders to net layers) was just starting to appear. Yet the foundation for a force that could fight its way across the Pacific was in place. New designs for ships and aircraft were being drafted and industry was beginning to expand production. There were plans in hand for dramatically increasing the number of trained sailors and officers. The concepts for taking the war to Japan had been explored and tested for a generation. There was a cadre of intelligent and skilled officers who could implement these concepts. The fleet was not ready for war in 1939. But it had the capacity to get ready, and that is what eventually mattered.

2
THE SHIP
THE NAVY AS A FIGHTING MACHINE

When Rear Admiral Bradley A. Fiske published the book with the title *The Navy as a Fighting Machine* in 1916, he was advancing an argument and not describing reality. He wanted his fellow officers and the civilians who led and influenced them to comprehend the complexity and power of the modern, mechanized Navy. As he put it, "The most complex organization in the world is that of a navy, due primarily to the great variety of mechanisms in it, and secondarily to the great variety of trained bodies of men for handling those mechanisms." What held this great organization together—what made it a powerful fighting machine—was the same set of "invisible wires of common understanding" that bound the members of a ship together. This "common understanding" was a comprehension of, and appreciation for, modern technology. Fiske wanted to persuade his brother officers to embrace this technology eagerly.

For Rear Admiral Fiske, the machine was a metaphor for the ship, and the ship a metaphor for the Navy. Did this mean that ships were lifeless things, the product of a faceless technology? Not by any means. Modern ships could be just as graceful, just as awe inspiring, as the great sailing ships of the past. As Fiske put it, "As surely as the mind and brain and nerves and the material elements of a man must be designed and made to work in harmony together, so surely must all the parts of any ship, and all the parts of any navy." This was an anthem of the machine age, and Fiske's book was a call to make the best of what that age had to offer in the way of power, innovation, and ingenious design.[1] Fiske did not see sailors as the servants of machines, nor indeed were machines the servants of the sailors. The relationship between them was that of the master carpenter to his tools, or the surgeon to his instruments. Workers in industry were having to adapt to the demands of the assembly line and to the prescripts of "scientific" management as embodied in time-motion studies. Not so on ship, where repetitive action mattered less than the use of skill and judgment, as sailors and their officers fine-tuned their machines.

True, stokers shoveling coal onto the grates beneath a ship's boilers were laboring, and sweating hard, to satisfy a machine. Moreover, their working lives were even worse than those of railroad firemen (who also fed coal to steam engines), because the latter weren't tied to their machines the way sailors were. But the Navy was moving from coal to oil as a source of energy, and oil was loaded, stored, and burned by machines under the control of men. It was also true that men had to clean out boilers—filthy, hard labor—but it was equally true that the Navy's own engineers were not content to accept outdated power plants and inefficient, even dangerous, machinery. In private industry, improved, safer working conditions often had to be forced on a reluctant management. In the Navy, by contrast, there were always men with an engineering bent who were eager to tap the latest technology. It was a strategy guaranteed to pay off in wartime. Warships in the interwar period, like warships today, were factories of death and destruction that floated—and had to stay afloat when damaged. Ships were like buildings, except that ships had to bear the stresses and strains imposed on them by the sea and the ravages of war. Ships housed, fed, showered, and entertained their crews. Like factories ashore, ships had power plants, machine shops, special storage compartments for all sorts of items, plumbing systems for fire fighting and sewage disposal, and miles of electrical wiring. Combat ships such as battleships, cruisers, and destroyers carried tons of specialized, complex machinery that allowed them to find and then strike targets with guns or torpedoes. Aircraft carriers were mobile airfields, with hangars, workshops, fueling stations, and large armories.

You can still visit one ship that was active during the entire interwar period: battleship *Texas* (BB-35) is now moored near the Houston ship channel. Although today painted in dark, wartime gray, *Texas* was bright, clean, and "shipshape" in her days as fleet flagship in the late 1920s and early 1930s. She's bulky, rather short (less than two football fields in length) for a battleship, and wide (106 feet at the widest part) compared to her overall length of 573 feet. Commissioned in March 1914, she appears today more or less as she did during World War II, with more light antiaircraft guns and topside armor shields for those guns than she had in 1929. But a tour will give you some idea of how warships of the interwar years were constructed, operated, and maintained.

In the engine room of *Texas* are two squat, massive reciprocating steam engines, but they aren't like the engines that drove steam locomotives in the same time period. Railroad locomotives usually had two pistons, one on each side of the engine for each set of driving wheels. Steam was released into the cylinder head, pushing the piston back, and a connecting rod and crank transferred the back and forth motion of the piston (which was also pushed forward by steam) to the locomotive's driving wheels. You can see these engines on static display in a variety of railroad museums, and there are even a few large steam locomotives still in operation.

By comparison, the two reciprocating engines of *Texas* were (and are) more like the engines in automobiles. Each steam engine has four cylinders, and the pistons in all four are linked to the same crankshaft, like the pistons in a car. This type of engine (see diagram, figure 1), is called a "triple expansion" steam engine because the initial intake of high-pressure (285 pounds per square inch), high-temperature steam (417 degrees Fahrenheit) from the ship's boilers pushes the piston in the high pressure cylinder down and then is used three more times to displace three more pistons in sequence. Steam from the high-pressure cylinder is vented into the next (intermediate, or I.P.) cylinder. After pushing that piston through the first half of its full stroke, the steam is vented again, this time to the two low-pressure cylinders, where the process is repeated. After expending its energy in the two large (83 inches in diameter) low-pressure cylinders, the steam exits the engine as exhaust,

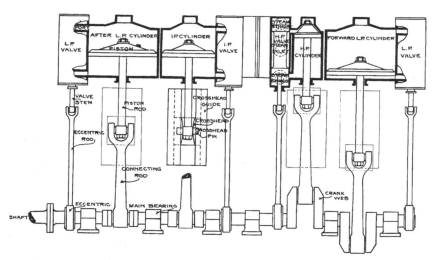

Figure 1. Four-Cylinder Triple Expansion Engine

where it is cooled, condensed, and then converted again into steam in the ship's boilers.[2]

The triple expansion reciprocating steam engines in *Texas* are not the only engines of the type that have been preserved. The Liberty ship *Jeremiah O'Brien*, homeported in San Francisco, also has a working triple expansion reciprocating engine, as does a similar vessel (*John W. Brown*) based in Baltimore. But the engines in *Texas* are unique because they were designed to fit below the battleship's armored deck and still generate twenty-nine thousand shaft horsepower (SHP). To fit them into the protected space deep inside the ship, the engines were reduced in height as much as possible. Space was at a premium because all essential volume, especially that which housed machinery, ammunition, guns, and the ship's command personnel, had to be protected. That is why the engines in *Texas* are squat, separated by a waterproof bulkhead along their length, and take up a significantly smaller space than her boilers.

It is sad that visitors to *Texas* can't see and hear and smell these engines in action. They gave the pulse of life to the ship when she was in commission. One witness to such an engine described an encounter with it this way:

> The engine room is stifling. The smell of oil and hot grease permeates everything. It is a cacophony of mechanisms, a labyrinthine world of condensers, cylinders, pipes, and valves—all arranged seemingly without the slightest logic to the uninitiated. The great engine is at center stage. Everything, everywhere is in constant motion, as if all the mechanical apparatuses ever invented had been assembled together in a bewildering arrangement of flailing rods, pistons, rocker arms, cranks, and tons of steel hurtling 'round and 'round. Every working part is bathed in oil, shining, glistening, working in unison with singular purpose.[3]

Later battleships had very different engines—turbines, where jets of steam were directed at blades attached to a shaft. As steam turbine engines grew more reliable and more economical, they increasingly—though not completely—displaced reciprocating steam engines, particularly in warships. Turbines were particularly suited to those ships, such as aircraft carriers and their escorts, that normally cruised at high speeds. But turbines posed a particularly thorny problem for engineers. Turbines run most efficiently at high speed. High-temperature, high-pressure steam will drive a steam turbine like a supercharged windmill; the energy in the steam becomes, through the turbine, the energy in a rapidly spinning shaft. But rapidly spinning ships' propellers waste energy; they work best at speeds far slower than that given to the turbine's shaft by the roaring steam. So some way had to be found to save the steam's great energy while rotating the propeller's shaft at the most efficient speed to push the ship through the water.

There were two solutions to this problem. The first was to have the turbine's rapidly spinning shaft turn an armature in a generator to produce electricity. The electricity could then be used to run a large direct current motor that would drive the propeller. The same electricity, stepped down through transformers, could power shell hoists, other motors within the ship, and the ship's electric lights. This solution also offered ship designers a chance to isolate the ship's turbines from her motors. The turbines powered a generator, but the only link between the generator and the motor that drove a propeller was an electric cable. This permitted the designers to increase the degree of compartmentation, or subdivisions, *inside* the ship, thereby making her more resistant to underwater damage. It also allowed the ship's engineer to shift from forward to reverse by simply reversing the polarity of the main electric motors. Battleship *New Mexico* (BB-40) was the first large ship in the Navy to be given this form of power plant, in 1916, but battleships 43 through 48 and the large aircraft carriers *Lexington* (CV-2) and *Saratoga* (CV-3) were also powered in this way.

The second solution to the problem of turbine efficiency versus propeller efficiency was to place a set of reduction gears between the turbine and the propeller shaft. These performed the same function as the gears in an automobile, but, in a large ship, the operating stresses under which they operated were immense. Each reduction gear had to be carefully machined from a large, metallurgically faultless forging, and there weren't many firms that could produce the forgings or cut the gears in them to the tolerance required.

The abundance and variety of machines in the Navy, and even within the same ship, forced the leaders of the service to train its would-be officers studying at the United States Naval Academy as engineers. A tour around *Texas* will show you why engineering was at the center of the Naval Academy's curriculum. From her windlasses forward (for hoisting her anchors), to her shell handling gear below her third deck, to her boat cranes amidships, and then back to her steering gear aft, *Texas* is just full of machinery, some of it quite complex even by today's standards.

Texas is also full of armor—specially treated steel plates and slabs designed to deflect or break up shells that strike them. You can see some of this armor clearly on the sides, back, and tops of her turrets, and you can walk on it as you tour the spaces along her second deck, such as the passageways leading to the cafeteria that feeds modern day tourists. What you will see there are regularly shaped pieces of very dense steel that are laid on the deck like thick squares of linoleum tile. *Texas* was designed in 1910, and her armor protection was based on the estimate that she would fight it out with any enemy battleship at a range of no greater than ten thousand yards (about five nautical miles). But the range of effective battleship gunfire was growing rapidly. By the time she was commissioned in 1914, battle range was already twenty thousand yards (just over ten nautical miles) in clear weather. That meant she had to be given additional armor on her decks to deflect shells plunging down on her at higher angles. You can see that armor today, painted deck red, almost as it was when she emerged from her reconstruction in 1927. You can identify it by rapping on it with your knuckles. It is so dense that it will not sound like any other metal surface you have ever struck.

The emphasis on machinery even extended to dining facilities. *Texas* was constructed on the assumption that food would be taken from the galley to enlisted crew spaces by younger sailors who slung their hammocks in those spaces. This was the traditional way enlisted men were fed. Officers, warrant officers, and chief petty officers had their own galleys separate from those of enlisted men, and officers were served by enlisted stewards, most of whom were African-Americans or Filipinos. But both cooking and serving became more industrialized in the 1930s. Carrier *Ranger* was, in 1934, the first large warship commissioned with a cafeteria, and the success of that form of dispensing food did away with the traditional method in ships built after her.

The key machinery in *Texas*, however, served her ten 14-inch guns. The guns were a technological marvel. As structures, they had to maintain their shape and not droop or twist significantly over their total length of 642.5 inches (53.5 feet). They also had to withstand immense pressures when the 420 pounds of smokeless powder ignited in their breeches drove their 1,500-pound shells out their length to emerge at twenty-six hundred feet per second. The recoil of the guns had to be constrained to forty inches by hydraulic cylinders, because space inside the ship's turrets was limited. The sheer weight of the guns—each weighed over seventy-one tons—and their mounts helped absorb the shock of firing.

Yet the guns had to be elevated and depressed quickly, so that their crews could reload them rapidly and then return them to maximum elevation. The 14-inch guns of *Texas* elevated at a rate of 4 degrees per second to a maximum of 15 degrees. The turrets that housed the guns weighed 532 tons *each*, and each had to turn smoothly and reliably. Moreover, the bearings on which they rolled had to be able to withstand the tremendous loads placed on them by the tons of weight in the turrets, guns, and gun mounts. If you stand in the working chamber below the 14-inch guns in a turret in *Texas*, you get a sense of the mass of metal around you. Guns, gun mounts, and turrets are even more massive in the preserved 16-inch gunned battleships, such as *Massachusetts*, because the weight of a large gun increases as shell mass grows, and shell mass increases with the cube of the diameter of the gun. And it is shell mass that gives the shell its punch.[4]

Shells and powder bags for the guns were stored in different magazines deep inside the ship. In *Texas*, shells were stored nose-down in special racks in the ship's magazines. When a shell was needed, sailors lifted it from its rack with an overhead chain hoist and then placed it in a cylindrical lift that served as an elevator. The gun crew in the turret raised the shell to the level of the gun's breech. There, a loader tipped it backward onto a special tray that extended into the just-opened breech of the gun. Using a powerful mechanical ram, driven by a hydraulic speed gear, the rammer operator shoved the shell into the gun's breech, seating it against the rifling in the barrel that would give the shell the spin that would keep it stable in flight. With the shell set in the breech, the rammer was withdrawn.

Four 105-pound silk bags of smokeless powder came up with each shell, but through a completely separate set of hoists. Below the waterline, in specially protected magazines, the powder bags were stored in airtight metal containers called "powder tanks." Once removed from its tank, a powder bag was rolled through a fireproof rotating scuttle (that worked like a revolving door) into a lower powder handling room. The bag was then placed in a special lift, or powder hoist, and boosted up to a special room (called a "powder flat") on a level below that of the turret guns. The powder hoist could be open only at the top or at the bottom; it could not be open at both the top and the bottom at the same time.

The great danger was that an enemy shell, bursting through the armor of the turret, would ignite powder bags not yet loaded into the gun, and that the flame and flash of their ignition would spread to the powder magazines below the waterline. If a magazine exploded, the ship would sink almost immediately, with terrible loss of life, as battleship *Arizona* did at Pearl Harbor in 1941, when a converted Japanese 41-centimeter armor piercing battleship shell dropped by a carrier bomber ignited her forward powder magazines. The process by which the powder bags moved from their magazine storage to the breech of the ship's 14-inch guns was therefore a series of movements through special doors from one isolated holding room to another, until the 105-pound bags were lifted manually from the level of the powder flat to the level of the breeches of the guns.

Once on the loading tray set in a gun's breech, the four bags were rammed by hand into the breech behind the shell. A primer was then set into the huge breechblock, and the block was closed and the gun elevated to its firing position. In battleships built after *Texas*, the greater weight of powder used required the gun designers to develop rammers that could both shove the shell into the breech and also push large powder bags in behind the shell without rupturing the bags. Using this combination of hoists, powered ram, elevating gear, and massive, swinging breechblock, trained crews could load and fire the heavy guns twice a minute.

Given the communications technology available to the crews, this was an extraordinary achievement. To protect the powder magazines, the steps of the loading cycle—and the people who made each step happen—were physically separated. Shells and powder bags were united only at the breech of a gun. Powder and shell magazines had sprinkler systems and could be flooded, and the turret had its own sprinklers. Shells were often stored in turrets, but powder bags never were, and no more than four bags were ever held at one time within the powder flat at the level below that of the guns. This severe compartmentation of shells and powder bags was essential to protect the ship, but it kept the magazine and gun crews from seeing one another as they worked.

The loading cycle, conducted and managed by men physically isolated from one another, was designed to continue without a break even if the ship were damaged. Electrical hoists, for example, were backed up by manual versions. The latter worked more slowly, but a slower rate of fire was clearly better than none at all. The gas ejector that blew air down the barrel after each firing, producing a characteristic puff of white steam that was supposed to blow any powder residue out of the gun, might lose pressure and fail. The gun captain would then have to be wary of any burning residue left in the breech. The basis for the whole complex system of men and equipment was drill—continuous practice, practice, practice—until the combination of men and machines worked as one.[5]

The big guns were always dangerous. In March 1925, Lieutenant Commander (later Admiral) W. H. P. Blandy presented a detailed lecture to Naval Academy midshipmen on the efforts to make the firing safer. He cited as one reason for this effort the case of "the terrible disaster on the U.S.S. *Mississippi* . . . off San Pedro on June 12, 1924." Like *Texas*, *Mississippi* also mounted 14-inch guns, three in each of four turrets. Blandy's remarks are worth quoting at length:

> The ship was firing to windward, and the gas ejector pressure was low in Turret 2. Seven salvos had been fired before the accident occurred, and on one of these the left gun of Turret 2 had fired prematurely, immediately after the breech was closed, while the gun was still in the loading position and the firing circuit was open. This event, strange as it may seem, did not cause any concern on the part of anyone, though it is quite likely that the same trouble existed in that gun as, a few minutes later in the right gun, caused the catastrophe. It was a grave warning that went unheeded.
>
> The shell and four bags of powder for the eighth salvo had been rammed in the right gun. The breech was still open when a small grayish ball of smoke and flame emerged from the breech, immediately followed by a large flash of flame which, with the accompanying gases, found its way throughout the turret as far as the lower handling room. . . .
>
> As a result of the fire, three officers and forty-four men lost their lives and nine other men were injured. . . .
>
> It is desired especially to point out that the court [of inquiry] found the cause of the *Mississippi* accident twofold—low gas-ejector pressure and failure properly to inspect the bore [of the gun] before loading. Of these two causes the latter is the one which should sink deeper into your memories.

Note his emphasis on the responsibility of the gun crew and gun captain—all enlisted personnel—to stay alert for any signs of danger, *to never allow their actions to be just mechanical.* Mistakes could be fatal then, just as they were years later, when, in April 1989, an error at the breech of one of the 16-inch guns of *Iowa* set off an explosion that killed forty-seven sailors.[6] Engines and guns were the big machines. They pushed *Texas* through the water and gave her the power to smash her opponents. But precision machines controlled by her crew guided her and linked her to other ships of the fleet. You can see some of these precision machines today, in the ship's radio room, for example, and on her navigation bridge. The latter contains the ship's helm, compass, engine order telegraphs, and rudder angle indicator. Above the navigation bridge is the flag bridge, and towering over both is the forward tripod mast.

The three levels of the housing supported by the tripod look more or less as they did in the 1930s. The topmost level then contained a "directorscope," a device that allowed the fire control men operating it to estimate the course and speed of a target ship. That information, initially computed in the second level of the tripod, was then sent to a plotting room deep inside *Texas*. Also sent to the plotting room was the range information on the target from the range finders in the battleship's turrets. The plotting room combined this information to calculate where the target ship would be when the shells of the battleships 14-inch guns reached her. Then the plotting room staff transmitted elevation and bearing information to a set of dials watched by gunner's mates manning the gear that elevated the guns and trained each turret. Those men, located in a space just below the guns, aligned their controls with the information from the plotting room. When a special instrument in the plotting room indicated that the ship was level, the firing circuit was closed and the guns fired.

Spotters in the top of the foremost tripod mast watched the target to see where the battleship's shells landed. They informed the plotting room if the shells had landed beyond ("over"), short of, or ahead or astern of the target. On the basis of this information and continuing readings of the range to the target given by the turret range finders, the plotting room staff adjusted the estimated range and bearing of where the target ship would be when the next salvo of shells reached it. That information was sent to the pointers and trainers elevating the guns and rotating the turrets; they adjusted the guns, more shells were fired, and the process continued. To make sure that the spotters could pick out their ship's shell splashes from those of other battleships, *Texas*'s 14-inch shells contained a dye that colored the towering fountains of spray they threw up when they struck the water.

Between World War I and World War II, this process became increasingly automated and centralized, though each turret's pointers and trainers could still work independently to aim and fire their two 14-inch guns. The 5-inch broadside guns, installed to ward off enemy destroyers, had been aimed "locally," or by their own gun crews, when *Texas* was commissioned, but the ship was later given directors analogous to the ones that directed the 14-inch guns. This equipment was operated from the third, or lowest, level of the foremast tower.

To a great degree, the intricate fire control equipment was invisible to most of the men on *Texas*. Some was located high in the foremast. Duplicate equipment was located in a truncated tower located behind the funnel. Other elements of the fire control installation were in the plotting room below the armored deck and in the backs of the turrets (the long range-finders). Sadly, most of this equipment—updated during the ship's service in World War II—was ripped out before *Texas* was turned over to the state as a memorial. There are also few photographs of the directorscopes, the large range finders in the turrets, or the equipment in the plotting rooms of the battleships from the interwar period.

How was this combination of men and machines organized and directed? First, by on-the-job training for officers as well as enlisted personnel. Second, through deliberate training and education at service schools. Third, by the *structure* of the ship's company. A battleship's crew, for example, was organized into departments and divisions. There were departments for gunnery, navigation, communications, engineering, repair, medicine, aviation (for the battleship's spotter planes), and supply.

Within each large department, such as gunnery, there were one or more divisions. In the gunnery department, for example, there would be divisions for the guns and for the fire control men. The gunnery division would be broken down even further into (a) the men who crewed the main battery turrets, (b) the men who manned the powder magazines, (c) the crews of the 5-inch broadside guns, and (d) the sailors who served the 3-inch or 5-inch antiaircraft guns. The communications department would have divisions for manning the ship's radios and for providing the visual (flag and signal lamp) signals. Engineering would have divisions for the main engines, the boilers, and auxiliary equipment. On a battleship, the ship's band was usually a division of her navigation department.

In the mid-1930s, the engineering department of *West Virginia* (BB-48) included six commissioned officers, four warrant officers, seventeen chief petty officers, and, according to the ship's "Recruit's Handbook," "about 300 other ratings, or about one fourth of the ship's company." The chief engineer was a lieutenant commander; his assistant was a lieutenant. Their department had four divisions. A lieutenant assisted by a chief machinist headed the "M" Division, which operated the ship's electric motors that drove the four propellers. Under them were five chief petty officers and eighty-seven other machinist mates, electrician's mates, and firemen. "B" Division fed the boilers, maintained the fresh-water distilling plant, and tended the ship's refrigeration units. Headed by a lieutenant, the 108 water tenders, firemen, boilermakers, and machinist's mates in the division worked directly under four chief petty officers.

"A" Division operated the rest of the machinery and performed repairs in the machine shop, foundry (yes, a real foundry), and blacksmith's shop. This division also watched over the oil fuel tanks and tended the engines of the ship's twelve motorboats and launches. Also headed by a lieutenant assisted by a chief machinist, this division had three chief petty officers and seventy-one subordinate ratings. "E" Division was, quite naturally, composed of electricians and firemen in charge of servicing the ship's internal lighting, searchlights, telephones, fire control instruments, and gyro compasses. The division officer was a lieutenant; he was assisted by two chief electricians or electricians. There were five chief petty officers and sixty-five other enlisted personnel.

At sea, the chief engineer held forth in the main control room below the ship's armored deck. The four division officers rotated as officers on watch. As the "Recruit's Handbook" noted, "An electrician's mate, first class or chief, from 'E' Division operates the switches and the throttle while a machinist's mate from 'B' or 'M' Division controls the steam being made by the boilers and also sends out orders given by the engineering officer of the watch to the various engineering department stations." *Everyone had a place and everyone knew his place.* Every sailor knew his rate (or standing in the ship's company), when he was to stand watch, whom he "messed" (ate) with and when, where he swung his hammock, what his battle station was, where he went in case of fire or collision, and even what boat he was supposed to abandon the ship in, if it came to that.

This was a structured, formally ordered world. By the Navy's reckoning, it had to be; most sailors were young, with the energy but also the brazen immaturity of the young. They needed guidance and training and discipline if they were to operate ships and guns safely and effectively. But it was not a rigid world, or a brutal one. Instead, it was designed to promote personal reliability so that men and machines would survive—hopefully triumph—in wartime. As *West Virginia*'s "Recruit Handbook" put it: "A man's conduct is a test of his reliability. The navy has no place for unreliability. . . . Watch standing is a test of a man's reliability. You will hear it said of a certain man 'He knows his job and he stands a good watch.' There is no higher praise."[7]

This emphasis on taking responsibility was complemented by a full schedule of athletic events, a voluntary regimen that the Navy came to sponsor under the tutelage of Navy Secretary Josephus Daniels (1913–21) and his successors. The larger ships had newsletters—some printed on quality paper, the others cheaply reproduced, but all dwelt on the achievements of the ship's athletic teams. Team competition fed team spirit. Successful teams also brought their supporters money, as crews bet on the outcomes of the competitions—in baseball, rowing, and other team and individual sports (such as boxing).

Man and machine were coupled by training, education, routine, habit, deliberate organization, and a standard of responsibility embodied by the senior enlisted personnel and their commissioned officers. Every ship was a collection of units organized around functions such as engineering or gunnery. An officer and a team of older enlisted specialists led each unit. Each unit had its character, its habits, and often a very distinct identity. Many units, or divisions, competed against similar divisions in ships of the same type for a coveted "E" for "efficiency" in engineering or gunnery or signaling. Winning such awards meant both prestige and some extra cash for the sailors.[4]

The coupling of men and machines on ship also tied both to the Navy ashore. The link was through what Commander (later Admiral) Robert B. Carney called "material administration." As he put it in a 1938 essay, "Skill and discipline are vital elements of victory, but the perfect functioning of material is the articulate expression of that skill and discipline in terms of fighting power." Put another way, "The best personnel training is of little value if the material of gunnery, engineering, and other departments cannot operate under service conditions without demoralizing casualties."[8] Keeping the ship's equipment in the best possible condition, however, called for a *system* "of organization, training, records, inspection," routine maintenance, and repairs.[8]

This system was based on planning, scheduling, detailed knowledge of machinery and material, tests, and *paperwork*. For example, when the Navy accepted a ship from a builder, the ship's engines and steering had already been thoroughly tested by Navy and civilian inspectors. The ship's new crew would have all the documentation they needed to familiarize themselves with their new home—diagrams of her wiring and plumbing, charts showing her turning circle at different speeds, thick booklets identifying all her compartments, and other papers that were, in effect, part of an owner's guide. Their job as crew members was to maintain the equipment given them and to keep records of inspections and maintenance. Officers were charged with making sure that the equipment—particularly guns, engines, and steering gear—was in good working order and that any changes to that equipment were thoroughly documented.

It was the documentation—from reports of maintenance to records of training—that linked the Navy afloat to the Navy ashore. And, because the Navy grew more and more technologically sophisticated year by year, the Navy ashore grew correspondingly larger and the burden of paperwork increased. Consider the guns on battleship *Texas*. The guns were constructed at the Naval Gun Factory in Washington, D.C. By 1939, the Naval Gun Factory and its associated ordnance laboratory employed over seven thousand engineers, technicians, machinists, and other workers, most of them civilians.

The guns and their shells were tested (as guns and shells still are) at the Naval Proving Ground at Dahlgren, Virginia, which employed almost three hundred people, again mostly civilians. Powder for the guns was developed, tested, and even manufactured at the Naval Powder Factory at Indian Head, Maryland (which still exists). Powder and shells were stored at eleven ammunition depots, from Lake Denmark, New Jersey, to the naval base at Cavite in Manila Bay.

There were also more than three thousand Navy Bureau of Ordnance (BuOrd in Navy parlance) employees at the torpedo station on Goat Island in Narragansett Bay, Rhode Island, and about one hundred fifty at the torpedo station in Keyport, Washington. Altogether, the twenty-four installations under the control of the Chief of the Bureau of Ordnance employed approximately fourteen thousand people. They were complemented by forty-five uniformed inspectors of shells, fuses, and fire control equipment in privately owned factories that dealt with the bureau. That made the Bureau of Ordnance a major industrial and engineering establishment. Between World War I and II, its specialists designed and produced new 5-inch, 6-inch, 8-inch, and 16-inch guns, as well as the shells they fired. The Bureau also designed and developed a new 1.1-inch antiaircraft gun and armor for the new ships that were built in the 1920s and 30s.

The Bureau was led by *line* officers—officers qualified to command ships at sea. For example, about half of the nearly forty Navy officers stationed at the Naval Gun Factory in Washington were line officers. The rest were *staff* officers—specialists with postgraduate degrees in engineering, chemistry, and metallurgy. Staff officers, recruited from among the Naval Academy's graduates with the highest course grades, did not have to go to sea; they were industrial, scientific, and engineering managers. But BuOrd was *always* led by line officers; the idea was to maintain the strongest possible link between the development of weapons ashore and their successful use at sea. As one Chief of BuOrd, Rear Admiral W. R. Furlong, put it in testimony to Congress, "The officers of the Bureau of Ordnance are quite different from those in any other Bureau except Aeronautics, in that they are both technical and operative. It is a distinction that few realize."[9]

He might better have said that it was distinction that few *outside* the Navy realized. Inside the Navy, line officers would have been quick to note that BuOrd always insisted on its prerogatives as the custodian of the Navy's then most powerful weapons. Indeed, the often imperious nature of BuOrd's line officer leadership is what led to the stories about the "Gun Club," the fraternity of gunnery officers who were said to dominate Navy tactics, leadership, and policy. There is some truth to this claim. For example, as historian Clark Reynolds has noted, the ambitious and talented "Captain Richmond Kelly Turner made the momentous decision to get out of aviation after ten continuous years in it," and John Towers, the most visible and certainly one of the most able of the surviving aviation pioneers, had to rely on the pressure exerted by President Franklin Roosevelt to gain flag rank.

The July 1, 1937, *Navy Register* lists forty rear admirals in the ranks of the Navy's line officers. Only seven of the forty were qualified as "aviator" or "aviation observer." Most of the seven, like Rear Admiral Frederick J. Horne, were aviation observers—officers who went through flight training late in their careers so that they could qualify to command aircraft carriers. A few, such as Rear Admiral Ernest J. King, were ranked as aviators, even though King was a late-comer to aviation, his early years as an officer having been spent in all sorts of surface ships, as well as submarines. Longtime aviator John Towers, then a captain, was certain that the Gun Club was against him and other "real" aviators. Towers was also certain that having only a very limited number of aviation flag officers would have harmful effects on the Navy if war came. He viewed the strong link between BuOrd and the fleet as an obstacle to innovation.

The point here is not to argue for or against the perception Towers had that aviators were deliberately thwarted in their efforts to reach the rank of admiral. Towers would have been the first to admit that he had benefited from the assistance of his own patrons, Rear Admiral Moffett, first Chief of the Bureau of Aeronautics, and Rear Admiral Emory S. Land, for a time Chief of the Bureau of Construction and Repair and later head of the Maritime Commission. What mattered throughout the Navy was not only an officer's patrons and opponents but also the links that tied ships at sea to the bureaus ashore.

Individual officers worried about the quality of their assignments, and about how promotion boards would evaluate their performance. The so-called shore establishment, which did not go to sea, was an *institution* created and modified over time to maintain the Navy's material and technological strength, regardless of what happened to particular officers or enlisted sailors. One source of tension within the Navy was the very different perspectives of individuals struggling for promotion and recognition within the fleet and the established leaders of the Navy's material bureaus, such as Ordnance, Construction and Repair, and Engineering.

The staff and line officers, and senior civilians, leading these bureaus were linked to the ships of the fleet through a network of ongoing messages and correspondence. These shore organizations were the ones that developed and acquired most of the Navy's equipment. They prepared the manuals of instruction and all the other documents that were necessary for the equipment to work properly. They were the custodians of the methods of material management and, therefore, pressed on the fleet their own notions of how that management should be done.[10]

You can get a sense of their power by recalling the very strong influence that the late Admiral Hyman G. Rickover—a master of material management—exercised over the Navy's nuclear-powered ships and submarines. Rickover had never commanded any ship in combat, yet his power, exercised through what amounted to a "bureau of nuclear engineering," spread through most of the fleet during the cold war because nuclear-powered ships and submarines could not go to sea without his approval. In the 1930s, as under Rickover in the 1970s, fleet officers often chafed at the routines imposed on them by the bureaus ashore, but that influence was an inevitable consequence of the growing technological sophistication of the Navy's ships, aircraft, and weapons.

3
THE WORK OF SAILORS

It is often said in the Navy that more damage than good is done by overhauling gear. This is true only when men who are doing the overhauling do not know their business. And it is a condition for which there is no excuse.

Instructions for Use in
Preparation for the Rating of
Gunner's Mate 3c (1939)

Sailors in the years between World War I and World War II by and large performed two kinds of important work. The first was fighting, which meant manning guns, firing torpedoes, attacking enemy ships and aircraft with carrier airplanes or seaplanes, and a host of other actions that brought explosive ordnance to bear on opposing forces. The second was maintaining the ships, submarines, and aircraft that took them to and into the fight. In peacetime, "work" usually meant maintenance, and most of the maintenance duties were blue collar, from sweeping and scrubbing decks to simultaneously interpreting and typing out radio messages sent rapidly in Morse code. In this sense, ships and shore stations were like factories, warehouses, and machine shops in civilian life. White-collar workers performed specialized staff functions, such as medical care, research, and accounting, and they also served as managers. Blue-collar workers did everything else.

As in civilian life, there were two working worlds—the formal and the actual. The formal world was by the book and went according to Navy regulations and tradition. The actual working world was something rather different. It had its own unwritten rules, and senior enlisted men enforced them. As former enlisted man Allan Bosworth put it, the actual world of the sailor—in his case, on battleship *Maryland* in the 1920s—was "a feudalistic system."[1] It rested on loyalties of junior enlisted men to their seniors and on the relations among the chief petty officers. The latter rose in rank because of their skills and because they could be trusted. All those who have ever worked a trade understand this.

The best situation for a new young man on the job was to have an experienced, levelheaded foreman to show him the ropes. A competent foreman—and a good chief—kept the officers (the bosses) off your back, quickly and surely taught you your trade, gave you the "inside dope," and "treated you square." Theodore "Ted" Mason described just such a man, the "near-legendary" chief radioman Thomas J. Reeves, whom Mason served under in battleship *California* (BB-44):

> He was a man who scorned the easy shore billet that could have been his for one of the toughest jobs in the enlisted navy: chief in charge of the combined ship-flag radio gang, Commander Battle Force. He ran the ninety-man C-D Division with a discipline that was firm without being oppressive, and a competence that was awesome. . . . The officers of the communication division were utterly dependent upon him, and knew it. Not a single one, to my knowledge, could copy a Fox schedule (fleetwide communication system) message, operate a key even at ham radio speeds, tune a transmitter, or make repairs to the radio gear. Nor were they expected to. The chief alone decided when and where you stood watch, what your battle station was, when you went on liberty, and when you were ready for a faster radio circuit or an advance in rating. Within his division, he was more feared and respected than the captain himself.[2]

The chiefs and their immediate juniors made ships and shore stations work through two time-honored *informal* tools: scrounging and cumshaw. At its worst, scrounging was stealing. At its best, it helped establish and maintain a process of quiet dealing and bargaining that shunted supplies to those who needed them. Cumshaw was what a sociologist would describe as an "exchange process" that built loyalties among the different fiefdoms within a ship. Brand-new pharmacist's mate Allan Bosworth described it this way:

> I . . . was painting the operating room when George Burton entered from the sick bay. He was our pharmacist's mate first class . . . and he looked shocked.
>
> "Knock it off!" George said in a tone that was both advice and command. "You don't have to paint this joint."
>
> "Captain's inspection tomorrow," I said. "White gloves."
>
> "Knock it off, I said. Ski will handle it for you."
>
> "Ski?" I asked. . . .

"I mean Walter Kerzwicki, painter first class—in charge of the paint locker," George said. "He's got some strikers working for him." . . . "Get smart!" he told me. "You can get this painting done cumshaw."

"How?" . . .

"Look," he said. "You've got two pints of alky in that locker. One's open for sterilizing instruments, and for surgical dressings—the minute you open it, that pint is expended. The full bottle is for emergencies, operations. Now, who's going to ask you how many surgical dressings you handle? Man falls down a ladder and cuts his knee, *you* fix him up, not the doctor. How about Morgan, the ship's cook first? You know him?"

I said yes. Morgan was the butcher, and had cut his hand slicing meat. I took stitches.

"Morgan likes a little shot of alky, now and then. You fix him up with that, and then when the chow in the mess don't look good, Morgan will fix you up with a steak. See what I mean? Cumshaw." . . .

Just then Walter Kerzwicki appeared, a lean dark man of about thirty. He shook hands with me, but addressed himself to George Burton. He pointed to his Adam's apple.

"Doc, that silver tube in me t'roat—it's rustin."

"Give me the key to the alcohol locker," George said.

He poured an ounce of pure grain alcohol into a medicine glass. Ski tossed it off. It must have burned fearfully, but Ski sauntered leisurely to the sink and, talking all the while, drank a medicinal ounce of water for a chaser. . . .

George reached for the expendable bottle again, and then suggested there was something Ski's stupid strikers could do. I finished the painting that week, but on the following Friday, three of his non-rated men painted the operating room from stem to stern, and left no brushmarks. I lifted no hand, except to pour Ski a couple of shots when he came to inspect their work.[3]

Yet the informal tools were always in the background. In front, especially in destroyers and submarines, was the craft a petty officer or chief had mastered. These were the skills of sailors and fighting men. Some of the most important of these were learned the hard way—by watching older men and then by imitating them, practicing again and again until a skill was mastered. Author and former enlisted man Marcus Goodrich has left us, in his novel *Delilah*, an unforgettable picture of destroyer sailors dealing with their eternal enemy—the sea—as they man whaleboats for a landing on a beach through heavy surf.

Barefooted, the six oarsmen took their places on the thwarts of each boat; the coxswain standing in the stern. Their shoes, into which their socks had been tucked, were hung around their necks by joined laces. At the command, "Toss Oars!" they swung their oars up vertically and held them there, while seven members of the Landing Party crawled into the bottom of each boat between the thwarts. . . .

Cruck [chief boatswain's mate] roared his orders; Bidot [quartermaster, first class] sang his. "Let Fall!" The oars came down to just above the surface of the water. "Give Way Together!" The boats slid swiftly in towards the beginning of the surf. . . . Just outside the well-defined line where the great, smooth calm of water mysteriously aroused itself and began to charge violently toward the land, the two boats paused. The men rested on their oars while Cruck and Bidot studied the problem before them.

Suddenly the standing Cruck braced himself and felt for a good grip, with his hands, right elbow and hip, on the great steering oar trailing out astern. The six oarsmen facing him, as they saw this, felt for holds with their bare feet, curling their toes down as if to grip, while their hands flexed preparatorily on oar handles. . . . The passengers crouching in the bottom of the boat had complete confidence in these men. They were the best boat's crew in the ship. . . .

"Give Way Together!" yelled Cruck, digging his steering oar deep into the sea. . . .

They stroked swiftly and steadily in with the surging water until Cruck, in a periodic turn of the head, saw roaring down upon them the first and greatest of the pursuing waves. Looking terrible in its great height and velocity it blotted out the seascape . . . and overtook them.

"Oars!" shrieked Cruck.

The oars came out of the sea, paused for a few seconds just above it, dripping blades parallel to the water and in line, waiting for the swiftly following command.

"Stern All!"

The blades of the oars turned, dipped. The straining bodies now pushed against the oars. The boat stood still for an instant before it reversed its direction.

Cruck, his feelings exaggerating this perilous stationary moment as his eyes glared back into the charging, monstrous mass of water, screamed wildly, raising his eyes instinctively to the sky:

"Stern All! . . . Stern All! . . . Christ! I'm out here with a gang of pansies!"

The boat, however, had gained momentum. It was backing water straight out to sea, straight at its great enemy, which the oarsmen could now see plainly. Towering in cold, dispassionate ferocity the wave scooped down upon them at terrific speed.

By the time the stern of the whaleboat had met the base of the wave, the boat was traveling fast enough to neutralize somewhat the speed of the sea. The boat stood comparatively still while the comber passed under it; but this is not what seemed to happen. As if it were going to loop the loop, the whaleboat appeared to dart up the massive, concave front of the wave towards the scintillating ridge of foam that had begun to sprout all along its length.

This was the moment on which hung the fate of all in the boat . . . if the whaleboat had been backed at a precise right angle into the wave at a speed sufficient to maintain that angle before the force of the wave, [it would] prevent her from being carried along in front of it. Otherwise, the boat would end for end, spilling . . . the helpless men into the sea . . . ; or the boat would jerk broadside on to the sea, be roared along before the wave out of control, like a piece of flotsam, to fill with water and capsize.

With Cruck fighting his oar in a raging, brutal aggressiveness that seemed to lend personality to the liquid monster that gripped it, the whaleboat leapt onto the top of the wave. . . .

As the whaleboat slid down the long, slanting back of the wave, the crew at Cruck's order now pulled vigorously with it. For the time that they could cling there on the wave with their oars, the boat traveled shoreward in a gale of speed. Soon, however, the wave left them behind. . . . Cruck roared the time for their stroke: "Yo! . . . yo! . . . heave!" . . . The battle was not over by any means. Behind them curled and thundered another monster almost as large as the first. Again the boat reversed its direction, met the enemy, was flung high in the air to come down precisely on the wave's back and speed shoreward. Time and again they thus met the immensities of water, escaped their ferocity and tricked them into becoming beasts of burden. The last one, much smaller and much easier to deal with than the others, carried the boat out of deep water onto the slope of the beach.

When Cruck felt bottom with his steering oar, he yelled, "Trail Oars," threw his oar at the water and leapt overboard. The boat's crew almost at the same moment dropped their oars into the water and jumped after him. The oars, on short trailing lines, dragged sternward, clinging close to the sides with the onward motion of the boat. The crew, nearly waist deep in water, seized the gunwales and with the help of the sea's rush dragged the boat up on the beach before the back-wash could develop.[4]

This was the skilled seamanship of the disciplined sailor, an art developed through trial and error and usually passed along from generation to generation of semiliterate men in the way that people ashore passed along the skills of hitching horses to a carriage. Perhaps the most obvious survivor of this traditional way of learning is instruction in the craft of tying knots. Perhaps the most useful survivor of the seaman's art is that of conning (directing the steering of) a ship.

It was the chief boatswains who were masters of the mysteries of seamanship. Assume, for example, that a battleship had to anchor in a tideway with two anchors to hold her against the current and any wind. One method for doing this successfully was worked out by Chief Boatswain J. P. O'Neil in the old battleship *Rhode Island* in 1908. (*Rhode Island* was sold for scrap in 1923.) The goal was to drop the port and starboard bow anchors in such a way that the ship was held between them. This was not a simple task. Anchors were heavy—almost ten tons each in battleship *Arizona*. Anchor chain (called "cable") was also heavy. Two-and-a-half-inch diameter chain weighed 375 pounds per fathom; three-inch chain weighed 540 pounds per fathom. *Arizona*'s chain weighed in at 630 pounds per fathom.

Assume the starboard anchor was "let go" first and rested on the bottom. The ship was then moved slowly upstream, without dragging the starboard anchor, to a point where, once the port anchor was lowered to the bottom of the harbor, the ship would drift back down to a point equidistant between the two anchors. This was only the beginning of the process, however. Stopping the maneuver there would run the risk that the ship, in swinging about her two anchor cables, would cross one cable over the other, or drift over one or both cables.

To avoid this, both anchor cables had to be secured to a common swivel. That swivel had first to be placed between links of the port anchor cable while the cable was still on deck—forward of the windlasses and flat on one of the steel runways that led from the windlasses to the port hawse hole. Then the heavy starboard anchor cable had to be unlinked, lowered through the starboard hawsehole, and pulled back up through the port hawsehole and attached to the swivel that was part of the port cable. Finally, the port cable had to be let out enough so that the swivel—now attached to both cables—was suspended below the ship's bow. In this position, the ship could turn in a circle about her own stem, and the radius of that circle would be the length of the ship plus the length of the cable attaching her to one of the anchors (see figure 2).

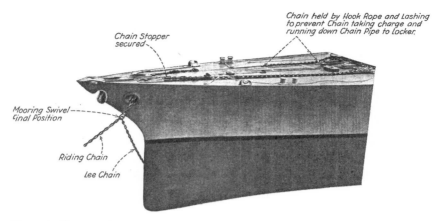

Figure 2. The mooring swivel is in place and the battleship is free to pivot around it without fouling her anchor chains. (From *Knight's Modern Seamanship*, 10th ed., 1941)

Mooring a ship in this way was a common maneuver, but doing it with the minimum of effort called for careful coordination between bridge personnel and the sailors rigging the swivel. It also depended on the proper working of the windlasses and on the soundness of the cables and the gear used to attach both to the swivel. Seemingly small matters could wreck the whole maneuver. A kink in a cable, for example, could cause it to jam in the pipe leading it to a windlass or to jump out of the drum of the windlass. To forestall kinks, anchor cables were stowed in tiers in special "chain lockers" deep in the ship. A ship's boatswain carefully inspected anchor cables and other "ground tackle," and Navy regulations required that every ship's first lieutenant keep a "complete log of every piece of ground tackle."[5]

Before steam power, hoisting anchors, like so much of a sailor's work, had been sheer manual labor. Steam engines, embraced by navies in the second half of the nineteenth century, provided a ready source of energy, and so eased the burden of a deckhand's duties. But the need for skilled seamen, capable of using a ship's own power to manipulate very heavy anchors and chains, remained. In addition, the need to operate and maintain a ship's engines and generators—devices so essential to a ship's efficiency and survival—depended on yet another class of skilled personnel: those who worked inside a ship, in her boiler rooms, machinery spaces, and machine shops.

When Admiral Fiske published *The Navy as a Fighting Machine*, he was literally describing how machines drove ships through the water, elevated and supplied a ship's guns, powered her searchlights and radios, and kept her crew warm and dry. These many machines—from boat cranes to clothes washers to the elevators that lifted heavy shells from magazines—worked off a ship's electrical and hydraulic power lines, and these in turn depended on the smooth operation of a ship's boilers and her engines. The men who fired those boilers and regulated her reciprocating or steam turbine engines had to be well trained and at ease with machines.

By the 1930s, many of those assigned to engine and boiler rooms had the intelligence and proficiency of machinist's mate Jake Holman, protagonist of Richard McKenna's 1962 award-winning novel *The Sand Pebbles*, which described life in a Yangtze River gunboat in the 1920s. Like all men who love machines, Holman even liked their smell—"burnt rubber and hot oil and steam and sometimes coffee." McKenna captured his man's character by noting that "Jake Holman loved machinery in the way some other men loved God, women and their country. He loved main engines most of all, because they were the deep heart and power center of any ship and all the rest was trimming."[6]

But Holman's experiences in his fictional ship were symptomatic of a larger struggle that was fought out in the interwar Navy. Younger, better-educated sailors confronted both less-educated seniors and the often archaic traditions of the naval service. More sophisticated machines required better-trained—and educated—sailors. But education marked a man in a blue-collar world. If he weren't careful, he could become an outcast, like Holman. Whether in a factory ashore or in an engine room at sea, the game was always the same:

> There was always a clique of old hands in an engine room, and they always wanted a new man to learn from them as much as they wanted him to know and wait his time for admission to the clique. It always disturbed them to see Jake Holman learning by himself. They were afraid he would learn too much and have power over them, and they were right. . . . They couldn't openly stop Holman from learning, because learning the plant was supposed to be good. So they always tried by the weight of their silent disapproval to force Jake Holman to stay as fumbling and ignorant as they were, and nothing in the world could spur Jake Holman on more than that silent disapproval. The machinery was always on Jake Holman's side, because machinery was never taken in by pretense and ignorance.[7]

Rear Admiral Fiske and his generation, aided by the Secretary of the Navy in the Wilson administration, Josephus Daniels, had set the Navy off on a revolutionary track, but the battles of that revolution were fought day in, day out in hundreds of machinery and electrical spaces throughout the fleet. One reason Jake Holman liked his specialty was because "machinery always obeyed its own rules. . . . Machinery was fair and honest and it could force people to be fair and honest." The proof of a method or an idea was in how well the machines worked, and they worked according to certain physical principles, not according to prejudices, and certainly not according to the word of an older or tougher hand—just because he was older or tougher. Yet Holman and others like him paid a price for their understanding of machines. It was the same price young men were paying all over the industrial world, as knowledge based on instruction and experimentation replaced tradition, and men came to be valued for their ability to *think* and not just use tools in time-tested ways.

Because so much work on a ship was still manual labor, however, even the best trained of the new generation of sailors had to win the respect of older hands through hard work. McKenna's Jake Holman, for instance, had to take his turn at shoveling coal into his gunboat's furnaces. Shoveling coal "had to be done with shoulders, arms, and a particular snap of the wrist, to spread a shovelful evenly wherever you wanted it. When a man's wrists gave out and he began flexing his knees and throwing the coal with his whole body, the fire would hole and hump on him. He would have to start spreading with the hoe, working twice as hard to burn the same amount of coal, and it was a vicious circle." Yet Holman, like all men who know what it feels like to labor physically, "enjoyed it all the more because there was a need for the work he did." Work itself brought men together even as differences in intelligence, skill, and experience pushed them apart.[8]

The prospect of battle also brought them together. As Marcus Goodrich noted, "Aboard a fighting ship, what appears to landsmen to be undue and exaggerated recognition is given to minute and seemingly trivial morsels of efficiency and competency. Based deep in the consciousness of every soul in the craft is always alive and restless the awareness of how much depends on each single man and lever."[9] Seaman Oree Weller, new to battleship *Arizona* in 1941, put it another way:

I was assigned first to the 6th division, whose berthing spaces were shared with the 5-inch/51 caliber casemate broadside guns. It was here that I first began to appreciate that the ship existed primarily as a platform for the guns. Amenities for the crew were always sandwiched in and were to not interfere with the guns. My own view was that the requirement was right.[10]

The Naval Institute's own *Bluejackets' Manual*, which contained knowledge that a seaman needed to have and which tried to teach him the Navy's ways, said this: "*Silence* is the first requisite of discipline on the well-drilled ship. Unnecessary noise of any kind makes confusion. Those in authority, and this includes the petty officers, are the only ones whose voices should be heard."[11]

Practicing to kill was also hard work—very hard work—and sailors who manned weapons and fire control devices were drilled in it constantly. Retired Captain Joseph Taussig remembered the 5-inch, 25-caliber antiaircraft guns drilling on battleship *Nevada*:

> The pointer elevated the gun either by matching the signals sent from the director, or by eye. The trainer trained the gun in azimuth by the same method. The fuze setter set a timing mechanism on his "fuze pots," in accordance with the director order, or the order of the gun captain. . . . A third loader would strip the protecting wires from the rim of the can [containing the shell] and tilt the can so the ammunition could be handled by a second loader. This man then placed the [shell] nose-down in one of the three fuze pots, which set the mechanical/powder fuze. The first loader would reach over, pick up a shell from the fuze pot, and place it on a tray under the chamber of the gun. The gun captain would shove a lever, and the shell would be rammed home by compressed air. Automatically, the breech would close, . . . the gun would fire, recoil, and eject the empty cartridge. The first loader would start the action all over again by placing another shell on the tray. This was an amazingly fast and efficient method. We could often load and fire twenty or more shells a minute over a sustained period. The enlisted men were drilled for interminable hours into teams of near-inhuman perfection.[12]

Albert Pelletier, a radioman on fleet flagship *Pennsylvania* in 1933, described short-range battle practice with the ship's 5-inch, 25-caliber antiaircraft guns:

> I was on the boat deck between guns number three and five and so was right in the thick of things. Gun number one made an E. An E required that the gun put eight shots into the bull's eye in 35 seconds. That was shooting. Gun number seven also got eight hits out of eight, but they missed the E by a couple of

seconds. The gun didn't eject one shell, and the gun captain had to pull it out by hand. . . . It was sure nice to watch them fire. The ring of fire around the muzzle when a gun fired was awesome.[13]

Three years earlier, one officer and four sailors were killed while practicing for a similar competition, and two officers and six enlisted personnel were severely wounded, when one of *Colorado*'s antiaircraft guns exploded. Work wasn't just work. It could take a man's life in a heartbeat.

Competitive teams were not just created through various forms of work. To sharpen team spirit, ships' crews competed with one another in a variety of sports, including rowing, baseball, and boxing. Unfortunately, the competition could sometimes get nasty, especially when ships' crews came ashore to find old rivals holding down spots in local bars. Marcus Goodrich described a group of tough destroyermen about to go on leave:

Ensign Snell . . . fell into the prescribed routine with which an Officer of the Deck on a large man-of-war dispatches a liberty party. As he moved along the double line of men . . . he noticed a long bulge below the left side of Heller's fashionably snug jumper.

"What's that?" he asked the Pharmacist's Mate.

"That's a shoe, Sir. I'm taking it ashore to be fixed."

"Take it out and carry it," said the officer. "That's no way to go ashore."

Heller stood there without moving.

"Take it out."

Heller . . . lifted his jumper to display a length of iron pipe. . . . Heller pulled out this deadly weapon and tossed it on the deck. . . .

"Any more of you got these things?"

They did.

Wembly . . . reached beneath his jumper, produced a home-made brass knuckles and . . . heaved it on the deck close to Heller's primitive blackjack. All down the deck men now emulated this gesture, until Ensign Snell found himself staring down at a sizeable heap of metal and wood.[14]

This wasn't typical, yet it suggests how the strain of shipboard life—its isolation from the freedom enjoyed by civilians and the inability to get away from those who got on your nerves—could make sailors itch for a fight. Anger that built up on ship could explode in wild behavior ashore.

Women—or, to be precise, the lack of their company—were another source of strain. McKenna defined that strain in very stark terms: "Girls were much more important to a crew's health than beer. . . . Girls helped to keep in its cage a certain Beast that was always trying to get loose in a ship." Sailors didn't have much of a reputation as trustworthy lovers, but they made up for it with a certain carefree gusto. Young women, many of whom had a hard time of it during the Great Depression, were willing to take them on. Ted Mason recalled the desperate search of his generation for romance:

> In navy towns . . . one looked almost in vain for beauty. Incarnate were all the evils of America's continuous neglect of its poor . . . bad teeth, poor carriages, lusterless hair, bowed legs, faces puffy with starch or gaunt from early malnutrition. Only occasionally would one see an attractive girl, and she, invariably, would be surrounded by uniformed Lochinvars. Not that the others lacked for attention. Here they were all Helens of Troy, and scarcely one would fail to find a sailor eager to make love to her.[15]

Enlisted life was an amalgam of hard work (much of the time), adventure (some of the time), conformity to the rules (unless on liberty), and subordination. About the often rigid bar between officers and enlisted men, author and former chief petty officer Floyd Beaver had one of his fictional sailors remark, "The privileges of rank galled me as much as they did anyone. Some guys never adjusted to the reality, in fact, and left the Navy as quickly as possible. Those of us who stayed on came to accept the reality of the gap between officers and men as a somewhat silly and inexplicable rule in a game we agreed to play. As the old chiefs were forever telling us: 'You wasn't drafted.'"[16]

Indeed, some of the best fiction about the Navy of this period, such as *The Sand Pebbles*, is really a study of one or several enlisted men trying to come to terms with an authority that grates on their self-respect. The same goes for memoirs, particularly Ted Mason's *Battleship Sailor*. This theme even found its way into Hollywood movies; in the Warner Brothers film *Here Comes the Navy* (1934), James Cagney plays a feisty, lighthearted Ted Mason-like character, suitable for a general audience. The real Ted Mason was a lot more complex: a tough, gritty, smart aleck, yet an intelligent kid who grew up under—or despite—the Navy's structured regime.

Times weren't all bad, by any means. Life at sea provided all sorts of distractions from routine that weren't available to civilians. Allan Bosworth, on battleship *Maryland,* was watching while sister ship *Colorado* fired from twelve miles off at a target raft towed 720 feet behind his own ship.

> Several hundred men were topside on the *Maryland,* watching the practice, which was very dramatic. First there was a burst of flame on the skyline, then a cloud of black smoke, and then the shells could be heard approaching with a roar like an express train, to explode and rip huge holes in the [target raft].
>
> But something happened. A sixteen-inch shell fell short by a mile or two, struck the water with a clap of thunder, and then veered straight for the *Maryland,* skipping the surface just like a flat rock that had been skimmed across a pond.
>
> All hands topside rushed to go below and get behind the ship's armor belt. The shell fortunately expended itself and sank a few hundred yards away. A large number of the *Maryland*'s crew came back topside just in time to see the same thing happen again. Sailors frantically rushing below collided with sailors coming topside, and the sick-bay staff was very busy treating cracked craniums, skinned knees, and bruises.[17]

Seaman First Class Charles Pollow had an even stranger story to tell. In 1937 he was a member of the crew of *Cuyahoga,* a "cutter support ship for the presidential yacht." Pollow served as one of three Navy personnel on the fishing boat used off Florida by President Roosevelt. Before the crippled president could begin fishing he had to be transferred from destroyer *Moffett,* and, as Pollow recalled in 1997, "I'm afraid FDR did not leave in a manner befitting the commander in chief. His aides carried him down the *Moffett*'s narrow ladder, and after watching the swells for a minute or so, they tossed the president into the waiting arms of another crewman and myself. I don't know what would have happened to our careers if we had dropped him."[18]

Some occupations aboard ship that might have seemed dull and less than worthwhile—such as mess cook—were not necessarily all that bad. It depended on how the individual sailors handled them. As mentioned in the last chapter, before the concept of the cafeteria was tested successfully on carrier *Ranger,* enlisted sailors ate meals in their division's living spaces. Mess tables were triced overhead, except at mealtimes, when they were lowered to the deck. Men ate sitting on benches. The duty of the sailors assigned to be mess cooks was to set up the tables, get the food from the galley, serve the meal, and clean up afterward. Radioman Pelletier on *Pennsylvania* found it a pretty easy job:

I had to get up at 0600. At 0630 I set up the mess tables and at 0700 served breakfast. It was all over, including the cleaning up, by 0830. There was nothing more to do until 1100, at which time I started setting up for the noon meal. That was finished by 1300, and then I was off until 1630, when I served the evening meal. At 1800 it was all over for the day. Friday morning . . . I had to get all of my gear ready for Saturday morning inspection. I rated liberty every night and had no other duties. As a result, I had plenty of time in both the morning and afternoon to study [for promotion].[19]

Larger ships usually had newsletters or actual newspapers written and published by their own crews. Usually edited by officers but full of short articles and notices written by enlisted personnel, some newsletters even carried cartoons. In *The Colorado Lookout* of June 21, 1930, for example, there is the usual captain's exhortation:

Every ship has her character, which is the sum of the traits of her officers and men. If these traits are loyalty, obedience, alertness, courage and self-respect, the ship will be smart and ready. . . .

Your country's honour [*sic*] is not upheld by machinery. Fights are not won by cold iron. It is the spirit of the ship that makes her a good fighter and this spirit is given her by the spirit of her crew.

But then there are the contributions of the sailors:

Fox says the ship tied up across the dock was named after him, but he has been informed that it is a destroyer and not a "pig-boat."

There is some kind of rumor out about Clark [the master at arms] and a little girl in a yellow dress and yellow hat. How's to give us the dope and what is this strange power you have over wimmen?

Myers [electrician's mate, first class] has the hardest time lately. He stumbles over any little thing, falls down and goes right to sleep until "knock off" at 3:30. Next thing we know he'll be carrying a pillow with him.[20]

Although edited and censored, the meanings of these jibes were clear enough. As a short note in battleship *Maryland's Catapult* observed, "It's discouraging to wake up in the morning and find that, even after all attempts you made, you are still not aboard your ship."

The better officers and captains knew how to deal with sailors who, though talented, were independent. Albert Pelletier watched an interesting back-and-forth exchange in 1933 between Radioman Second Class Victor A. Maling and

Pennsylvania's captain. Maling had been required to send the dispatch of a visiting newspaperman to a commercial radio station ashore, but he had violated regulations by using the opportunity to send his own private message to a friend. That message, it turned out, had alerted the press that the battleships were about to enter San Francisco Bay—something the public was not supposed to know until the ships actually appeared, and the admiral commanding was not happy. Pelletier recalled that the admiral

> had tracked down the culprit and directed the captain to court martial him. Maling went to mast, and the captain informed him of the admiral's order— that he could expect a court martial. The captain, however, was an old shipmate of Maling . . . and had great respect for Maling's expertise. Accordingly, he told him in private that he had no choice but to order a court martial, but since the admiral failed to set a time limit, he . . . would take his time. In the meantime, however, Maling would be restricted to the ship.

Soon thereafter, a serious earthquake rocked Long Beach. Telephone and telegraph lines were down, and *Pennsylvania's* captain, having Maling "conveniently aboard," ordered the radioman to set up the ships' field radio ashore.

> Maling immediately made me a part of the party. Nine of us took the set over into Long Beach and set it up in the park. Because of Maling's expertise, we were on the air to the ship within the hour . . . we became the primary means of communication from emergency parties. . . . Maling had been able to see his wife during this operation, and when it was over he was the proud recipient of another commendation to put on the facing page of his court martial specifications. He also received one other bit of good news: the court martial was canceled, and he again had a clean slate.[21]

And so it went—the work, the routine, the rules, the rigors, and the sometime adventures of life at sea. And, of course, the hunger for the shore—for the women, the good friends initiating a young sailor in his first stiff drink, and the excitement to be found in cities like San Francisco. In the 1930s, young men traded independence for a paying job in the Navy—not a mean bargain at that time; and some stayed on, attracted by the opportunities that Navy life could offer them. After all, even in the early 1950s—to say nothing of the '20s and '30s—travel out of one's home town or county was a rare event, and names such as "San Francisco" and "New York" evoked visions of power, glamour, wealth, and great energy. The Navy was a ticket to all that. It was, moreover, an institution that had in common with industrialized civilian life the two-faced world of the factory and machine shop— the world according to the book, and the real world, the one you learned as a young man, working alongside and under men like Jim DeLuce, the best foreman the elder of us ever had. At its best—and the best was all too rare in civilian life, sadly—this was a world a man could be very proud of, indeed.[22]

4
THE WORLD OF THE OFFICER

Do not refer to the captain by name. He is The Captain.

Recruit's Handbook, USS West
Virginia (1935)

The form of address tells you everything. The specifics of a captain's responsibilities were printed in *United States Navy Regulations* (1920), and they were exacting, indeed:

> The commanders of all fleets, squadrons, naval stations, and vessels belonging to the Navy are required to show in themselves a good example of virtue, honor, patriotism, and subordination; to be vigilant in inspecting the conduct of all persons who are placed under their command; to guard against and suppress all dissolute and immoral practices, and to correct, according to the laws and regulations of the Navy, all persons who are guilty of them; and any such commander who offends against this article shall be punished as a court-martial may direct.[1]

The *Navy Regulations* listed all of the following offenses as warranting— "as a court-martial may adjudge"—the death penalty: mutiny, the disobedience of "lawful orders," striking a superior officer, supplying information to the enemy, desertion in wartime, betraying a trust in time of war, sleeping on watch, leaving a post before being relieved, "willfully" stranding a Navy ship or running it on the rocks, destroying public property, "pusillanimously" crying "for quarter" in battle, cowardice, neglecting orders during battle or the approach to battle, neglecting to clear for action, not using "utmost exertions to join in battle," failing to encourage "inferior officers and men to fight courageously," failing to pursue an enemy, and failing to "afford all practicable relief and assistance" to ships of the United States or allied navies during combat.

The responsibilities of the captain of even a small ship were great; his formal authority was commensurate. On his own, subject to no immediate formal review, a captain could deny a subordinate his freedom and his normal privileges. On his own, a captain could exercise the "right of self-preservation," which included "the protection of the State, its honor, and its possessions, and the lives and property of its citizens against arbitrary violence, actual or impending." *Navy Regulations* recognized that the "conditions calling for the application of the right of self-preservation can not be defined beforehand, but must be left to the sound judgment of responsible officers," but who could say what was "sound" and what was not? No wonder Captain W. J. Holmes noted, "The skipper of a ship is like the mother of a very young baby. Nothing can ever relieve him of the certainty of his responsibility. Even when he sleeps his vigilance never relaxes."[2]

The *Navy Regulations* again and again refer to cases where officers, especially captains, must employ their own judgment; and, at its best, the education and training of a Navy officer prepared him for that duty. For example, the Naval Academy at Annapolis was not accredited as an academically worthy college until 1933. Prior to that time, graduates did not receive a bachelor's degree, not even in engineering, which was the heart of the school's curriculum. What midshipmen did receive was an introduction to their peculiar calling—the foundation of which was the ability to make responsible decisions that subordinates would obey.

What a would-be officer encountered at Annapolis was an institution designed to instill a sense of unique responsibility in a young man who would soon be given the right to command others. But before you can command others, you must learn to command yourself. There were two paths to self-command offered young men in the United States in the 1920s and 1930s by private colleges and by schools such as the Naval Academy. One path led to the maturity of the mind by way of the great intellectual traditions of Western civilization. The other path—the way offered by Annapolis and West Point—left intellectual maturity for later in life and stressed gaining leadership skill through the rigor of athletic competition, practice at the officer's crafts (such as navigation), and the pressure of indoctrination. Annapolis offered young men not so much an education as preparation for a life of responsibility and command. Essential to that preparation was both high standards—inside the classroom and out—and competition.

The Naval Academy was only the beginning of this preparation. Upon graduation, young officers—ensigns—were sent to ships such as battleships for two years in order to master the routines of shipboard life, to demonstrate their potential as officers, and to get some understanding of what the Navy was like. Many fresh ensigns from this period were eager to get into the new fields of aviation and sub-marine service, but all had to serve their time as junior officers on battleships and cruisers before they could move on to train as pilots or submarine officers.

It was a good time and a bad time for these young officers—good because of the friendships formed and lessons learned, bad because of the "spit and polish" required in the "battleship Navy." *Navy Regulations* provided for inspections of individual ships by senior officers, and those officers were required to write, at the end of their inspections, "a concise statement of the condition and efficiency of the ship and whether special credit or discredit should attach to the commanding officer in connection with her condition and efficiency." The results of inspections strongly influenced an officer's career, especially the career of a ship's captain.

In consequence, manuals such as *Watch Officer's Guide* (1935) prompted junior officers with injunctions such as these:

All ladders and gangways should be kept strictly up to the mark, and the dress gangway should be immaculate.

A ship is known by her boats. The boats should be a credit to the ship and to the officer of the deck.

Enforce strictly the etiquette of the quarter-deck. Except for necessary work or drill in progress there, see that it is kept immaculate, and that its ceremonial character is strictly maintained.

The officer of the deck must make his salutes and reports dignified, smart, and in accordance with the best naval practice. He must avoid any semblance of informality, familiarity, or casualness, in dealing with officers, men, or visitors.[3]

As if this weren't enough, there were the many practical details that junior officers had to master, including how to sound alarms, how to close water-tight doors, how to anchor, how to shift from powered to hand steering, and how to deal with emergencies such as a man overboard. Junior officers had, in their initial positions, to master the process of understanding how their ships worked—how the ship's main steam and electrical machinery operated, where gear was stowed, where essential compartments were located, and how communications within the ship functioned. They also had to learn the rudiments of personnel management, including assigning sailors to watches and duties. A junior officer also had to learn "the tactical data and maneuvering qualities of his ship," including the "advance and the turning circles of his ship with full rudder and standard rudder, and with one engine stopped or backing."

Junior officers had to learn *how* to learn. If they were fortunate, more senior officers would provide them with models of how to act, how to teach, and how to command. Admiral I. J. Galantin had just such an experience in his two years (1933–35) as a new ensign on battleship *New York*:

> There was time and opportunity to learn much of human relations, of men's aspirations and motivations—the elements of leadership. Our formalized junior officers' training course came under the supervision of . . . splendid [regular] officers . . . , but much of our learning would come from working under officers who, through determination and ability, had progressed from enlisted status. I found these men . . . a mature, stabilizing, and understanding force in the ebb and flow of the ship's training and disciplinary problems. . . .
>
> The rigid pattern of custom and conformity [he found in *New York*, though] dull [and] repetitious, [was offset by] the steady accumulation of experience of the sea, of safety and survival in a capricious environment that imposed its own demands on personnel and materiel alike. As midshipmen, our summer cruises had given us inklings of this, but now direct responsibility for men's lives, for their performance under stress, for the safety of the ship, imprinted more deeply certain habits of thought and action that are the hallmark of seamen worldwide. Perhaps these are summarized in two words: responsibility and forehandedness.[4]

This is precisely what was supposed to happen. The process began at Annapolis, where classroom training, a rigorous athletic program, and hazing by more senior midshipmen was combined with summer cruises on ships such as battleship *Arkansas* (BB-33), where midshipmen gained some experience in the work of sailors and the responsibilities inherent in command. Midshipman (later Vice Admiral) Lloyd M. Mustin showed he grasped the concept of responsibility while serving as gun captain of a 5-inch, 51-caliber broadside gun on *Arkansas* during her 1933 summer cruise.

His gun had fired, recoiled, and returned to the loading position. Mustin had opened the breechblock, the enlisted shellman had inserted the shell, the rammerman had seated the shell in the firing chamber of the gun, and the powderman had stepped forward to insert a bag of powder behind the shell.

[But] he did not follow through with that powder charge. He stepped back before it was all the way in the chamber. . . . As he stepped clear, I swung the breech closed. This crushed the rear end of the powder bag, and the breech would not close. So I swung it back open . . . sang out for silence . . . reached in and pushed the remainder of the bag into the chamber and swept all the loose powder up with my fingers out of the threads of the screw box, and threw that all in there, put in a new primer . . . closed the breech, and said, "Ready."[5]

Mustin and his enlisted comrades were lucky. The mix of smokeless powder and black powder from the back of the ruptured powder bag might have spontaneously ignited.

Had he a sense of the danger? Yes.

I knew it, but I didn't stop to think about it, and the reason, of course, is one that . . . had been made amply clear by our instruction at the Naval Academy . . . that is, in these battle functions your people have got to be so trained and so disciplined that they will do what's right regardless, without pause to weigh the consequences, because there's no time to pause and weigh the consequences. . . . Do it that way because we've found out in letters of blood that to do it some other way costs lives. . . . It was an example to me pretty early in my career of what careful, meticulous, thorough training will do.

Unknown to Mustin, one of *Arkansas's* officers, Lieutenant Thomas H. Hederman, had witnessed the little emergency at the gun, and he had praised Mustin in a report sent back to the Naval Academy. Hederman's action, later made known to Mustin, taught the future vice admiral two other lessons in leadership: (1) the need to observe, and (2) the value of praising work done well or courageously.

After graduating from the Naval Academy, Mustin was blessed by being sent to heavy cruiser *Augusta* (CA-31), where he served first under Captain James Richardson (later Commander-in-Chief, U.S. Fleet) and then under Captain Chester Nimitz. The latter had a profound influence on the young ensign. Nimitz insisted that the ship's officers lead *Augusta's* athletic teams. Because *Augusta*, then serving, as Mustin put it, "on the China station," needed to be able to send armed parties of Marines and sailors ashore, Nimitz also insisted that his officers instruct the crew rigorously in the use of small arms. And he showed them how. As Mustin recalled, Nimitz "conducted the affairs within [his command] in such a manner that all of the young officers coming up were . . . exposed to these tools for developing and exercising leadership. And, of course, these were all small opportunities for them to display it . . . under the eagle eye of Chester Nimitz, who then reflected things accordingly in fitness reports he was writing."

To Mustin, Nimitz was the ideal officer—leader, teacher, tactician, and judge. When *Augusta* anchored in Shanghai, for example, Nimitz brought out Americans—both military and civilian—with experience in China and knowledge of the country's history to lecture to his officers. Yet Nimitz was also extremely demanding. "Any tendency of an officer to be somewhere other than with his men when something [was] going on in the *Augusta* soon led to that officer no longer being in the *Augusta*. . . . Nimitz was very direct and completely ruthless," recalled Mustin. The results were predictable: awards for the ship's crew, for engineering and gunnery, and high marks in inspections. In December 1934, *Augusta* returned to Manila from an extended cruise in the southwest Pacific. Almost immediately, the ship and her crew were subject to a once-a-year admiral's inspection. "She went through it with sensational success," according to Mustin, and "frankly, no one was surprised. It wasn't a great hurry and flurry getting ready after getting back into port. We had been ready all along."

Ensign William J. Ruhe (later, a much decorated captain) had a very different experience serving in destroyer *Roe* (DD-418) in 1941. Through the early and mid-1930s, new ensigns were sent to larger ships—battleships, aircraft carriers and cruisers—to begin their climb up the ladder of command. By the end of the 1930s, however, many fresh ensigns were sent to the new ships that had been built to bring the Navy to "treaty strength." One such was *Roe*, commissioned in 1940. Her captain's leadership left much to be desired, as Ruhe remembered so lucidly in his 1995 memoir, *Slow Dance to Pearl Harbor*.[6]

In March 1941, *Roe* was participating in a night exercise involving a number of ships. Ruhe, officer of the deck, "began seeing the wakes of four ships in column proceeding up and parallel to the *Roe*'s starboard side. Their wakes seemed about a thousand yards off." Ruhe suddenly "realized that the wakes of the second and third ships in the column seemed dangerously close to each other." Warning his captain of a likely collision, Ruhe was dismayed to note that his superior officer "merely grunted." On impulse, the young ensign activated the radio telephone: "This is a small boy. . . . I hold four small boys in column on my starboard beam fairly close aboard about a thousand yards away."

The captain told him to stop: "Ruhe, you can't send a message like that—in the clear without a proper call-up." When Ruhe continued, saying, "The bow wake of the third ship in column is within fifty yards of the stern of the second ship," his superior admonished him sharply. "You're making me the laughingstock of the whole fleet," he said. Ruhe, who felt that "saving two ships from a collision came first," broadcast another curt warning. The captain "clamped his hand over mine to prevent me from sending any more messages. 'This is crazy, Ruhe,' he growled, 'You don't know what you're doing. . . . Stop it! . . . You've got to learn proper voice procedures. . . . You're no help on this bridge.'"

But Ruhe had been prescient. "Within ten minutes there was startlingly a brilliant shower of sparks. . . . The destroyer *Somers* had climbed up the stern of the *Warrington* in a disastrous collision." Ruhe's captain's response was typical of the man's overall behavior: "We kept out of trouble, Ruhe. Didn't we? But you sure have to do some quick learning of voice procedures before any more of these exercises are held." Ruhe's thoughts were closer to those contained in the little book, *Naval Leadership*: "No question should ever be decided without considering *primarily* its effect on the efficiency of the fleet for *war*."[7]

This imperative extended throughout the ship. In his unfinished novel, *The Sons of Martha*, Richard McKenna offers a fictional glimpse of an engineering officer making the point to enlisted sailors under his command:

> I want to tell you a story, as it was told to me in an engineering class at Annapolis . . . many years ago the cruiser *Bennington* was making her annual speed run for the record and by the end of the second hour they realized, if they had no breakdown . . . , they would log the highest sustained speed ever for a ship of their class. All over the ship they were excited and keeping their fingers crossed, because . . . they loved her and they wanted her to score big. Then, about a minute before the run officially ended, a watertender called main control and reported low water in number six boiler. The chief engineer shouted back into the voice tube, "Wait one minute and then secure!" . . . Ten seconds later number six boiler blew up. The shock weakened the other boilers and within forty seconds they had all exploded. . . . By the time the minute was up, that fine, great ship was sinking, and a hundred good men were dead with the flesh scalded off their bones. . . . The instructor then asked us who was responsible. . . . One midshipman gave the answer that was obvious to all of us, that the chief engineer was. . . . The instructor shook his head. . . . The watertender sank that ship. He should have secured the boiler instantly and afterward reported the fact to nominally higher authority. If any officer was at fault, it was the one who advanced that man to the rating of watertender.[8]

McKenna's point was that engineering, with its potentially fatal steam and sparks, was different than even gunnery. There was "no sure way to interpose an officer's judgment and authority between a man and his duty." As his officer tells his men, "It is my duty to withhold the responsibility for operating machinery from any man who is unfit to bear it. I cannot learn that about a man from a written examination alone. I must depend upon my judgment of human character and I must draw also upon the judgment of chiefs and petty officers who have long since proven their own fitness." This leader finishes by calling his subordinates to their duty: "If I do not have fit men below, no amount of written orders and [punishments] will make them so. If I do have fit men, the highest tribute I can pay them is to trust them unhesitatingly with my professional reputation and the safety of our ship." This was the special, reciprocal relationship between officers and enlisted men: competency engendered trust, and trust encouraged even higher performance.

After the hurdles offered by the Naval Academy and the hard, initial experience of command, Navy officers wrestled with the selection process. "Selection" meant that the supposedly superior officers would be promoted "up," while the average officers would be shunted aside and then forced to retire. This was different from the case in other professions. For example, in law, medicine, or religion, the less able were often not at the head of their profession's leading institutions, but neither did they face the prospect of being forcibly retired while still in early middle age. In the nineteenth century, promotion to higher command in the Navy was a function of seniority. If an officer survived and did relatively well, he could be sure of what amounted to a reward for faithful (if not illustrious) service. He most likely would not make admiral, but his survival in some official billet was almost guaranteed.

In the years before World War I, Congress and the Navy cast aside this tradition of promoting by seniority. The notion of selection was first applied to promotion to the rank of rear admiral and was gradually extended down the chain of command. As Navy Secretary and reformer Josephus Daniels put it in 1917, "Promotions in all grades, from ensign to admiral, [should] be by selection."[9] The argument was clear: the Navy's officer corps did not exist to sustain its members; they existed to maintain the Navy. But how could selection be fair? How could boards of more senior officers fairly and effectively decide who among the younger officers deserved promotion?

How indeed? The need for standards by which to judge individual *line* officers drove the Navy to require them to serve a certain portion of their time at any given grade level (lieutenant, lieutenant commander, and so forth) at sea, where their performance could be tested. Staff officers were exempt from the requirement to serve at sea, though they had selection standards of their own to meet. Congress, which embraced the concept of selection early in the twentieth century and then maintained a running dialogue with Navy leaders about it, not only approved the legislation requiring selection and governing its application, but also provided liberal retirement pay that reduced the bitterness of officers who were passed over.

The history of the shift from promotion by seniority to promotion through selection has been documented in great detail by Naval War College professor Donald Chisholm in his *Waiting for Dead Men's Shoes* (2001). It is a complex, often undramatic, but vital story of naval officers and members of Congress attempting to balance the needs of the Navy against the needs of those who chose to commit themselves to the service of their country. The story was made both more fascinating and frustrating in the 1920s because of the "bulge" created by the cohort of non-Naval Academy graduates brought into the Navy during World War I and a second "bulge" that stemmed from the decision to restrict most aircraft pilot training to officers.

These bulges were large numbers of younger officers who, as they advanced, threatened to so dominate the upper echelons of command that the even younger officers rising behind them would have no chance at holding high rank. The solution was selection and the forced retirement of those not selected for higher command. Put another way, even talented officers had to be moved aside to make way for the younger generation.

W. J. Holmes has left a fictional but poignant description of just such a talented officer "passed over" while others were "selected up":

> He was a big man in a white linen suit that fitted him just a little too quick, as though it had been tailored when he was about fifteen pounds lighter. His light-colored hair was getting a little thin on top. His face was round like a full moon, and there was a sort of puffy look under his eyes.... [He] had a flushed appearance as though he had been drinking a little too much. I wasn't impressed.[10]

When offered sympathy by a contemporary officer who was selected up, the passed-over lieutenant commander made light of his plight: "Think nothing of

it. . . . We can't all be admirals. The selection board has to let the ax fall somewhere." Holmes told his story to show his readers that even a passed-over officer
could be an accomplished leader—that selection, though necessary in a service
where higher command opportunities were limited, was not a method without
faults. He also told his story to remind his readers to beware of first impressions.

There were, fortunately, compensations for the increased pressures that
officers were under. One was ship handling. Holmes's passed-over lieutenant
commander was good at it:

> The [tanker] was lying head to the wind, and there was plenty of clear water
> astern of her. The captain took the [destroyer] around in a wide sweep. It
> seemed to me that he held his speed on the approach overlong. We weren't
> more than two hundred yards astern of her when he stopped his engines. We
> came coasting in at a good clip, the sides of the [tanker] seemed to be sliding
> by like the view out of an express train window. The skipper walked over to the
> engine order telegraphs and flipped them back to Full Astern. It was like put-
> ting the brakes on a speeding automobile. He stood there, watching the deck
> of the tanker. At just the right moment he flipped up the handles to Stop. On
> the deck the lines were already going over.

As Holmes noted, "There is nothing a crew appreciates more than a good
piece of ship handling."

A classic among Navy destroyermen was a slim volume entitled *On a
Destroyer's Bridge*, by Commander H. H. Frost, published first in 1930. Frost
drew on his own extensive experience and that of others who commanded the
twelve-hundred-ton, 314-foot World War I destroyers in order to encourage
creative ship handling. In a chapter titled "Shoving Off from Other Ships," for
example, he advised his readers to "first get the ship carefully into the proper
position, and then execute one continuous maneuver ahead or astern. You can't
stop halfway, and the quicker you get clear the better. It's like stealing second—
he who hesitates is lost." The simile was both clever and apt.

"One of the thrills of a lifetime," according to Frost, "was to hold my breath
when the [destroyer] *Peary* passed the [destroyer tender] *Black Hawk* in the
Suez Canal. The latter was making about twelve knots and the *Peary* ran past
us at twenty. We could have thrown a biscuit across. It was a superb maneuver—
one of those *beau gestes* that every real destroyer captain loves to make. But
once is enough!"

Frost's book covered every conceivable maneuver, from cruising in formation to maneuvering among fields of ice. He had this story to tell about chasing down unarmed but live torpedoes during an exercise: "A torpedo was having a grand spree and we stopped to watch it from a distance which seemed safe. It curved around and straightened out for the bridge. It broached fifty yards short, dove beautifully under the ship and came up fifty yards on the other side. Let's hope all are as well trained."

The practical lore in the book was complemented by Frost's wry sense of humor: "During the last phase of a typhoon the Asiatic Destroyer Squadron tried to anchor in the lee of [Corregidor]. The wind was force-seven. The rain was blinding—that is not a figure of speech. Night was falling. The water in the lee was calm. We ran in close to the land and let go the anchor and sixty fathoms [360 ft.] of chain in twenty-five fathoms of water." But the bottom sloped so much that the anchor just slipped down the slope, leaving the ship at the mercy of wind and sea. Drawing in most of the anchor chain, Frost's destroyer, with the anchor hanging just below her bow, again approached Corregidor's lee shore. Unfortunately, the second attempt to set the anchor firmly on the sloping bottom also failed. "We then gave up attempting to anchor on the bank and let go in thirty-five fathoms [210 ft.] where the bottom was level." This time the anchor held. "By this time it was about 2100. Just as we were settled for the night the order came for the squadron to proceed into Manila. We piled into that small harbor at 0100 in one beautiful melee. Oh, what a night!"[11]

A telling anecdote, a clever sea story, and a wry comment were also compensation for the stress of command at sea. James Leutze, in his biography of Admiral Thomas C. Hart, captured one such engaging moment. Hart was known as a strict disciplinarian. While serving as Commander, Cruisers, Scouting Force, the admiral periodically inspected the ships under his command. Once, stepping on to a cruiser's bridge, "he seemed just as formidable as ever" to a young ensign at attention:

> To test the alertness of the engine-room crew, [Hart] walked over to the voice tube and shouted into it: 'If eggs are five cents apiece, how much would a dozen cost?' To the horror of the ensign, the reply came back: 'Shut up, you dumb S.O.B. Don't you know we're being inspected?' Hart showed just a twitch at the corners of his mouth. 'They are alert,' he announced.[12]

Yet no smile, no pleasure in conning a ship, no satisfaction in training a new generation of officers could obscure the reality of command responsibility expressed so pointedly in *Navy Regulations*. Marcus Goodrich portrayed that hard reality in *Delilah*:

> The Captain never can be just a man from Illinois who sleeps in rumpled pyja-mas, makes mistakes about history and uses his finger, when he thinks no one is looking, to push food onto his fork. Familiarity, when it is permitted to pre-vail, if it does not breed the proverbial contempt, certainly breeds between the giver and receiver of an order, an order that may lead to death or frightful mutilation, at least two things impairing the confidence, the aggressiveness and the speed with which a battle crisis must be met.
>
> First, in the giver of the order, it breeds a realization that if he takes this step, which in his judgement is exigently indicated, it may convert into a gory horror that tall, ruddy-faced man who has the next chair at dinner. . . . The order may be given; but the doubts, emotional stresses and temptations to rationalization, set up then, distract from the almost inhuman concentration on the development of the battle that must prevail, if those already dead in the struggle are not to have died in vain and the battle is to be won.
>
> Second, in the receiver of the order, familiarity breeds the constant reminder that the giver is merely a human being like himself, that the tactics on which he bases the summons to death may be as faulty as his familiar table manners. . . .
>
> The order to engage the enemy may come from . . . a man familiarly describ-able in terms of human failings . . . but these defects are hidden and made non-tainting behind the limits and barriers within which the man has been isolated and consecrated. . . . It was no crowd of cronies that responded with lethal alacrity to the command, "Damn the torpedoes! Go ahead!"[13]

The link between captain and crew, though, was two-way. It was best expressed by the traditional adage that a captain went down with his ship. As in so many things, Marcus Goodrich put well the reciprocal relationship between the captain and those he commanded. Watching his crew, *Delilah*'s commander felt "the same feeling of warning, with that impression like the recognition of a covenant, that had come to him every time he had called . . . for some rigorous performance. To these men . . . , these tested men who knew every eccentricity of her life, every weakness, every individualized strength, he somehow was inextricably committed." At its peak, the relationship between captain and crew was a moral one. They gave him loyalty and obedience. He gave them his energy, his dedication, and, if necessary, his life.

A naval commander's could be a hard life, and numbers of Naval Academy graduates either left it for what for them was more rewarding work or were compelled to retire because their seniors on selection boards didn't think they were fit for higher command. But it could also be a varied, exciting, and intensely rewarding life.

Rear Admiral Rufus F. Zogbaum, who commanded carrier *Saratoga* in the early 1930s and whose parents were prominent in New York artistic circles, had a naval officer's career that seems somewhat incredible in retrospect. As gunnery officer on armored cruiser *Pennsylvania* in 1911, he supervised the construction of the temporary platform used by pioneer aviator Eugene Ely in the first landing of an airplane on a warship. Two years later he was serving as an admiral's aide in Italy; then he took command of a destroyer under Captain W. S. Sims as the latter led a revolution in destroyer tactics; in the early summer of 1914, blessed by "the finest weather England had known in half a century," he was in London, ardently but patiently pursuing the hand of a clever Englishwoman. In the early part of World War I, while the United States was still neutral, he served in the eastern Mediterranean. After war was declared, he commanded one of the first six destroyers sent to Queenstown, Ireland, to reinforce the Royal Navy.

After serving as a convoy escort commander during the war, he commanded groups of destroyers in Italian waters, in the Adriatic, in the Baltic, and in Turkey. Fluent in French and thoroughly cosmopolitan, he and his equally sophisticated English wife became friends with a rich variety of expatriate Americans and prominent Europeans, including the former prime minister of Hungary and writer Edith Wharton. Zogbaum's privately published memoir, *From Sail to Saratoga*, fairly sparkles with stories of the many interesting and colorful characters he and his wife encountered during their European adventures. He even took destroyer *Reuben James* up the shallow, twisting Guadalquivir River to Seville, Spain. Returning to the United States to serve as executive officer of battleship *Oklahoma* (BB-37) and as a member of the Naval War College faculty, Zogbaum became a qualified naval aviator at the age of forty-nine, and then commanded seaplane tender *Wright*, experimental aircraft carrier *Langley*, and—finally—carrier *Saratoga*.[14]

This was the potential that a Navy career held out to its best officers—excitement, command, travel, and adventure. It was the kind of life beyond the dreams of most young men, the kind of life that had always lured so many restless young men to the sea. It could be—and usually was—hard on the women who married and followed such young officers. It was the wives who raised the children and followed their men to distant, sometimes inhospitable ports.

Some, though, had adventures in their own right. Louise Johnson Pratt, wife of the future Chief of Naval Operations, Admiral William V. Pratt, traveled on her own and with their son in Europe both before and after World War I. Described as "spirited" by historian Gerald Wheeler, Louise Pratt was independent and intelligent. Writing to her thoroughly professional husband—then commanding cruiser *Birmingham* in the Caribbean—from Paris in February 1914, she teased him with these words: "I don't see why it is necessary for you to have anyone else on board but yourself—no crew, no first officer, no navigator is any use for as far as I can see you can do the entire work yourself—and it is only an extra expense to Uncle Sam to have all those men on the ship."[15] The Pratts were extraordinary but not necessarily the exception to the rule, though it is wise to remember that the first wife of John Towers, the Navy's pioneer aviator, found Navy life—even life with the charismatic Towers—too demanding for her liking, and she and her pilot husband divorced after eight years of marriage.[16]

In the 1970s, historian Peter Karsten produced a careful, thoughtful study of the Naval Academy graduates who led the steam and steel Navy from its beginnings in the 1880s through its experiences with new technologies during and after World War I. The title of his book, *The Naval Aristocracy: The Golden Age of Annapolis and the Emergence of Modern American Navalism*, reveals its main theme—that the primary function of the path to command that began with schooling at Annapolis was to reinforce a set of values that most young midshipmen already possessed. Those values could be summed up in three words: commerce, Christianity, and constitutionalism.

Young men entered the Naval Academy accepting that the "business of America was business," even though, by embarking on a naval career, they were turning their backs on day-to-day business values, particularly the pursuit of personal wealth. They also accepted high church Protestantism, with its emphasis on hard work, on a belief that a few were "chosen" and most were not, and on social responsibility. Finally, they were conservatives of a republican sort; they usually disparaged partisan politics but never thought they had the right to usurp the power and authority of their civilian masters. They wholeheartedly accepted the Constitution they were sworn to defend. By and large, they were "national darwinists," and believed that nations competed in a world arena that gave rewards to the strong and punished the weak.[17]

What so marks the interwar Navy, though, is its shift *away* from the narrow band of values that historian Karsten described. Three factors undermined what he argued was a tight linkage between the social values of naval officers and the social backgrounds from which they came. The first were the reforms of Josephus Daniels, Woodrow Wilson's Secretary of the Navy. A figure of great controversy in his time, Secretary Daniels was instrumental in changing the way sailors were perceived by others and by themselves. His recruiting slogans were "Join the Navy and Learn a Trade" and "Every Battleship a School." He argued that educating enlisted men was a critical part of leadership, that the Navy needed to draw on better educated young men (especially from the Midwest so that the Navy would have a national rather than a regional character), and that more places in the entering class at the Naval Academy should be opened to enlisted men selected by competitive examinations. The Navy school system for enlisted men that he created was ahead of anything like it in any other navy in the world. That he also made the Navy "dry" did not add to the low regard in which he already was held by many commissioned officers who thought his reforms would undermine their traditional authority.

Daniels's effort to improve dramatically the capabilities of enlisted sailors was helped along by the coincidence of technology, specifically by the substitution of oil fuel for coal. "Coaling ship" was a kind of nightmare, and shoveling coal was very rough work. Captain Frederick A. Edwards was a midshipman on battleship *Michigan* in 1920, when "about every ten days or so we coaled ship." The work itself was bad enough, but the aftereffects were just as bad:

> The coal dust permeated throughout the ship. Our lockers were closed and sealed with papers to keep out the coal dust, but when you got your clothes out for inspection, the 'whites' were stained with black streaks. You hosed the ship down and scrubbed it the best you could. . . . It took even longer to clean up than it did to coal ship. Then, depending upon the schedule, we did it all over again.[18]

Sailors constantly busy with coaling, and later with cleaning up the mess coaling always left, had neither the time nor the energy to study. The switch to oil freed them from drudgery and gave them time to learn.

The introduction of oil fuel was one of a number of new technologies that required Navy officers to recruit, train, and lead more intelligent enlisted men. The greater use of electricity, radio communications, the development of the submarine and the airplane, and the constant improvement in the power and sophistication of ships' steam plants forced average naval officers to stay on their toes and offered incentives to the really bright ones to improve their technical and scientific knowledge.

Anyone who doubts the impact of technology on the Navy's officers should consult Rear Admiral David Taylor's *The Speed and Power of Ships*, first published in 1910. Taylor and his contemporaries bootstrapped the Navy into the twentieth century. Taylor himself built the first towing tank in the Navy and the Navy's first wind tunnel. He held the title of the Navy's chief constructor (ship designer), was a president of the Society of Naval Architects and Marine Engineers, and was the vice-chairman of the National Advisory Committee for Aeronautics.[19]

Under him, and under his contemporaries in the Navy's bureaus of Ordnance, Steam Engineering, and Yards and Docks, there developed a cadre of scientifically knowledgeable and wonderfully competent engineers who, within often severe budget constraints, kept the Navy at the forefront of technological innovation. In World War I, for example, the Royal Navy had clearly led the U.S. Navy in areas such as fire control, radio communications, and aviation. By 1941, the tables had turned.

The third factor that moved the Navy away from its "aristocratic" status was the influx of new kinds of officers and enlisted men. The non-aristocratic officers entered the Navy largely through the Reserve Officer Training Corps (ROTC, created in 1925) and the Aviation Cadet Program, established in 1935. Though the path to major command was closed to almost all young officers *except* Naval Academy graduates, the Navy moved gradually and steadily during the years between World Wars I and II to open its officer ranks to talent that did not pass through the indoctrination that marked the course of "study" at Annapolis.

The nature of the enlisted force changed because of the Great Depression. With most educational and economic opportunities closed to bright, energetic young men, thousands sought refuge in the Navy, giving the service some of the most capable enlisted men in its history. Great numbers of these men did not see their officers as living "a removed, privileged existence almost beyond aspiration . . . supervising every detail of their existences."[20] The more creative officers, such as Chester Nimitz, learned how much potential there was in these new men and thereby prepared themselves for the great influx of civilians in the coming war. The Navy, opened to democratic and modern ideas by Secretary Daniels, gradually abandoned the strict line (a "caste" barrier, to use the words of Marcus Goodrich) between officers and enlisted men and became the service depicted in such classics as *The Caine Mutiny* and *Mister Roberts*.

And always, as today, the captain was the one man responsible for his ship. In August 1916, armored cruiser *Memphis* (ACR-10) was suddenly literally buried by a massive tidal wave in the harbor of Santo Domingo, in the Dominican Republic. Her captain was the talented, articulate Edward L. Beach Sr. In his autobiography, Beach acknowledged that "my noble, splendid ship, *Memphis*—in the face of overwhelming, destroying force, though herself destroyed, yet by the soul of the U.S. Navy which built her and which had guided and controlled her on the day of her destruction—saved all but 20 of the 850 lives on board at the time."

What did he mean by the phrase, "the soul of the U.S. Navy"? Beach explained:

> Naval officers had designed that ship; had ordered every rivet that was driven; had made the drawings of every detail of machinery and hull; and the ship had been built under the immediate supervision of naval officers. The officers and men on board had been trained for their duties by officers of the Navy under Navy Department direction. These officers had inherited the traditions and experiences of our Navy. . . . And the men on board the *Memphis* on 29 August 1916 had maintained these traditions by their own conduct and actions.[21]

This extraordinary testament was a combined description and affirmation of the roles and the ideal values of the officers of the Navy in the years before World War II.

Tennessee and *Nevada* shoulder their way through moderate seas in the 1930s. This is the photograph that started this book. Both ships illustrate the defining characteristics of American battleships of the time: heavy firepower and a wide beam—just wide enough to fit through the Panama Canal. James C. Fahey, who wrote a short but very useful illustrated guide to the Navy in 1939, called battleships "the gauge of Sea Power."—*Navy Department, National Archives*

The Norfolk Navy Yard gave *Idaho* (BB-42) a dramatic makeover: a redesigned superstructure, new boilers, a very visible (along her waterline) "blister" to increase her underwater protection, 30-degree elevation for her 14-inch guns, new antiaircraft guns, and, of course, new catapults for her three spotting planes. Her silhouette was dramatically different from that of the modernized *Texas, Nevada,* and *Arizona,* with their towering tripod masts.
—*Navy Department, National Archives*

Oklahoma (BB-37) firing her ten 14-inch guns to starboard in 1919. She and sister *Nevada* set a pattern for all the battleships of her generation: heavy guns, great steaming endurance (from oil fuel), moderate speed, and protective armor concentrated "where it mattered." *Nevada*, however, had steam turbine engines. *Oklahoma*'s were reciprocating—the largest such engines in any U.S. Navy battleship. —*Navy Department, National Archives*

Oklahoma about fifteen years later. Very large tripods have replaced the cage masts because of her new and heavier fire control equipment. Her 14-inch guns now elevate to 30 degrees, and her 5-inch broadside guns have been moved a deck higher. She also has a new battery of eight 5-inch antiaircraft guns, plus three seaplanes for spotting gunfire and two aircraft catapults. She epitomizes American battleship design: speed has been sacrificed for defensive armor and steaming range. —*Navy Department, National Archives*

North Carolina (BB-55) was the first of the battleships authorized by the Naval Parity Act of 1934. Though built to the tonnage limit set initially by the Washington Naval Treaty, she carried nine 16-inch guns at a speed significantly greater than that of the existing ships of the battle line. Work on her began in 1937, though she was commissioned just before this photograph was taken in April 1941.
—*Navy Department, National Archives*

Indiana was one of four new battleships armed with 16-inch guns and designed with armor protection against 16-inch shells. *North Carolina* had been designed with protection against 14-inch shells. Construction of *Indiana* did not begin until November 1939, and she was not commissioned until April 1942. This photo shows her fitting out at the Newport News Shipbuilding and Dry Dock Company in Norfolk, Virginia.
—*Navy Department, National Archives*

Heavy cruiser *Augusta* (CA-31) being completed at Newport News Shipbuilding and Dry Dock Company in 1930. Ordered in 1927 and launched at the beginning of 1928, she was commissioned in January 1931. The British naval commentator Hector Bywater called such heavily armed (8-inch guns) but lightly protected cruisers "eggshells armed with hammers."
—*Mariners' Museum, Newport News, Virginia*

Heavy cruisers of the Scouting Force maneuvering off the California coast in 1939. This is Division 5, with *Chicago* (CA-29) closest to the camera. Next distant is *Portland*, and behind her are *Louisville* (CA-28) and *Chester* (CA-27).
—*Navy Department, National Archives*

Astoria (CA-34) was one of a class of seven successors to the six Northampton-class cruisers that were commissioned between 1934 and 1937. Though displacing about the same tonnage as the Northamptons, *Astoria* and her sisters were much better protected. The faces of the turrets of the former, for example, were protected by 2.5 inches of armor. In the latter, the corresponding figure was 8 inches. All of the eighteen "treaty" heavy cruisers saw service in World War II, and seven were sunk in battle. —*Navy Department, National Archives*

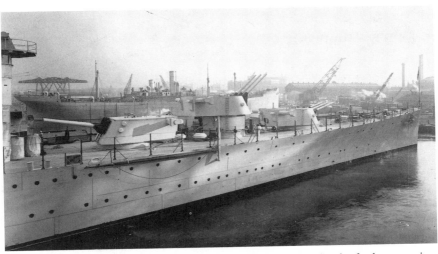

The three forward 6-inch gun turrets of light cruiser *Helena* (CL-50) shortly after her commissioning in September 1939. The volume of fire from her fifteen 6-inch guns made her a threat to even the heavy cruisers, whose 8-inch guns packed a greater wallop but had a slower rate of fire. The firepower of these ships was instrumental in convincing the U.S. Navy to accept the argument of the Royal Navy at the London Naval Conference of 1930 that 6-inch gun cruisers could be substituted one-for-one for the 8-inch gun type. —*Navy Department, National Archives*

Atlanta (CL-51), namesake of the last class of American light cruisers officially constrained in size and firepower by international agreement. The ship is shown at her builder's yard about a month after her launching in September 1941. Armed with sixteen dual-purpose 5-inch guns, eight torpedo tubes, and sixteen heavy antiaircraft machine guns, *Atlanta* and her sisters were designed to serve as the tactical replacements for the older Omaha class light cruisers.
—Navy Department, National Archives

Destroyer *Dunlap* (DD-384) cuts through the water two months after her commissioning in 1937. Authorized by the Naval Parity Act of 1934, *Dunlap* was named for a highly decorated Marine brigadier general. This photograph projected the Navy's image of the new destroyers whose tonnage was limited by the London Naval Treaty of 1930: high speed coupled with firepower, with powerful engines driving guns and torpedoes.
—Navy Department, National Archives

Destroyer *Jacob Jones* (DD-130) in a dry dock at Mare Island, California, after a collision with another destroyer. The ship was named after a captain who became famous as the commander of frigate *Macedonian* in battles with the Barbary "pirates" in the early part of the nineteenth century. Destroyers often carried out high-speed maneuvers at night and through smoke screens. Collisions were the inevitable result.
—*Navy Department, National Archives*

940-30   U.S.S. JACOB JONES
DRY DOCK Nº 2 MARE ISLAND, CAL.
NOVEMBER 18, 1930

U.S.S. IDAHO (BB42)
ON ARRIVAL FOR MODERNIZATION
NEAR HEAD ON VIEW
NORFOLK NAVY YD.   PORTS'H, VA
SERIAL No. 834-31   1 OCT. 1931

Idaho docked in Norfolk, about to begin her modernization. In the distance is a Northampton-class heavy cruiser. *Idaho* has a very spare superstructure and light cage masts for her obsolete spotting equipment. Her 14-inch guns only elevate to 15 degrees, and her forward casemates for 5-inch broadside guns have already been plated over because the guns in them could not be worked in a heavy sea.
—*Navy Department, National Archives*

Above *Idaho*'s bridge in this 1936 photograph is a "range clock," which told the battleship ahead of her in formation the range at which her guns were shooting. Above that are her secondary battery range finder, main and secondary battery spotting optics, and the new director for her 5-inch antiaircraft guns. *Idaho* and sisters *New Mexico* and *Mississippi* (BB-41) were the last battleship modernizations of the 1930s. Plans to modernize the Tennessees and Colorados were set aside because the Navy could not risk having them out of commission while they were being rebuilt. —*Navy Department, National Archives*

A 16-inch gun being lifted out of its turret on battleship *Maryland* (BB-46) at Puget Sound Navy Yard in December 1927. It took just three hours and twenty minutes to lift out the old gun and replace it with a new one. This is an example of the "material management" so necessary to keep the Navy's ships in a ready condition. Note the aircraft catapult on top of the superimposed 16-inch turret.
—*Navy Department, National Archives*

The loading crew of a 6-inch, 53-caliber gun on light cruiser *Memphis* stand by the breech of their gun, waiting to begin the loading cycle. The men who elevate and traverse the gun are hidden from view inside the circular armored casemate forward of the breech. The sailor just to the right of the breech with the earphones is the plugman. He'll open the breech to begin the loading process. The sailor holding the long pole will ram the shell home once he's convinced that the bore of the gun is clear of burning powder. The powderman holds the long cartridge bag, and three shellmen hold 105 lb. shells. —*Navy Department, National Archives*

The gun's breech is open and the bore is clear. The trayman on the far left will use a metal tray to protect the threads of the breech from being damaged as the next shell is inserted into the breech. Though three shells are exposed, only one charge of powder has been removed from its protective case. The tall pillar at the lower left is an elevator for the cans containing the powder cartridges. —*Navy Department, National Archives*

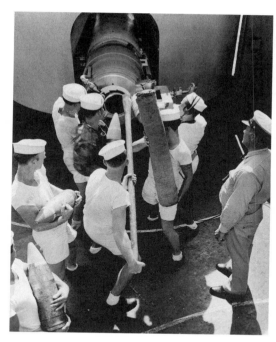

The first shellman is about to insert his shell. Note that he wears a special leather jacket to absorb any oil or Vaseline still coating the shell. You can just see the plugman swinging his left forearm across the inside of the breechblock. He's wiping the "plug" clean of any residue from the previous firing. The rammerman is prepared to seat the shell once it's placed in the breech.
—*Navy Department, National Archives*

The tray's been withdrawn, the shell's properly seated, and the powderman is inserting the cartridge. The second powderman is standing next to the starboard 6-inch casemate. The third powderman is ready to pull a closed cartridge can from the rack of ready charges. The first shellman already has the next shell cradled in his arms.
—*Navy Department, National Archives*

This is plugman John Cofer of *Memphis*, boatswain's mate, second class. He uses the towel wrapped around his forearm to wipe the face of the "plug," or breechblock. Around his waist is a belt holding ignition primers. He will put one into the breechblock with each shell and powder cartridge. The plugman made sure that the breech was properly closed and latched. He was one of the few members of the gun crew allowed to speak while the gun was being loaded, and he was the only one—besides the gun captain—allowed to handle the primer that set off the cartridge inside the breech. —*Navy Department, National Archives*

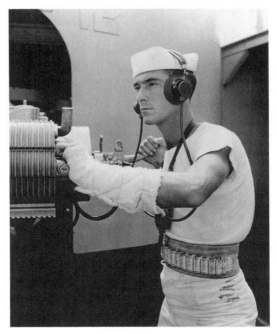

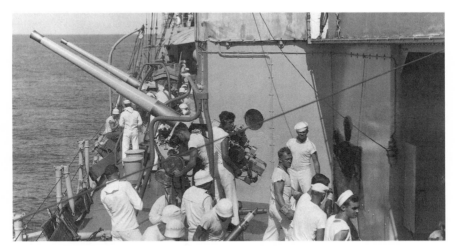

Gunners serving a 3-inch, 50-caliber antiaircraft gun on *Milwaukee*, a sister of *Memphis*. These guns were elevated and traversed by hand. The 3-inch shells were fused to explode at a particular altitude. Shell and powder cartridge were "fixed" together, unlike the separate shell and cartridge fired by the ship's 6-inch guns. There are more shellmen supporting this gun than the 6-inch because the rate of fire for this weapon was greater. Expended cartridges are visible on the deck to either side of the breech. Some of the sailors have turned down their white hats to shield their faces and ears from the sun. —*Naval Historical Center, courtesy of Mr. Franklin Moran*

Like most light cruisers of her vintage, *Memphis* was mostly guns and engines—powerful enough to smother a destroyer with her 6-inch guns and fast enough to slip away from any threatening battleship. This photograph shows six of her original twelve 6-inch guns—two in a gunhouse forward and four in single casemates just before the bridge. Behind and above the gunhouse is a single 3-inch antiaircraft gun. Just above it is the range finder for the 6-inch guns, and immediately above that is the height finder for the 3-inch antiaircraft guns. —*Navy Department, National Archives*

A lieutenant commander, armed with a .45-caliber pistol and his dress sword, and sporting a gas mask, on the bridge of battleship *Oklahoma* in 1925. The Navy took the possibility of gas attack on ships very seriously in the 1920s and '30s, though little was said about it publicly.
—*Naval Historical Center, courtesy of Captain C. M. James*

Officers, assisted by enlisted personnel, "shooting the sun" in a Navy publicity photograph from the 1930s. They are using sextants to determine the altitude of the sun above the horizon at a specific time. They will use that information to determine the ship's position. The summer white uniforms were standard for both officers and enlisted men, but compare these with the working dress of the gun crew of *Memphis*. —*Navy Department, National Archives*

Led by *Idaho* (her hull number, 42, is painted on top of her forward superimposed 14-inch turret), battleship divisions of the Battle Force form a column from a line of divisions and salute President Franklin D. Roosevelt during a fleet review near San Diego, California, in October 1935. This is the kind of maneuver that the battleship divisions (three ships per division vs. the four of the 1920s) practiced constantly so that they could carry it out despite the confusion and damage resulting from the gunfire and bombing that would take place during an actual engagement.
—*Navy Department, National Archives*

Conning a four-stack destroyer, as described by Cdr. H. H. Frost in his *On a Destroyer's Bridge*, could be dangerous as well as exhilarating. This is *Graham* (DD-192) at the New York Navy Yard after being rammed and severely damaged by the merchant ship *Panama* in December 1921. Though *Graham* appears undamaged in this view, the dark horizontal stain down her side shows how deeply she settled in the water after she was struck. Named for a former Secretary of the Navy, *Graham* was judged not worth rebuilding, and her hulk was sold for scrap in September 1922.
—*Navy Department, National Archives*

5
THE TACTICS OF A BATTLE LINE ENGAGEMENT

In the years after World War II, the prewar Navy was criticized by a variety of commentators for having outmoded tactical ideas—for being dominated by the "gun club," a clique of "battleship admirals" who stubbornly refused to acknowledge the power of carrier aircraft and submarines. It took Japan's attack on Pearl Harbor, or so the story goes, to break the hammerlock these conservative officers had on the fleet's thinking. The truth is far more complex than that.

In the interwar period the Navy's concept of warfare at sea was dominated by the ideas of the naval officer and strategist Alfred Thayer Mahan (1840–1914). Mahan placed supreme emphasis on a single climactic fleet engagement—the battle that would give the winner the freedom to use the seas at will. Consequently, U.S. Navy officers, like their peers in Japan and Britain, looked forward to waging one decisive battle between whole fleets. In this battle the U.S. fleet would face an enemy fleet, most likely that of Japan, somewhere in the open ocean, distant from land bases, and the outcome would be decided by combat between those ships capable of dealing out and resisting the heaviest blows. Triumph in this duel would give the U.S. Navy control of the sea and ultimate victory ashore.

In pursuit of this goal the Navy faced a complex problem. Through most of the interwar period the fleet was restricted in size and fighting power by the naval limitation treaties and the parsimonious appropriations of Congress. These factors combined to make it impossible to utilize the industrial power of the United States to out-build potential adversaries in peacetime.

The advancing pace of technology further complicated an already complex situation. Airplanes, for example, rapidly increased in range and striking power. Submarine torpedoes became more powerful and gained greater range; what had once been a threat only to stationary or slowly moving warships became a powerful threat to the battle line. Battleships increased in potency as well. Although new construction was forbidden by treaty, existing ships became more powerful with the addition of state-of-the-art fire control systems and improved armor-piercing shells.

How could the Navy fight and win a major fleet action in the face of new technological threats and the treaty limits on the size and number of ships? To piece together an answer to this question, Navy officers studied carefully the battle of Jutland, the only fleet action fought between the British and German navies in World War I. The Royal Navy's failure to bring its overall numerical superiority to bear on the German fleet and crush it became a subject of considerable attention at the Naval War College in the 1920s. Successive War College classes arrived at three primary reasons for the failure: poor approach dispositions, inadequate coordination and communication among the British formations, and the Royal Navy's inability to seize the offensive and control the pace of the battle.[1]

Senior American naval officers considered it essential that their fleet not make the same mistakes in any war with Japan. How could that be done? First, fluid maneuver in the face of the enemy would be ensured by the development of new tactical formations. Second, the need for aggressive offensive action would be ingrained in the Navy's officers through study at the War College and during tactical exercises at sea. For this to work as desired, however, some means had to be found to coordinate the actions of their ships in battle. Back and forth communications during the battle itself would not do. Such communications, through signal flags, had been prone to error during the battle of Jutland. To solve this problem of coordination, the Navy needed to promote a common understanding among its officers. It had to develop a tactical doctrine.

At the beginning of the interwar period, the Navy lacked an effective tactical doctrine. The doctrinal principles in place were very basic and provided little guidance for officers in battle. There was an acknowledged need for an improved doctrine. The Navy's 1923 *War Instructions*, for example, noted that victory would be aided by "indoctrination of the forces, so that there may be mutual understanding of the intentions and plans of the commander in chief and so that there may be coordination in the means and methods employed in carrying out the tasks assigned and of the necessary procedure when without orders."[2] However, the *War Instructions* of 1923 provided little detail to senior officers as to how such indoctrination was to be accomplished. During the interwar period, accomplishing it would become a major focus of fleet thinking and exercises.

The development of a common doctrine began with the adoption of a common vocabulary. In 1922 the Navy described its vision of a future naval battle in a War College pamphlet, *The Naval Battle*, written by Captain (later Admiral) Harris Laning. Laning divided the battle into distinct phases: advance, approach, and engagement.

During the advance phase, the specific location of the enemy would be uncertain. Because of the fluid nature of naval combat, it was essential that the fleet be arranged in a formation that would prevent the most valuable ships—the battleships and the auxiliaries of the fleet train—from blundering into surprise contact with the enemy. The specific term the Navy used was "security." A secure formation was one with enough screening vessels—cruisers and destroyers—dispersed far enough from the center of the formation to provide adequate warning of the approach of enemy ships, aircraft, or submarines from any direction.

The ideal solution to providing adequate security was arrived at almost as soon as Laning and his colleagues began thinking in terms of doctrines to govern the advance, approach, and engagement of *fleets*. A circular disposition was invented with the most important ships—battleships, the auxiliaries of the fleet train, and later carriers—at the center. Concentric rings of cruisers and destroyers would screen the larger ships and give warning of impending attacks. Earlier cruising formations, as these dispositions were called, had been rectangular in shape. Rectangular formations required more complicated maneuvers when changing course, and were less well disposed to provide security in all directions.

What the staff and students at the Naval War College recognized was that technology had given them ships of enormous power. Battleships could smash one another at distances greater than twenty thousand yards (over twelve statute miles). But this new technology had a catch: It had to be coordinated, and coordinated quickly, or a weaker enemy could escape, as the Germans had at Jutland. The British commander at Jutland had thirty-seven modern battleships and battle cruisers to his German opponent's twenty-one, yet he was unable to translate that advantage into an overwhelming victory. The U.S. Navy would likely have a 12–9 advantage in any fight with the Imperial Navy of Japan, and it would have to do better than the British.

With the exact location of the enemy uncertain, scouting was an extremely important activity during the advance and the approach phases of battle. At the end of World War I, cruisers did most of the scouting. Cruisers were powerful enough to fight their way past destroyers screening an enemy formation and had the fuel endurance to steam independently in advance of the main fleet formation. The aircraft of the day lacked the necessary endurance to be effective scouts. As a result, cruisers and even destroyers were frequently deployed in scouting lines.[3]

The ships in the scouting line would steam in a broad line abreast formation, with each scouting unit separated by slightly less than twice the limit of visibility, far out of sight of each other. Scouting units would be composed of one or more ships, depending on the specific mission. If simple reconnaissance was the primary goal, each scouting unit would be composed of a single ship. This would allow the scouting line to cover a large area and, it was hoped, locate the enemy. Once the enemy was located, the scouts would concentrate and shadow the enemy formation; they might also attack, especially if they could get at their quarry at night.

If attack was the goal of the scouting line, scouting units would be composed of several ships. The specific number of vessels varied depending on the exact mission, but the basic theory remained the same—to place enough ships in the scouting unit to give it the power to attack immediately once the enemy had been sighted and its position reported. The contact report was extremely important; it would permit the other scouting units located along the line to head toward the enemy formation and attack in turn.

Destroyers often performed this "night search and attack." Occasionally, a cruiser would be added to each scouting unit to help the destroyers break through the enemy screen, but the destroyers more frequently went in alone. In the fleet problems these attacks were very effective at locating and attacking enemy formations, but the difficulty of assessing damage in the confusing night melees that resulted also made it difficult to estimate just how effective these attacks were.

As the capabilities of airplanes increased, they were more frequently employed as scouts. However, one major limitation remained. They could only be used during the day and in relatively good weather. For this reason, daylight scouting lines based on cruisers continued well into the 1930s. It was only in the aftermath of Fleet Problem XX in 1939 that the obsolescence of the daylight cruiser scouting line was finally recognized; the scouting line of the "Black Fleet" was decimated when it ran afoul of a concentration of "enemy" cruisers supported by an aircraft carrier.

Even with their limitations, the potential capabilities of aerial scouts and the effect they would have on a future naval battle were well recognized by the early 1930s. In the 1922 edition of *The Naval Battle*, aircraft had two primary

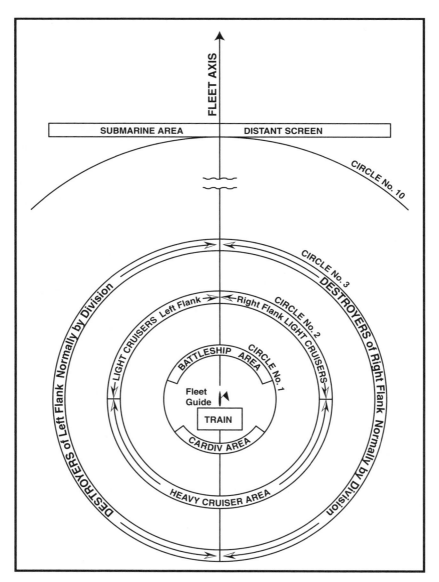

Figure 3. Typical Cruising Formation

roles, the defense of the U.S. (or "Blue") fleet and harassing attacks on enemy capital ships. Their utility as scouts was seen as extremely limited. In the 1933 revision, however, Laning gave aircraft a vastly expanded role:

> A Battle Force requires tactical scouting of far greater range than is provided by the outlying surface craft in our cruising dispositions. Such tactical scouting, in ordinary weather, can be done by aircraft; hence, having adopted a somewhat concentrated cruising disposition for the Battle Force in cruising or advancing towards the enemy, we must also provide means for air tactical scouting that will let us know of any enemy forces within several hundred miles of us.[4]

Advance warning of an approaching enemy formation could also be given by signals intelligence. The Navy placed great emphasis on the ability of radio direction finding to locate enemy formations. Low-frequency direction finding was relatively simple; the necessary equipment already existed in the 1920s. As high frequencies came into use, there was a need to develop high-frequency direction finders, but it took time for the Navy to develop them. Experience with experimental high-frequency sets in the fleet problems illustrated their effectiveness, and by 1939 high-frequency direction finding (or HFDF) was being used to locate not only enemy formations but individual submarines and airplanes as well. HFDF proved to be an important weapon in the Navy's arsenal during World War II.

After the location, size, and strength of the enemy formation had been determined, the approach phase would begin. Initial assumptions held that the approach phase would start when the opposing fleets were relatively close together. Cruisers (designated by the letters CA or CL) and destroyers (represented by the letters DD) of the scouting line would be in contact with the enemy. While they sought to fix its exact location and determine the composition of its force, the officer in tactical command (OTC), who was responsible for the conduct of the battle and generally the senior officer present, would shift the fleet into an approach formation and head toward the enemy.

In shifting to an approach formation, the fleet would reorient itself. Again, great emphasis would be placed on security, but as the general location of the enemy had now been determined, screening vessels would be redistributed toward the front. With the formation heading toward the enemy, contact in the rear was less likely, and it was essential that there be enough light forces far enough ahead to give the battle line time to deploy into battle formation before coming into gunnery range.

During the approach, the battle line would steam in parallel lines of divisions, three battleships (represented by the letters BB) in each division. From this arrangement, each division could quickly turn to port or starboard in succession. Such a turn would bring the ships into a single line, with their broadsides facing the enemy. From there they could bring all their guns to bear on the enemy's formation.

And such guns! In 1939, the battle line consisted of twelve battleships (not counting battleships *New York*, *Texas*, and *Arkansas*, whose guns lacked the range of those on the other twelve). Among them, these twelve ships carried one hundred and four 14-inch guns and twenty-four 16-inch guns. Together, these 128 guns could fire armor-piercing shells collectively weighing almost 105 *tons* to ranges beyond thirty thousand yards (seventeen statute miles), and they could fire this huge mass of shells twice a minute. The goal of doctrine was to focus this crushing firepower on the enemy fleet's key units before the enemy could do the same. It was essential to find and track the enemy, force the enemy commander to array his forces, and then deploy the battle line quickly so as to concentrate its firepower.

Once airplanes began to become effective scouting platforms, the approach phase increased in length and importance. The distances at which two fleets could sight each other increased dramatically. The approach, once measured in hours, could now take days. With the opposing fleets outside of gun range, aircraft were the most effective means to deliver a blow, and airplanes came to dominate the approach phase. Aircraft also forced submarines to dive to avoid detection, which meant that submarines would find their role as scouts reduced and their role as scavengers—cleaning up damaged units after a battle—emphasized.[5]

Airplanes could do more than scout. They could attack enemy ships; lay smoke screens; and spot for battleship gunfire, allowing it to be far more accurate and effective. Gaining the freedom to use airplanes in all these roles might prove decisive in battle. Achieving aerial superiority over the enemy became one of the most important activities of the approach phase. This could most effectively be accomplished by locating the enemy carriers and wrecking their flight decks, rendering future flight operations impossible.

The fleet problems illustrated the vulnerability of aircraft carriers to aerial attack, as well as the advantages that could be gained from achieving aerial superiority during the approach. In Problem X (1930), the Black Fleet's smaller carrier force gained control of the air when planes from *Lexington* located and attacked the

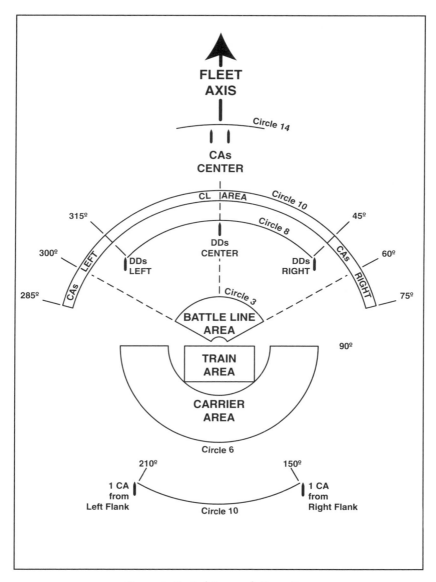

Figure 4. Typical Approach Formation

Blue carrier forces. *Saratoga* and *Langley* (CV-1), Blue's carriers, were both ruled disabled by umpires, and Blue was left at a severe disadvantage because Black's battleships used aerial spotting to good effect during the main engagement.

The approach phase in the fleet problems was dominated by this quest for aerial supremacy. The same was expected to hold true in wartime. Carriers were extremely deadly to each other, and the first side to get in an effective strike had a great advantage. To free the carriers for aggressive offensive scouting, commanders in the fleet problems often detached carriers from the main body, assigning them the task of locating and destroying the enemy carriers. This tactic proved more flexible than grouping the entire force together, but it exposed the entire fleet to defeat in detail. However, the advantage of securing domination of the air outweighed the risks, and by the eve of war carriers were operating independently in fast task forces.

Carriers had become a decisive striking arm *during the day*, but the threat they posed to one another was thought to be far greater than the danger they posed to a battleship formation. Experiments in the Fleet Problems showed time and again that, even when making determined aerial attacks, the small carrier fleet allowed by the Washington Naval Treaty could not reliably halt the advance of a battle fleet without battleship support to fall back on. Therefore, the final destruction of the enemy would have to be left to the guns of the battleships. This would come in the engagement phase.

The engagement would begin once the battle line was just outside maximum gun range. The battleships would deploy, with each ship in each three-ship division turning to port or starboard in succession to bring all the ships into a single line with broadsides facing the enemy. Deployment had to be done at just the right moment. In 1937 Laning observed:

> The deployment should be made before the battle lines come within effective range of each other. It should be made as late as is commensurate with being fully deployed when gunfire opens. Too early a deployment may require a reorientation of one's own forces before the battle lines close to gun range. . . . On the other hand, if the deployment is too late, the enemy may obtain an advantageous concentration of fire.[6]

As the battleships deployed, the remainder of the fleet would shift into a battle formation. Destroyers and light cruisers would concentrate at the head and the rear, screening the flanks of the battle line. The normal ratio was to place two-thirds of the light forces in the van, guarding against attack from ahead, and one third to the rear. Attacks from the rear were less likely due to the formation's speed. Through the 1920s and 1930s, as fleet officers gained more experience with their developing fleet tactical doctrine, the specifics of deployment and concentration were refined (see battle formation diagram).[7]

During battle, the main objective would be the destruction of the heart of the enemy fleet, the enemy battle line. All ships would work toward this end. Battleships would employ gunfire. Light cruisers, firing their many 6-inch guns, would intercept enemy destroyers as they advanced for a torpedo attack. Heavy cruisers, with their longer-range 8-inch guns, would take the enemy battleships or—especially—battle cruisers under fire. Destroyers would seek a favorable opportunity to charge at the enemy battle line and attack it from close range (several thousand yards) with torpedoes. If light cruisers were available, they would lead the destroyers' advance, using their firepower to open holes in the enemy screen through which the destroyers would pass.

Airplanes would perform in a variety of roles. They would continue to scout, keeping tabs on the enemy fleet and its movements. Fighter planes would engage enemy aircraft and prevent them from attacking or spotting for battleship gunfire. Aerial smoke screens would be laid to isolate portions of the enemy line or conceal the advance of a destroyer attack. Torpedo bombers, level bombers, and dive-bombers would attack enemy ships, concentrating initially on aircraft carriers, battle cruisers, and battleships. Specialized observation aircraft, launched from the battleships, would spot their fire to ensure that it was accurate and deadly.

By the end of World War I, the systems used to control the fire of battleships had become very sophisticated. At the heart of these systems were well-trained sailors, complex mechanical computers, and automatic electromechanical communication systems. These elements all worked together to identify targets, predict their movement, and rapidly bring them under accurate gunfire.

The gunnery officer initiated the process. He would designate the target by sighting upon it with his periscope. Target bearing information was automatically transmitted electromechanically from the periscope to the main battery director atop the foremast. Within the director the "pointer" would locate the target and track it with his telescopic sight. The precise bearing to the target was automatically transmitted from the director to the computers located in the plotting room deep within the ship.

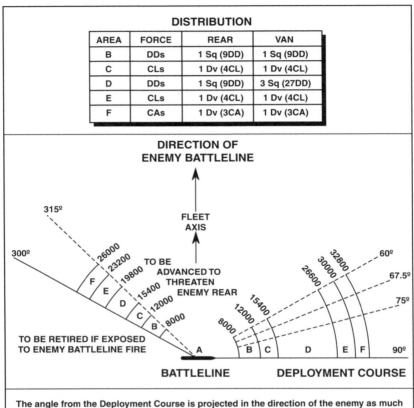

Figure 5. Typical Battle Formation

In the plotting room, the main fire control computer received the target bearing from the director and combined this with the "director offset"—the slight difference in bearing introduced by the specific target angle—for each of the main turrets, resulting in the correct target bearing for each of them. This information was automatically transmitted to the turrets.

At each turret, target-bearing information arrived at a dial in front of the "trainer." He would train the turret until the current bearing matched the target bearing indicated on the dial. The turrets would now be facing the target, and the large stereoscopic rangefinders in the officer's booths at the rear of each turret would be used to estimate the range to the target.

Back in the plotting room, the range estimates from each of the turrets, along with the estimate of the "spotter" in the main director, would be plotted, averaged, and entered manually into the fire control computer. The spotter's estimate of the target's course and speed would also be entered by hand. The firing ship's course was introduced automatically through a gyrocompass. With this information, the computer had enough data to generate advance range and deflection, predicting where the target would be when the shells arrived up to a minute later.

Advance range and deflection were converted automatically to specific gun elevation and gun train orders for each turret. The gun train order arrived at the trainer's station and the elevation order at the station of the pointer. The trainer would again rotate the turret until the turret bearing matched the bearing order presented on his dial. The pointer would elevate the guns until the current elevation matched the elevation order, also displayed on a dial.

At this point, the guns were ready to fire. The turret officer indicated to the plotting room and main battery director that his turret was ready by turning on his "turret ready" light. Once all of the turret ready lights were illuminated, the pointer in the main battery director closed the firing circuit so that all the guns would fire simultaneously the next time the main deck was parallel with the horizon. Together the men and machines of the fire control system could direct battleship gunfire accurately to ranges beyond thirty thousand yards.

At these ranges it was extremely difficult to spot the fire accurately from the positions in the masts—the spotting tops—of a battleship. At thirty thousand yards only the superstructure of the target would be visible; the hull would be hidden below the horizon by the curvature of the earth. With only a portion of the target visible it became extremely difficult to tell if shells were being fired at the correct range. At closer ranges spotters could use the target's waterline as an aiming point. When the waterline was visible, determining whether shells were being fired at the correct range was relatively easy for a trained spotter. At longer ranges, the accuracy of even the most skilled spotters fell off rapidly.

Accurate spotting of the fall of shell was an important part of battleship gunfire. Each time a battleship fired its guns, the shells fired made up a salvo.

Although all the shells from a single salvo were aimed at the same point, the multitude of variables involved—powder temperature, shell weight, wind, movement of the firing ship—would cause the shells to land over a large rectangular area. This area was called the *pattern*; it was the smallest rectangle containing the points of impact of all the shells in that salvo.

Patterns tended to be much larger in range than they were in deflection; that is, they were relatively long, but very narrow. This was because the variables affecting the flight of a shell had a greater impact on the distance it flew than on the direction it traveled. As the range to the target increased, the time of flight of the shell increased and the many variables had more time to influence the flight of the shell. Thus pattern sizes increased in both range and deflection as the range to the target increased.

Within the pattern, shells were distributed according to the laws of probability. This meant that over repeated firings (as would happen in battle) relatively few shells fell at the edges of the pattern and the majority concentrated in the center. The chances of a hit were therefore maximized when the pattern was centered on the target. However, the maximum number of shells in a battleship salvo varied between just eight and twelve. This limited number of shells made it difficult to determine the center of the pattern reliably. Although it was more likely that the majority of shells would be concentrated at the center of the pattern, probability ensured that this was not always the case. Consequently, the Navy emphasized firing all guns for each salvo in an effort to reduce this potential error.

This emphasis on maximizing the number of guns firing in a single salvo led to unexpected problems. The blast from one gun could interfere with the accuracy of others fired at the same time if the guns were close together. This would result in increased dispersion and "wild shots"—shells landing abnormally far from the center of the pattern. Occasionally, shells were even observed to "kiss"—to brush against each other—in flight on the way to the target. The problem was solved by the introduction of delay coils, electrical devices designed to allow a slight pause in the closure of the firing circuit to ensure that neighboring guns did not fire exactly at the same time. After their introduction, accuracy noticeably improved.

It was the job of the spotters in the mast tops to observe the fall of every salvo and report the necessary adjustments to the individuals working the computers in the plotting room underneath the ship's armored deck. Spotters had to be familiar with the distribution of salvos, understand the variations within them, and accurately determine the location of the center of the pattern. If the pattern was not centered on the target, they had to call for adjustments in the ship's fire to shift the aiming point. Estimating the location of the center of the pattern and bringing it on target was very difficult at long range.

Aerial spotting provided the ideal solution. From the air it was easy to determine the center of the pattern and its position relative to the target. Initial experiments with aerial spotting were very promising. In 1919, battleship *Texas* conducted a long-range firing exercise using aerial spotting. Lieutenant Commander Kenneth Whiting, an experienced aviation officer, told the members of the General Board that the increase in gunfire effectiveness with air spotting was likely to be as great as 200 percent.[8] Later estimates at the Naval War College predicted even greater effectiveness; in 1935 it was assumed that at a battle range of twenty-nine thousand yards air spotting would deliver six times as many hits as observation from spotters in the mast top positions.[9]

The potential was not lost on the Navy. Tactical exercises came to emphasize the decisive effect of long-range fire with aerial spotting. In Fleet Problem X (1930), *New Mexico* opened fire at the extreme range of thirty-five thousand yards. She was actually incapable of firing to that range at the time, but all battleships were considered to be armed with 16-inch guns and capable of long-range gunfire during Fleet Problem X in order to test the feasibility of the new tactics. In the mock combat of Fleet Problem XI (1930), the opposing fleets opened fire at thirty-two thousand yards. Fleet Problem XIII (1932) witnessed *Nevada* firing at thirty thousand yards. During Fleet Problem XVI (1935) fire was opened at thirty-eight thousand yards (almost twenty-two statue miles). In Fleet Problem XVII (1936), maximum gun range was considered to be thirty-five thousand yards; during Fleet Problem XX (1939), fire was *opened* at that range.

Simulations conducted at the Naval War College exhibited slightly shorter opening ranges, often because of visibility limitations written into the scenario. In Tactical Problem III-1934-SR of 1933 the battle lines engaged each other at ranges out to twenty-seven thousand yards; maximum visibility was twenty-eight thousand yards. Operations Problem II-1935-SR (1935) saw engagement ranges of twenty-seven thousand yards. In Operations Problem III-1935-SR (1935), visibility was restricted to twenty-five thousand yards; ships fired to that range once targets came into view.

Opening fire at extremely long range was stressed in the Navy's tactical publications. The *War Instructions* of 1934, still in effect well into World War II, stressed the benefits that could accrue from opening fire at these great distances: "Fire should be opened, normally, at the maximum range at which an effective fire can be delivered under the conditions which exist at the time. The advantage of an initial superiority is so great that every effort should be made to establish early hitting."[10]

Technology had made accurate gunfire at these extreme ranges a possibility; steady improvement during Long Range Battle Practices had shown the Navy's battleships could hit at these extreme ranges, but the emphasis on attacking aggressively at the outset of an engagement was not new. The advantage of hitting early had been recognized by the Navy long before. As the War College's 1922 pamphlet on main battery fire control had noted:

> The ultimate mission of a ship is offensive. It was built to fight. Not only was it built to fight, but, given reasonable powers, it is best used to begin the action as early as possible and continue it with unabated vigor until the enemy is defeated. . . . The ultimate object to be obtained is the destruction of the enemy. This is obtained by producing damage to his material and accomplishing the destruction of his personnel, or their disorganization by damage to his morale. In order to do this it is necessary to begin to hit as early as possible before one's own apparatus and personnel begin to suffer damage.[11]

Laning's *The Naval Battle* provided the framework for the Navy's developing doctrine, but the foundation was an emphasis on aggressive offensive action designed to seize the initiative and keep the enemy off balance. This principle was emphasized repeatedly in the Navy's tactical publications. Gunnery exercises focused on it as well. For example, in both Short Range and Long Range Battle Practices it was important to score hits early. By getting on target rapidly, a ship could achieve a much higher score than another ship that achieved an equal or even greater number of hits but got on target late. Getting on target late in an exercise meant fewer points.[12] The doctrine was: rapid, accurate gunfire at the longest possible range and at the earliest stage of an engagement.

This emphasis on aggressive action as a matter of doctrine also influenced Navy research and development efforts. The desire for quick and accurate gunfire spurred the development of radar and its integration into fire control systems.

The fire control systems themselves—the computers, electromechanical transmission systems, procedures, and skill of the men—were the subject of continual improvement and increasing automation. Servo mechanisms were invented to allow fire control directors to control heavy guns; this made the pointer and trainer within each turret redundant in ships built on the eve of World War II. Methods for spotting and gunlaying were improved; specific methods for firing at night were developed, increasing the accuracy of gunfire at close range in low visibility.

The introduction of radar into fire control systems was a natural outgrowth of this trend. Unfortunately, early radar sets lacked the ability to give accurate targeting information on their own. Their wavelengths were too long to provide sufficiently accurate target bearing data; but the range information they provided was more accurate than visual methods, particularly in conditions of low visibility. This made the investment in radar well worthwhile.

In the words of Admiral Frank H. Schofield, Fleet Commander-in-Chief in 1932, "I am of the opinion that we are stronger, quicker, and more effective when acting on the offensive than on the defensive."[13] It is easy to misunderstand the meaning of this statement. Schofield is not referring to an offensive stance at the strategic or tactical levels; he is indicating a preference for aggressive offensive action designed not only to cause the enemy physical harm but also to reduce his effectiveness by keeping him off balance, no matter what the tactical or strategic situation.

The actual conduct of the War in the Pacific illustrates the wisdom of this position. Consider the action off Samar Island in the Philippines, fought during the battle of Leyte Gulf in October 1944. The destroyers and destroyer escorts of Task Unit 77.4.3—the famous "Taffy 3"—had a defensive mission, to preserve the small aircraft carriers that were the heart of their formation. In this defense, they attacked the oncoming Japanese battleships and cruisers relentlessly. Although on the tactical defensive, their actions were decidedly offensive. Aided by a series of desperate U.S. aerial attacks, the destroyers and destroyer escorts managed to disrupt and confuse the Japanese attack; rather than seek further action within Leyte Gulf, the Japanese withdrew. Concerted offensive action was emphasized in all tactical situations.

Once a common vocabulary had been established, and the need for aggressive offensive action embraced, the formulation of a coherent doctrine moved ahead—despite restrictions on funding for exercises and for research and development. In 1930, the Navy produced the first in a series of doctrinal publications designed to increase the ability of the OTC to coordinate his forces in battle. *Tentative Fleet Dispositions and Battle Plans* was an important step forward; its templates for a variety of dispositions and battle plans were the basis for a vast playbook designed to ensure coordination in battle.[14]

Here is how it was designed to work. The fleet commander would draw up a series of plans and dispositions for situations he expected to encounter. These plans would be based on those provided in *Tentative Fleet Dispositions and Battle Plans*. There would be formations for cruising, approach, and battle. Plans would cover a variety of potential circumstances; sea state and the direction of the wind—the sea's terrain—would be accounted for, as would the composition of the enemy's force.

Ship and formation commanders would familiarize themselves with these plans; they were expected to understand the object of the plan as well as their own specific role within it. When it came time to execute a specific plan, the OTC would send out the associated signal. It would be brief and contain no additional instructions. Like a quarterback calling a play at the line of scrimmage, the OTC would set the plan in motion. It would be up to his teammates—subordinate ship and task group commanders—to be familiar with the plan and execute it appropriately.

The new format for plans and dispositions was tested during Fleet Problems X and XI in 1930. Vice Admiral W. Carey Cole, commander of the Blue Fleet, offered the following comment:

> The "Tentative Fleet Disposition and Battle Plans, 1930" give to us the greatest single advance in fleet tactics I have known in my years of service in the fleet. It affords to the O.T.C. an extraordinary increase in the flexibility of control from the beginning of tactical scouting through the general engagement. . . . Our greatest danger lies in an inflexible adherence to a conception of the enemy's strength and disposition made even under the best conditions of visibility for tactical surface and air scouting, but made with the fleets separate by forty to sixty thousand yards. We must have the tactical forms to admit of quick change, and the flexibility of mind to use them.[15]

Later tactical publications refined the initial concepts, but the major focus remained the same. The OTC would draw up and call the plays, leaving their execution to individual ship and formation commanders. Victory would hinge on their ability to carry out the plan. To balance this responsibility, they were given the freedom to act on their own initiative in furtherance of the plan's objective.

In the face of treaty limitations, the most powerful unrestricted weapon the Navy possessed was the skill and training of its officer corps. To leverage the full effect of their talents, the Navy encouraged their initiative and trusted them with the freedom to act on it. In the summations contained in the report on Fleet Problem XV of 1934 the Commander-in-Chief, Admiral David F. Sellers, explained this perspective:

> The Commander-in-Chief considers that our officer corps is the most intelligent and best educated of any in the world. It is our greatest naval asset today. He desires that it be used to maximum advantage in battle. Therefore, he expects that every battle situation shall be judged strictly on its own merits, and not upon instructions printed long before. Decisive, positive, aggressive action suited to the actual situation, must be the guiding idea of every flag and commanding officer.[16]

Battle plans were designed to meet the needs of a specific situation. But there was a fear that a plan, once set in motion, would be so rigidly accepted that officers would overlook potential opportunities. To reinforce the need for tactical flexibility Sellers eschewed battle plans entirely for Fleet Problem XV (1934).

> The second idea I have endeavored to emphasize is that of flexibility. As O.T.C., I commence a battle exercise with an entirely open mind. I have no set plan. . . . The Battle Line and its attached forces are handled in accordance with the situation that develops, whatever this may be. By the use of general signals it is possible to operate the Fleet in any way desired. Every situation is judged by its own merits. This is the only principle of naval tactics that is always applicable.[17]

Sellers was particularly interested in challenging his subordinates by having them deal with a constantly changing situation such as they would face in wartime. The goal was to encourage officers to recognize the fluidity of a combat situation and teach them that through their own aggressive actions they could control the pace of combat, imposing their will on the enemy. Once the battle began, effective control of the entire fleet from a single location would become difficult if not impossible. The OTC would have to trust subordinates too carry out the details of his plan. With the plan set in motion, success or failure—victory or defeat—would be in the hands of subordinates. The plan would coordinate their actions; their skill would have to provide the rest.

In parallel with the increasing emphasis on the initiative of subordinate commanders and commanding officers, the Navy began to stress the increasing importance of all arms to success in a major engagement. The battle line formed the basis for tactical thinking, but gunfire alone could not win the battle. The combined weapons of the entire fleet would be necessary. Laning, in the 1933 revision of *The Naval Battle*, stated it this way: "With so many weapons carried on such different types of ships it is apparent that if we are to get the maximum effect of all weapons and make our blow the sum total of the blows of all, there must be perfect coordination between the types carrying them."[18]

Coordinated attacks became an important part of the Navy's tactical thinking toward the mid-1930s. The combined weight of aerial attacks with bombs and torpedoes, destroyer attacks, and battleship gunfire was expected to quickly overwhelm the enemy battle line. The pervasive influence of this theme can also be seen in the design of new equipment. The scout bomber—the Douglas SBD Dauntless of wartime fame and its predecessors—was a product of the emphasis on aggressive offensive action. It was a plane designed to be able to scout with a bomb load, so that it could attack immediately on sighting the enemy. With the decisive influence aerial superiority could have on the battle, it was essential that enemy carriers be located and attacked as soon as possible. The SBD validated this concept at Midway.

In Fleet Problem XV (1934), carrier planes attacked soon after the battleships opened fire on the "enemy" fleet. This attack was very well timed and considered quite successful. Such coordination required planning and exact timing, but it was assumed that the benefits would make it well worthwhile. Fleet Problem XX (1939) also saw aerial attacks on battleships during the fleet action. By the ruling of the umpires, one battleship (*New York*, BB-34) was destroyed by a combination of battleship gunfire and aerial attacks. Dive-bombers and torpedo bombers inflicted severe damage, the majority of it early in the action. Battleship gunfire finished her off.

By combining attacks the Navy hoped to multiply their effectiveness. Airplanes were fragile. It was thought that they would not be able to fly through antiaircraft fire and score enough hits on a maneuvering battleship to do effective damage. But in a fleet action, the enemy battleships would have to steam a steady course or reduce the effectiveness of their fire. Radical maneuvers would make it difficult for the fire control systems of the day to predict the future location of the target. Battleships had to maintain a relatively steady course for accurate fire, as had *New York* in Fleet Problem XX (1939). This provided an ideal opportunity for attacking aircraft. If the enemy battleships maneuvered, they could avoid the attacking aircraft, but their fire would become wild. If they didn't maneuver, the airplanes could more easily torpedo and bomb them.

Battleships would also benefit from the combined attacks. Airplanes could harass the enemy ships, not only by dropping bombs and launching torpedoes, but also by strafing their superstructures with machine gun fire. These attacks would injure enemy personnel, particularly the spotters high up in the masts, responsible for controlling the enemy gunfire. With them incapacitated, enemy battleships would find it far more difficult to hit their targets.

Like aircraft, destroyers were also considered quite vulnerable in the face of battleships. In simulations at the Naval War College, destroyers were decimated when they approached the enemy battle line in good visibility. Staff presentations stressed this vulnerability and emphasized that destroyers would need support if their attacks were to succeed. Support could be provided by battleship gunfire or by cruisers leading the destroyers into the attack. Together, as a cohesive unit, the combination of ships and planes of the fleet, working toward a common goal, would ensure victory.

By the late 1930s the Navy's goal of developing a common doctrine to guide the conduct of its officers in battle had largely been achieved. A framework had been developed that would allow the Navy's units to coordinate their efforts in the heat of battle without the need for centralized control. The principal elements of this doctrine—aggressive offensive action, individual initiative, and the use of a battle plan—were hallmarks of the Navy's effective operations in the Second World War. But this doctrine—developed, it will be recalled, to remedy the problems of battle command and control revealed during the battle of Jutland—was not without flaws.

The emphasis on a single major fleet engagement served the Navy well in large actions, but this emphasis came at a price. Minor tactics—the tactics of individual ship types operating in small formations—were consistently neglected in the interwar period. Laning noted this deficiency in *The Naval Battle* in 1922 and again in 1933. The failure to prepare commanders for small battles between task groups of cruisers and destroyers proved very costly during the initial fighting in the Solomon Islands in 1942 and early 1943.

The Navy also found it difficult to impart the necessity of tactical flexibility to students at the Naval War College. In simulations, officers often failed to adjust their battle dispositions in the face of changing circumstances, preferring to stick to the staff-solution even when adjustments were obviously necessary. It appears that the flexibility encouraged by the Navy's doctrine was often a victim of the effectiveness of its own sample dispositions.

The Navy's concept of night combat was limited by the fact that Japanese forces would likely have the initiative. It would be the U.S. fleet that would be steaming west, across the Pacific; and Japanese air and naval forces would inevitably try to take advantage of the night to stage raids to whittle down the strength of the American force. The simulations at the Naval War College and the fleet problems highlighted this danger, and Navy forces prepared to fight at night. But they were not properly prepared by their own training for the kind of combat they faced in the narrow waters off Guadalcanal in 1942.

Night combat doctrine reflected the emphasis on the decisive battle. It was expected that destroyers on both sides would use the cover of darkness to seek out the enemy main body and attack with torpedoes. The Navy's destroyers were well practiced in this night search and attack. At the same time, the battle line would attempt to use maneuver and early warning by screening vessels to avoid the uncertainties of night action. These circumstances did not hold in the initial fighting in the Solomons in 1942, and consequently Navy officers found themselves at a disadvantage in comparison with their Japanese opponents, who *were* implementing their prewar doctrine.

But these specific failings were more than offset by the advantages of the prewar doctrine. The emphasis on aggressive offensive action proved its worth time and again, particularly in carrier operations. The victory at Midway was a replay of the aggressive approach phase tactics worked out in the fleet problems. Reliance on individual initiative and a decentralized command structure allowed the Navy's officers to make the most of transitory opportunities and attack the enemy when it was most vulnerable. The use of a battle plan ensured that these acts of individual initiative would further a common goal, and the planning itself served to prepare officers for their staff responsibilities in wartime.

At the beginning of the interwar period, the Navy lacked an effective tactical doctrine. By the end of 1939, this deficiency had been rectified. A coordinated doctrine, one developed in the era of the battle line but equally applicable in its absence, was ready to guide the Navy to victory against Japan in the Second World War. The ensuing battles, both those dominated by the aircraft carrier and the confused night actions ruled by the torpedo, would be won through the application of the principles mastered during the years that Navy officers struggled to apply modern technology to naval engagements.

6
NAVAL AVIATION

The primary function of the main body of carriers is certainly to
increase the major attack power of the fleet. . . . The use of heavy attack
planes from carriers is comparatively undeveloped and the results of
endeavors in this direction should be such as will warrant placing fleet
carriers in exactly the same category as battleships for improving the
striking power of the battle line.

> Rear Admiral William A. Moffett,
> Chief of the Bureau of Aero-
> nautics, to the members of the
> General Board of the Navy, 1931

Navy aviators returned from their experience in World War I convinced that aviation would play an essential role in future warfare
at sea. Senior officers, many of whom had trained under sail,
agreed with them. After months of hearings in 1919 on the future of Navy
aviation, the admirals sitting on the General Board counseled Navy
Secretary Josephus Daniels that "fleet aviation must be developed to the
fullest extent. Aircraft have become an essential arm of the fleet. A naval air
service must be established, capable of accompanying and operating with
the fleet in all waters of the globe." The board went so far as to recommend
that the Secretary of the Navy ask Congress to authorize "one carrier [for]
each squadron of capital ships" plus "a liberal appropriation" for "experimental and development work . . . in each yearly program."[1]

Secretary Daniels was willing, but Congress was not forthcoming. Only one
carrier was authorized, and it was a converted collier. Even in 1919, visionary
Navy aviators such as Cdr. John Towers could foresee fleets of large carriers supported by many squadrons of land-based long-range bombers. But before that
vision could begin to become a reality, some hard questions had to be
answered. What was the future of aircraft development, for example? Would
carrier aircraft soon gain the horsepower and range to carry heavy bombs and

torpedoes in quantities that would give a carrier's air complement the ability to smash enemy battleships? Were carriers, loaded with ordnance and aviation gasoline, too vulnerable to attack? What was the future of lighter-than-air craft, such as rigid dirigibles and blimps? Would seaplane bombers supplant carriers? Members of Congress had watched the size and cost of battleships creep ever higher, and they wanted some assurance that aircraft, aircraft carriers, and other elements of naval aviation would be worth the high cost of acquiring and supporting them.

As they endeavored to answer these questions to the satisfaction of members of Congress, Navy aviators also had to deal with the issue of whether all military aviation in the United States should be consolidated in a separate "aviation department" or a separate air force. Military aviation pioneers such as Brigadier General William Mitchell of the Army argued forcefully that future wars would be fought and won in the air by long-range bombers that bypassed enemy ground forces and struck at the heart of the enemy's industrial might. Modern war was industrialized war, so why not strike at the industrial base? Mitchell and his military and civilian supporters also argued that surface navies were obsolete. Only submarines could hope to hide from the firepower that aircraft could deliver.

Navy aviators faced a crossroads. On the one hand, siding with General Mitchell and pressing Congress for a separate aviation service like Britain's Royal Air Force would guarantee that aviation would receive resources and recognition. On the other, the kind of military aviation that Mitchell advocated was land-based. It emphasized long-range bombardment. Navy aviators had experienced the value of long-range patrols against submarines in World War I, but they had also carefully watched their British allies develop carriers and carrier aircraft as strike weapons, fighters, and scouts. Following Mitchell's lead would take them *away* from carriers, and away from the fleet.

Nineteen twenty-one was the decisive year. Mitchell had campaigned so hard against the battleship that it was decided to allow his Army bombers to attack German ships handed over to the U.S. Navy as war reparations. After a comic opera buildup in testimony to Congress and in the major newspapers, Mitchell and the Navy squared off over destructive tests against the German battleship *Ostfriesland* in July 1921. In violation of the rules for the tests, Mitchell's bombers swamped the stationary *Ostfriesland* with heavy bombs at low altitude, and film crews and still photographers caught the unmanned ship in her death roll.

But the Navy had the last laugh. While Mitchell and his airmen were planning to sink *Ostfriesland*, Congress created the Bureau of Aeronautics (BuAer) for the Navy, and Rear Admiral William A. Moffett was made its head. Moffett, a former battleship commander and superb bureaucrat, led the bureau until his death in the crash of airship *Akron* in April 1933. In July and August 1921, Moffett began his career as BuAer chief by convincing the Joint Board of the Army and Navy, chaired by General John J. Pershing, that Mitchell's pronounced obituary for the surface Navy was premature.[2]

Moffett also wrote much of Navy general order No. 65, which defined the new bureau's authority to cover (a) the development and production of aircraft, (b) advising the Chief of Naval Operations on "all aeronautic planning, operations, and administration," and (c) recommending how pilots would be selected, assigned, and promoted. Moffett used that authority to protect and expand naval aviation. He had no intention of allowing Mitchell to steal "his" aviators or commandeer for the Army's sole use the exciting image of flying that the young military aviators projected.

Moffett was aided by the results of the war games and simulations conducted by the classes of the Naval War College in Newport, Rhode Island. The president of the War College was the famous Navy reformer, Rear Admiral William S. Sims. Sims wanted the War College, already a center for innovative tactical and strategic thinking, to address the impact of new technologies—particularly aviation—on operational and tactical problems likely to face the fleet in any future war, particularly one with Japan, which Navy war plans assumed was likely. To make the games and simulations conducted by the War College classes more realistic, Sims and his staff solicited information on existing and *future* technology and tactics from the fleet and from the Navy's material bureaus. Moffett and his subordinates cooperated enthusiastically, allowing the students at the Naval War College to evaluate aviation as it was likely to develop and not just as it was.

Within a few years, the officers in BuAer, at the Naval War College, and in the fleet worked out a special relationship. Moffett's BuAer staff would provide the War College classes with information about aircraft, aircraft carriers, seaplanes, and so forth. This information would be used in the college's war games. Results considered provocative or interesting would then be tested in large fleet exercises or fleet problems. The results of the fleet problems were assessed within the fleet but also passed on to the staff of BuAer and the staff of the Naval War College. The result was a cycle of ideas (from BuAer), paper tests (the games and simulations at the War College), and then real exercises (the fleet problems), with the results of the real exercises feeding yet another round of the cycle.

But for this cycle to work effectively, fleet aircraft had to be able to conduct effective operations at the same pace as other units. The first carrier, *Langley*, was experimental; she had to become fully operational. The officer who led the effort to make her so was Captain (later Admiral) Joseph M. Reeves, a graduate of the Naval War College class of 1925. Reeves had carefully studied the war games conducted by his class, and he had decided that the key to making carrier aviation a potent military force was what later came to be called the *effective air effort*. Carriers needed to carry lots of aircraft, and they needed to be able to fling those aircraft in heavy waves at an opposing force in order to saturate the enemy's defenses. Yet when Reeves took command of the fleet's aircraft in the fall of 1925, *Langley*'s small complement of fourteen aircraft could not be launched or recovered back aboard quickly. The effective air effort was correspondingly weak.

The problem was that the American airmen were using British flight operations techniques. This meant that only one aircraft was on deck at a time, whether for takeoffs or landings. After a plane landed, it was lowered to the hangar deck before the next one was allowed to land. Reeves challenged *Langley*'s crew and the fleet's pilots to find a faster way of getting airplanes into the air and then, their missions complete, back down again. He was after a high sortie rate; he wanted the fleet's aircraft in action. That was the only way they could demonstrate their military value. In December 1925, it took thirty-five minutes to land ten aircraft; by August 1926, those same aircraft could be taken aboard in *fifteen* minutes. On August 9, 1926, *Langley*'s fighter squadron number 1 completed 127 landings in a single day, and Reeves noted that she could carry and operate twenty-eight aircraft and was therefore a fully operational combat ship.[3]

How was this transformation achieved? The key innovation was a wire barrier that separated the landing area at the stern of the carrier from the forward part of her flight deck. If a plane landed safely, its tailhook caught an arresting gear wire and it halted at the back of the flight deck. Plane handlers then unhooked it from the wire and pushed the plane forward, over the lowered barrier wires. Then the barrier was raised and the next plane was brought aboard. If the oncoming plane missed the cross-deck arresting gear wires, it would plow into the barrier but not into any aircraft parked forward of it. Once all of the landing aircraft had been recovered, the barrier was again lowered, and all the planes were pushed to the stern of the ship where they could be rearmed and refueled in preparation for the next mission.

By the fall of 1926, *Langley* operated like a modern carrier. Her flight deck crew was trying out different colored jerseys so that each man's role on the flight deck could be identified instantly. Senior enlisted men in yellow jerseys made sure the arresting gear wires were at the proper height above the deck, and younger sailors unhooked each aircraft's tailhook from the arresting gear once it had come to rest on the after end of the flight deck. Junior enlisted personnel in blue shirts moved aircraft around the flight deck under the direction of the yellow-jerseyed petty officers. Other sailors, wearing purple, tied down stationary aircraft. The men who fueled and armed the planes wore red cloth caps called "helmets" that covered their hair and ears. Fire fighting crews wore solid red outfits.

By the 1930s, watching a carrier conduct landing operations was like watching a football game. One team, in green, backed up the landing signal officer (LSO), who guided each airplane in for a landing. Once that plane had landed and had been unhooked from the arresting gear, the blue-shirted plane handlers took it in hand as it taxied over the lowered barrier wires. They made sure it was moved as far forward on the flight deck as possible. After recovery operations were complete, the blue shirts moved the planes aft, where the red helmeted refuelers and ordnancemen prepared the planes for the next mission, or where, after operations were complete, the purple shirts tied them down.[4]

One young reserve officer observing flight deck operations caught this atmosphere well: "On good days, on days when everything is going just right aboard, and when the planes are taking off within their few second intervals— on those days a carrier sings. She is a symphony of engine thunder and colored signals. She is ballet almost."[5] By the spring of 1939, the trained flight deck teams routinely launched seventy-four aircraft (a carrier's full air group) in twenty minutes and recovered all back aboard in forty minutes. Some flight crews shaved these numbers to eighteen and thirty-five minutes, respectively.

But carriers were only one part of the blossoming of Navy aviation in the 1920s. Because they were so good at extending the "eyes of the fleet," aircraft were placed almost everywhere. Tests in 1919 on battleship *Texas* had shown that gunfire spotted by aircraft was significantly more accurate than gunfire spotted from a ship's masts, and so all the fleet's battleships and the newer cruisers were given floatplanes that were catapulted off, performed their missions, and then were recovered after landing in the water alongside the ship that carried them. There was an effort to fit a destroyer with an aircraft catapult and seaplanes, but existing destroyers were too small to hold all the necessary equipment, such as aviation gasoline for the planes. Destroyers were also too "lively" in rough seas.

Submarines were another matter, however. Even a small submarine could carry an airplane in a watertight hangar. The plane's wings could be folded for storage. Once the submarine surfaced, its crew could unfold the aircraft's wings, and the sub could submerge until its deck was just under water. The airplane, equipped with floats, could then "swim" away from the submarine, take off, and scout a wide area. Submarine *S-1*, equipped with a small watertight hangar that housed an equally diminutive seaplane, tested this concept successfully in the summer of 1926. However, the value of the information provided by the small scouting aircraft was not thought worth the various costs and risks associated with converting or building a submarine to carry it.[6]

Because of the success of German airships in World War I, some Navy aviators, including Rear Admiral Moffett, thought that the Navy had a great future in lighter-than-air operations using both blimps and dirigibles. The problem that it might solve, as in the case of the submarines, was scouting at sea. For the sub, the problem was tactical—finding ships to attack and sink. For the fleet commander, the problem was strategic—finding the enemy's main fleet. The rigid dirigible, with its great range, promised to solve the fleet commander's problem. A number of Navy aviators had flown British- and French-made airships in World War I, and they returned to the United States convinced that the future of airship operations was bright, especially because the Navy had developed the means to replace the very flammable hydrogen used in World War I with the somewhat heavier but nonflammable helium.

That seemingly bright future was first clouded and then destroyed by a series of tragic accidents. The elder of us recalls seeing the absolutely huge, awe-inspiring dirigible hangar in Akron, Ohio, as a boy (where the giant airships *Akron* and *Macon* were built), and hearing his father talk about the crash of the airship *Shenandoah* (ZR-1) in a thunderstorm near Zanesville, Ohio, on September 3, 1925. *Shenandoah*'s commander, Lieutenant Commander Zachary Lansdowne, was an Ohio native, familiar with the violent storms of the Midwest. But *Shenandoah* and the other rigid airships could not climb over such storms, and the primitive weather forecasting of the time could not provide the slow-moving airships with sufficient warning to avoid such violent weather.

Los Angeles (ZR-3), built in Germany in 1924 and flown to the United States across the Atlantic, had a very successful career that spanned more than seven years. During that time, the airship made 331 flights of over forty-three hundred hours and also "logged almost 2,000 hours moored at masts out in the open." *Los Angeles* demonstrated that a large airship could moor to a special mast, rigged to modified tanker *Patoka* (AO-9), and could even refuel from a carrier. *Los Angeles* was also the test bed for a special trapeze that allowed aircraft to "hook on" while the airship was flying. This same trapeze was fitted to both *Akron* and *Macon* to enable them to recover the specially designed scouting aircraft that each carried *inside*.

Akron and *Macon* were fantastic machines. Each was 785 feet in length, with a maximum diameter of over 132 feet (for a length/diameter ratio of 5.9–1, rather similar to the length/breadth ratio of a battleship). Eight twelve-cylinder engines, rated at over forty-four hundred horsepower, drove these helium-filled giants at speeds ranging from forty-six to seventy knots, to distances over seven thousand nautical miles. Each airship could carry five Curtiss F9C "Sparrowhawk" aircraft, armed with two 30-caliber machine guns for self-defense. The planes, one of which is in the collection of the Smithsonian Institution's Air & Space Museum in Washington, D.C., could range out to over 150 miles from the airship, allowing the very large mother ship to hide behind clouds while her brood of scouts went hunting.

The whole point to these amazing creations was to find the Imperial Japanese Fleet at trans-Pacific distances. The aerial distance between Pearl Harbor and Saipan, then a major Japanese possession in the Marianas Island group, was about thirty-three hundred miles. At forty-six knots speed, *Macon*, with four scouting aircraft aboard, could just get there in about eighty hours. But she *could* get there. Compare that performance with the World War II–era Consolidated PBY-5A "Catalina," which cruised at less than 120 mph out to about a thousand miles (and then back again along the same path). *Akron* and *Macon* were 1924 concepts authorized by Congress in 1926 and commissioned, respectively, in 1931 and 1933. Both were lost accidentally. Neither flew more than eighteen hundred hours. They were magnificent failures, described by historian Richard K. Smith as "the first multimillion-dollar weapons system born of twentieth-century technology which was terminated without being tested in combat."[7]

But lighter-than-air survived for another generation, and multiple non-rigid airship squadrons served in World War II and even into the cold war. None of the wartime models, however, had the majesty of *Akron* and *Macon*. The two huge airships were stately and awe inspiring, while, as writer Fletcher Pratt noted, the motion of one of the smaller blimps was

> like a space ship just in from Mars, with an even motion, elegant and rather disdainful. Seen from within or from just below, it has the manners of a drunken elephant. It lurches, reels, staggers along crabwise over the ground, part of the time with tail aloft, the rest with nose up to forty-five degrees. It rides the ocean of air as a ship does water. When it strikes one of those waves which are air bumps, instead of slamming through it like a plane, it climbs slowly up one side with waggling tail and as slowly pitches down the other, heaving uneasily.[8]

But it's well to recall that such Dumbo-like blimps were the first U.S. aircraft to use acoustic homing torpedoes against enemy submarines in World War II.

One development dominates all others in the field of Navy aviation in the 1930s: the growing power, range, and ordnance-carrying capability of Navy aircraft, especially *carrier* aircraft. The most obvious sign of this important change was in the airplanes themselves: monoplanes gradually replaced biplanes. But what was happening—slowly at first and then rapidly as the 1930s came to a close—was that airplanes were becoming ship killers. The weight of *accurately* delivered naval ordnance shifted, almost suddenly, from battleships to carriers.

The newer battleships such as *West Virginia* (BB-48) could throw a huge amount of ordnance—over eight tons twice a minute. But at very long range—over thirty thousand yards—they could not count on getting hits with their shells at a rate of more than 5 percent. Five percent of sixteen thousand pounds (eight tons) is eight hundred pounds. By 1941, one dive-bomber carrying one bomb weighing one thousand pounds could knock a carrier's flight deck out of action—and do it at a range of over 150 nautical miles. Two such strikes could ignite the highly flammable aviation gasoline in a carrier's aircraft and turn the ship into an inferno, putting it out of action. Yet it wasn't the quantity of ordnance that a carrier's attack planes carried that mattered as much as it was their ability to deliver that ordnance accurately over long distances against *enemy carriers*, thereby gaining air superiority with one successful attack. Some comparisons will illustrate the trend.

In 1929, the two-seat Curtiss F8C-4, used as a bomber, was powered by a 450-horsepower engine, had a gross weight of approximately four thousand pounds, flew at about 145 mph, and had a range of less than four hundred miles carrying two 100-pound bombs. The Curtiss SBC-4 of 1937 had, by comparison, a 950-horsepower engine, a gross weight of between sixty-five hundred and seven thousand pounds, a maximum speed of 237 mph, and a range of 590 statute miles carrying a 500-pound bomb. The monoplane Douglas SBD-2 of 1941 could carry one thousand pounds of ordnance almost one thousand miles under ideal conditions.

Fighters also grew heavier and more powerful: the Boeing F4B-1 of 1929 was powered by a five hundred–horsepower engine, had a gross weight of 2,750 pounds, a maximum speed of 176 mph, a range of 371 statute miles, and a rate of climb of 1,724 feet per minute. The Grumman F3F-3 of 1938 had a 950-horsepower engine, a gross weight of approximately forty-five hundred pounds, a maximum speed of 264 mph, a range of 980 statute miles, and a rate of climb of 2,750 feet per minute. And the F3F was a *biplane*. Grumman's F4F-4 of early 1942, a monoplane, had a maximum speed of 318 miles per hour and a service ceiling of almost thirty-five thousand feet. In 1940, BuAer tested the prototype of the famous Vought F4U Corsair, which weighed about ten thousand pounds, driven by an engine of over two thousand horsepower, and which could outfly any land-based fighter in the U.S. inventory.[9]

The figures for aircraft performance, however, overstate what the planes could do in combat. Aircraft range was particularly influenced by how carriers sent their air squadrons into battle. Navy carriers operated their aircraft from the flight deck, which meant that all the aircraft for a strike against an enemy carrier would be spotted aft at the time of takeoff. The fighters, because they could get airborne with a shorter run down the flight deck, were first to take off. Then they had to wait while the rest of the squadrons took off and formed up. While they were circling their carrier, the fighters were burning gas—as were the dive-bombers that followed them into the air. Once the slower torpedo bombers were airborne and organized, the whole air group could head for the enemy.

What this meant was that the effective combat range of carrier air groups was at best about two hundred miles in 1941. That was as far as the loaded aircraft could go, drop their ordnance, and then return to their carrier. Fighters, which usually climbed above their own bomber formations to better protect them from attacks by enemy fighters, had even less effective range. But this was still a dramatic improvement over the early 1930s, when, in fleet exercises, carriers had to steam so close to "enemy" formations to launch or recover air squadrons that they risked being "shelled" by fast-moving heavy and light cruisers.

In the 1920s and '30s, engine and airframe technology, deliberately stimulated by the Navy and Army, stormed ahead, making aircraft obsolescent almost as soon as they were fielded. Tactics lagged, perhaps inevitably. In the summer of 1926, Captain Reeves, then serving as commander of the fleet's aircraft squadrons, assembled them in San Diego so that the pilots could spend three months doing nothing but working out systematic fighter and attack aircraft tactics. The result was a new set of "Aircraft Tactical Instructions."[10]

Fighters, for example, were instructed to operate in groups of three, composed of a section leader and two wingmen. Fighter pilots were directed to attack targets at relatively close range (several hundred yards) using "deflection shooting," where the attacking pilot approached his target from the side and aimed his machine guns at where his target was heading, not at where it then was. As aviation historian John Lundstrom observed, "A pilot trained in deflection shooting was extremely versatile, as he could attack from virtually any angle up to full deflection with a reasonable chance of hitting his target."[11]

But would such tactics, and the training that inculcated them, work with the newer aircraft, especially the heavier monoplanes and their high dive speeds? The answer, as Lundstrom has shown, was no. In 1939, the Commander, Aircraft, Battle Force, Vice Admiral Charles A. Blakely, directed two fighter squadrons to do what their predecessors had done in 1926: work out the best way to win at air-to-air combat, but using two-plane teams instead of the three-plane sections. As a 1927 report on aircraft tactics had argued, "Air tactics are, at present, in a very undeveloped state and their rapid development is mandatory. An annual period of air concentration, similar to the one just completed, is the best method of fostering such development." But in fact the Navy's method for developing and teaching air tactics was to do it at the squadron level. Though this practice made for cohesive, capable squadrons, it did not set the stage for the kind of fundamental reassessment that Vice Admiral Blakely ordered up in 1939.[12]

Few of the younger aviators worried about it. Most knew that even routine peacetime flights could be deadly. A pilot could accidentally kill himself with an instant's inattention. Early aircraft had open cockpits, and pilots often suffered from cold and fatigue. Bad weather was another threat; and night formation flying was extremely hazardous. But flying was exciting. Despite casualties, there was always a line of young men clamoring for the chance to fly.

Yet the Navy's Bureau of Aeronautics, working with industry, lowered the risk of accidents as it purchased and fielded aircraft that were more reliable, thereby increasing the hours both pilots and aircraft were safely in the air. That the rate of accidents per aircraft hours flown declined dramatically from the early 1920s to the late 1930s, *despite* an increase in the weight and size of aircraft, can be seen in table 1. The rate of fatal accidents per hours flown also dropped from the early 1920s to the middle and late 1930s, even as the number of pilots and flying hours increased. Put another way, the quality of flying improved even though there were more pilots to train and there were a lot more pilots and aircraft in the air.

The percentage of a pilot's time in the air devoted to training was high. In 1936, the proportion of total flying time for both Marine and Navy aviators that was taken up by training was almost 42 percent. In 1938, the percentage was about 41 percent. In 1939, even with an increase in the number of pilot trainees, it was over 34 percent. An important dividend of this attention to training was that the Navy knew how to develop pilots. Senior aviators such as John Towers knew that the number of aircraft and pilots would jump once war

Table 1: Hours Flown vs. Accidents, 1922–1941

Year	Pilot Hours Flown	Aircraft Hours Flown	Number of Pilots	Accidents per 1,000 Aircraft Hours Flown	Fatal Accidents per 1,000 Hours Flown
1922	42,590	39,808	NA	2.864	.275
1928	156,850	137,286	820	1.857	.138
1935	323,759	283,350	1,601	1.239	.049
1939	652,024	542,664	3,265	0.866	.053
1941	1,322,466	1,107,738	4,550	0.739	.060

Source: "Table I—Flight Statistics—Trends, U.S.N.—Aeronautical Organization— H.T.A., (Fiscal Years 1922–1941 Inclusive)," from File "DCNO Air, Administrative History, Vol. XV," Box 70, World War II Command File, Naval Historical Center.

Table 2: Trainers as a Percentage of All Aircraft, 1925–1939

Year	Total Planes	Combat Planes	Training Planes	% Trainers to All Planes	% Trainers to Combat Planes
1925	860	491	188	22	38
1929	1,038	664	205	20	31
1935	1,456	1,041	170	12	16
1939	2,098	1,316	262	12.5	20

Source: "Appendix 4, Aircraft on Hand, 1920–1965," *United States Naval Aviation, 1910–1995,* by Roy A. Grossnick (Washington, D.C.: GPO, Naval Historical Center, and Navy Department, 1995), pp. 447–48. The numbers include both Navy and Marine aircraft, and include planes in storage and planes assigned to reserve units.

threatened. What he and his colleagues developed in peacetime was a training program that, with some modifications, could crank out the required number of skilled fliers required during wartime. In effect, they learned how to "industrialize" the training process.[13]

This meant, however, that the Navy had to purchase and maintain a lot of specialized training aircraft. To make it possible for the Navy to have those aircraft and still field a strong combat aviation force, the overall number of aircraft had to be high. The relationship between numbers of training aircraft and numbers of *all* aircraft can be seen in table 2. In 1920, the Navy classified all of its planes as combat aircraft. There was no distinction between training and operational aircraft. By 1925, both the Navy and the Army had purchased special aircraft for training purposes. The number of "trainers" had jumped quickly and sharply. By 1929, as the Navy purchased more aircraft as a consequence of the long-term authorization of 1926, the number of training aircraft dropped as a percentage of all aircraft on hand and of combat aircraft. The percentages stabilized by the mid-1930s, so that the number of aircraft procured for training stayed at about the same relative level through 1939. This is an indication of a mature training program—one that can grow in parallel with the increasing need for both pilots and operational aircraft.

The advent of more carriers in the late 1930s (there were five in commission by the summer of 1938) turned out to be a mixed blessing. This might seem surprising. After all, the aviators had pressed for more and better aircraft carriers ever since *Langley* had joined the fleet in 1922. However, it wasn't clear just how multiple carriers and multiple air groups should operate together. For example, battleships had operated in divisions of four in the early 1920s and then in divisions of three in the 1930s. Organized by these divisions of four or three ships, the battleships could shift formation quickly, and, if necessary, each division could operate as a separate command. Could carriers adopt a similar organization? That depended on how their air groups were handled.

Was it better for each air group, composed of fighter, bomber, and torpedo squadrons, to attack a separate sector or portion of an enemy force while other groups from other carriers focused on different portions of the total enemy force? Or should the groups from separate carriers attack the same targets in consecutive waves? Carrier doctrine emphasized the attack; the carrier that struck first usually sank its opponent and gained air superiority. So how should a force of multiple carrier air groups attack? Simultaneously, with the groups bunched all together as a massive striking force, or sequentially, in waves?

This was a serious problem. Command and control of carrier air squadrons and air groups *in the air* was very uncertain. In an emergency, a carrier would push her aircraft into the air as quickly as possible, even if they didn't fly off her deck in the order best suited for forming up and moving to attack an enemy carrier force. Even if there were no emergency, squadrons often became separated once in the air, and using radio to try to pull them together risked alerting the enemy.

Moreover, one of the most serious operational problems facing carrier commanders was finding the enemy. That's why the Bureau of Aeronautics developed scout bombers, aircraft that could scout and then, if they found an opposing carrier, move right to the attack, hoping to catch her combat air patrol by surprise and planting a bomb on her flight deck. In any air group attack on opposing carriers, the tactical doctrine emphasized a coordinated strike by torpedo and dive-bombers, with American fighters protecting the bombers by driving off enemy fighters. But there was a tension between attacking immediately on sighting an enemy carrier and taking time to form up for a coordinated attack.

Prewar fleet exercises had shown how difficult it was to overcome these problems, and they had not been surmounted at the beginning of World War II. At the battle of Midway in June 1942, for example, carrier attack squadrons lost contact with one another and attacked piecemeal. Other squadrons didn't even find the Japanese carriers. But the basic doctrine of attacking first with whatever squadrons could strike at the enemy was sound, as was Rear Admiral Moffett's decision in 1922 to recruit naval aviators from the ranks of young officers. As squadron commanders, they would, he knew, have the confidence and the maturity to know when to commit their forces in an uncertain situation.

In 1939, the question facing the Navy's leading aviators was whether they could command a *fleet*-sized force of carriers, with multiple carrier divisions and many carrier air groups. If they could not, then they also could not in good conscience shift the bulk of the fleet's firepower from battleships to carriers. Vice Admiral Ernest J. King, who was Commander, Aircraft, Battle Force in 1939, realized that this was a problem that had to be solved before war began. Through exercises, he and his subordinates developed techniques and doctrine that he believed would allow as many as nine carriers to be maneuvered as a task group, and as many as twelve air groups to be coordinated in repeated attacks against an enemy force. It is this development that laid the conceptual foundation for the great carrier fleet of 1944 and 1945.[14]

Once having completed a thirty-day basic course, cadet pilots (mostly Naval Academy graduates) learned to fly through a rigorous training program at the naval air station at Pensacola, Florida. To complete the course successfully, they had to show that they could fly floatplanes, carrier aircraft, and multiengine seaplanes. Successful graduates were turned loose on the fleet. The survivors quickly realized that they still had a lot to learn.

In 1935, Lieutenant (later Admiral) John S. Thach was a Martin P3M-1 seaplane pilot flying with Patrol Squadron 9 (VP-9) based on seaplane tender *Wright*, in Alaskan waters. He recalled later that on the way to Dutch Harbor,

we passed by an island that was near the tip end of Unimak Island. We went on a few minutes more, and all of a sudden we were in the worst looking blizzard I've ever seen. You could just dimly make out the plane ahead of you in this formation of six aircraft. We held our course for about an hour hoping to run out of this thing, and then the skipper decided we'd better turn around and go back.

The last place we had seen before going into this storm was a kind of clay-looking cliff that was a different color than the rest of the rocks. We turned around, and in about seven minutes there we were right back again at this cliff! The wind had come up to about 60 or 70 knots, and our cruising speed was 80, so we had just been almost standing still in that blizzard.[15]

And that was just the first of a series of adventures on that particular trip. To provide more pilots for the fleet aircraft increase authorized by the Naval Parity Act of 1934, Congress agreed to the Navy's proposal to allow recent college graduates to qualify as "aviation cadets" and receive training as pilots in exchange for three years of service with the fleet. One of these cadets, Robert A. Winston, wrote an engaging memoir of his experiences in training and then in the fleet. He was, to put it mildly, moved by the experience of being catapulted into the air in a Vought O2U seaplane at Pensacola:

There is no more outrageous sensation . . . than that of a catapult "shot." During the first one that I sat through, I surely thought the world had come to an end. One minute I was sitting in the rear cockpit, . . . watching the preparations below me. I saw the catapult chief open the breech of the firing mechanism and shove home a five-inch shell nearly a yard long, filled with smokeless powder. I felt the plane shake and strain as the pilot in front of me opened his throttle wide, and braced my head against the pad behind me. Out of the corner of my eye, I saw the chief jerk the lanyard. Then time seemed to stand still—an unearthly sensation of rigid immobility and suspended animation.[16]

He was airborne.

But simply being airborne wasn't enough. Winston, and so many others like him, wanted both the excitement of flying and the sheer joy of piloting a wonderfully responsive machine. One such was Boeing's F4B-1:

Taxying [sic] out on the runway. I eased the throttle forward, intending to make a conservative take-off. Before the throttle was halfway open, I was astounded to find that the plane was fifty feet in the air and climbing with no apparent effort. . . . At first I over-controlled badly until I found that this plane could really be flown with the fingertips. I stuck my left hand out into the slip stream to see how strong the wind felt, and to my amazement the little ship immediately went into a gentle left turn. Experimenting further, I found that I could actually turn the ship in either direction with the wind resistance from my outstretched arm . . . this was incredible. It responded to the slightest touch. . . . It was almost like having a personal set of wings. I looped, dived, zoomed and spun the little ship around the sky, feeling it out and growing more delighted each minute with the way it handled . . . at last I was really flying![17]

Neither of the fathers of Navy aviation, Rear Admirals Moffett and Reeves, were hell-for-leather pilots. Indeed, both had commanded battleships before learning to fly. But they understood how unique the extraordinary pilots were, and they gave them enough rope. Moffett directed that a pilot's honest mistakes were not to be counted against him, and the chief of BuAer encouraged Navy pilots to break records and participate in air shows and air races. The stern looking Reeves was just as tolerant, as crack pilot Daniel W. Tomlinson IV learned:

Old "Whiskers" Reeves, as we called him, wanted to put on a demonstration of an attack on the flagship in the Pacific Fleet. So in October 1926, we went out from San Diego with [Curtiss] F6C Hawks and made this dive-bombing attack, and it really shook them up. When we got back from the exercise, we were laughing. We could look down and see people ducking and lying down on the bridge. We came down a little bit low. Those things made the damnedest roar you ever heard.[18]

Tomlinson was a hot shot, a natural. He was also a prankster. On a 1928 deployment to Hawaii, he was determined to avenge some embarrassing moments that a Navy squadron had suffered at the hands of Army pilots from Wheeler Field the year before. As he recalled telling his squadron, "We're going to take those crummy army pilots to town." With better airplanes this time around, "that was exactly what we did . . . we ran . . . them right back to Wheeler Field before we let go of them. We had fun. The tables were turned. That irritated the army pilots to no end." In revenge, an Army aviator buzzed the Navy planes as the latter were lined up for Saturday morning inspection, "missing the airplanes by five or ten feet, the pilot thumbing his nose as he went by." More adventures followed.[19]

But it wasn't all fun, by any means, as Robert Winston discovered as his squadron punched through a rainstorm in an effort to return to carrier *Lexington.*

Not until we spiraled down close to the water did I realize how much the ship was rolling and pitching. I had never seen her tossed around like this before. . . . The plane ahead of me was almost up to the ship. I saw the stern ramp rise yards above it, then drop far below. A moment later the plane was down, but instantly there was a blast of white steam from the ship's stacks—the signal for a deck crash. I pulled up and out to one side. . . . Circling again for another approach, I was again warned away . . . *my turn was next.*

This time the deck was clear, and I concentrated on the approach. At first I was high, then I over-corrected and approached too low—a sure form of suicide. A little more throttle, and I was back up in proper position. Now I was over the stern, which was luckily level for the moment. Chopping the throttle off, I held my breath and eased the stick back. There was a jolt as the wheels struck the deck, a jerk as the landing hook engaged the arresting gear, and I was safely aboard. . . .

At last I could relax. I exhaled slowly, and then the reaction set in. My knees began to shake so that I could hardly keep my feet on the brake pedals.[20]

All the planes got aboard. "Five planes were badly damaged, two of them wrecked beyond repair, *but not a single man had been injured.*" (Emphasis in original.) In such conditions, with their carrier pitching wildly, pilots could envy their counterparts who were assigned to the huge airship, *Macon.* Lieutenant Harold B. Miller, later a rear admiral, flew F9C "Sparrowhawks" from both *Akron* and *Macon.* He judged hooking up to them "the easiest thing in the world."

We would fly alongside that number one engine, which was about where the trapeze was, about twenty-five feet below the ship and maybe twenty-five aside from there. Then with our rudder, we would just skid under the ship slowly.

Now, you're under the ship and behind the trapeze. . . . At this point, the pilot has to change from normal horizon flight by looking up, so he is now flying on something that's up above him. . . . It was so simple because you had only one task to do, and that was to decrease the distance between the trapeze and your hook. . . . The hook was spring-loaded, so at that point when you hit it reasonably hard, it would lock . . . and you knew you're locked on, although there were a couple of times when I thought I was locked on, and I'd sit back fat, dumb, and happy and just fall off. That was no problem either.[21]

All in a day's work, obviously. Surviving *Macon*'s crash in February 1935 was another matter. Severe winds collapsed one of *Macon*'s tail fins, and the craft lost altitude.

We landed on the water in a horizontal position, just as gently and as softly as you please. People had broken out life rafts and dropped lines from [*Macon*], and the order was given to abandon ship. Those with any sense lowered themselves into the life rafts, and some didn't even get wet. . . .

Some of us stayed on board. . . .

Those in boats pulled off a quarter or half a mile away and huddled in a group out there. Here we were high and dry on [*Macon*], thinking how stupid they were. Then, the first thing we knew, instead of being horizontal in the water, the ship suddenly assumed a very slow upward movement to a vertical position. Instead of being fifty feet from the water, we were four hundred feet up in the air.

Macon was about to sink slowly by the stern, as her large saucer-shaped bags of helium collapsed one by one. Eventually, Miller and the other survivors clinging to the nose of the airship decided to abandon their perch and swim for it. As they did so, navigation flares still within that portion of the airship's envelope that was above water ignited gasoline vapor. "On the outside of the envelope was the red, white, and blue star of the national insignia, and the inside was all aflame. The silhouette of the star was the most beautiful sight I had ever seen."[22]

By the mid-1930s, naval aircraft were as colorful as decorated Christmas trees. In 1939, for instance, each carrier's squadrons had distinctive tail colors—bright white for *Saratoga*'s, for example, and green for *Ranger*'s. A squadron of eighteen aircraft was divided into six sections of three aircraft, and no two aircraft in any squadron bore exactly the same colors or markings. Each section leader's aircraft had a distinctive colored stripe around its body; the engine cowling was painted the same color. The second man's plane in that section had only the top half of its cowling painted that color. The third man's plane had only the bottom half painted. The section leader's plane also had opposed diagonal stripes of his section's color painted over the central part of the orange upper wing (for biplanes). This helped the other two pilots in the three-plane section keep formation on their leader.

Patrol planes and the spotters catapulted from battleships and cruisers were almost as colorful. By the late 1930s, the colors given these aircraft were also standardized. All had bright orange on their upper wing surfaces. Their engine cowlings were painted like those of carrier aircraft—a full coat for the section leader and partial coats for the second and third planes. They also had distinctive stripes around their midsections, behind their wings. Vertical tails and rudders were painted in solid colors or stripes. The rest of the plane was silver; white stars with red centers in a field of blue—the national insignia—were painted on upper and lower wing surfaces and on each side of the noses of larger aircraft.[23]

Many, many years later, Admiral Thomas H. Moorer, who had served as both Chief of Naval Operations and Chairman of the Joint Chiefs of Staff, recalled this golden age: "I still have many fond memories of those years between the wars, when there seemed to be more room, more tolerance for the individual, for creativity, and for freedom of expression. Every day on board ship, or flying long distances over the ocean, brought new challenges and adventures the likes of which we will never experience again."[24] It was a happy adolescence.

However, like most adolescents, naval aviation had its problems. Early carrier aircraft, for example, were fragile. Recall Robert Winston's account of his squadron's landings on *Lexington*. Planes got broken a lot; pilots less so. But the waste of machines and pilots added to the high cost of carrier aviation, and it wasn't clear in the early 1930s that carrier aviation was *the* essential war-winning weapon. Those who doubt this should watch the 1932 movie *Hell Divers*, with Clark Gable and Wallace Beery, and ask whether the F8Cs filmed flying off *Saratoga* were all that impressive.

Larger and heavier carrier aircraft might be faster and carry more ordnance, but larger carriers had to be built to contain them. Admiral Reeves once put it very succinctly when he said that carrier size (expressed as tonnage) was a function of aircraft size and weight, and aircraft size and weight went up as the need for longer-range aircraft with heavy ordnance loads became imperative. And they *were* imperative, because the Imperial Navy of Japan had its own carrier force augmented by squadrons of land-based bombers. For the U.S. Navy to fight its way through Japanese defenses in the western Pacific, it would have to have the best possible aircraft, and those larger, heavier aircraft would, in turn, require larger aircraft carriers. There was no getting around it. Carrier aviation was expensive—and would become even more expensive as time went on.[25]

Moreover, seaplanes and land-based bombers could carry heavy ordnance loads great distances, and many bomber advocates thought that these large aircraft could brush off enemy fighters and overwhelm enemy fleets with bombs dropped accurately from high altitudes. It wasn't clear in the mid-1930s that the future of war at sea belonged to carriers and their squadrons. As it happened, land-based *high altitude* bombers such as the B-17 were not good ship killers, but the Japanese Imperial Navy did develop long-range, heavily armed land-based torpedo and level bombers, and the squadrons of these planes posed a grave danger to surface ships without adequate fighter escort.

The future of naval aviation held both great promise and great uncertainty. The latter is the primary reason why the Navy did not rush to construct fleets of carriers once the major arms treaty restrictions were abandoned in 1936. But an adequate foundation of technology, training, and tactics was there. So was the aggressiveness for which naval aviators were (and still are) notorious. It was put very well in the Naval Academy's aviation textbook in 1933: "Consideration of self-protection must be abandoned once the actual attack is begun. From this stage on, the paramount governing idea should be to drive the attack home in the shortest possible time, regardless of outside interference." Backed by the nation's immense and sophisticated industrial base, this aggressive approach to military aviation, which was based on careful thought and extensive experiments, was an essential element in the U.S. Navy's success in World War II.

Two O2U-1 floatplanes of Observation Squadron 5 on *Maryland* in 1929. One is mounted on one of the ship's two catapults. The other is about to be moved by one of the ship's aircraft handling cranes. The planes seem flimsy compared with the massive turrets with their 16-inch guns, but the biplanes were an essential part of the ship's armament.
—*Navy Department, Naval Aviation History Office*

Destroyer Squadron 20 staging a mock attack through a smoke screen laid by aircraft in 1936. The destroyer closest to the camera is *Farragut*, commissioned in June 1934. Destroyer squadrons practiced such mass attacks so that, in battle, they could overwhelm the enemy's battle line with a swarm of torpedoes. —*Navy Department, National Archives*

Battleships getting under way in the late 1920s. Three patterns of superstructure are shown: the heavy cage masts of the Maryland class, the large tripods of the Nevadas and Pennsylvanias, and the narrow cage mast of the obsolete *Arkansas* (BB-33). —*U.S. Naval Institute Photo Archive*

West Virginia's 16-inch guns fire a salvo in 1931. Her armor-piercing shells weighed 2,100 lbs. *each.* The special shells used for target practice caused less wear on the guns' rifled liners. The cost of one eight-gun salvo was $3,600. Between 1924 and 1935, *West Virginia* won the fleet gunnery trophy for battleships five times.
—*U.S. Naval Institute Photo Archive*

Battleships of the battle line deployed in a column, with main guns trained to port. Leading the column is *Colorado* (BB-45), whose eight 16-inch guns could strike targets at a range of seventeen miles. Note her wide beam, which gave her both stability and a full measure of underwater protection against torpedoes.
—*U.S. Naval Institute Photo Archive*

Carrier *Saratoga* enters a smoke screen laid down by her escorting destroyers on a picture-perfect day in October 1934. In a clash of battle lines, carriers needed to be good at running and, if necessary, hiding. In 1934, carrier aircraft still had limited range, and a carrier attacking an "enemy" formation often had to steam relatively close to it to launch and recover her strike aircraft. —*Navy Department, National Archives*

Destroyer *Williamson* (DD-244) refueling at sea from heavy cruiser *Indianapolis* in November 1934. It was routine for battleships, carriers, and heavy cruisers to refuel accompanying destroyers at sea—especially the older destroyers such as *Williamson*, which had about half the endurance of the destroyers built during the 1930s. What was *not* routine was refueling at sea from the Navy's own tankers, which could not refuel warships at a speed high enough to avoid creating an easy target for a submarine. —*Navy Department, National Archives*

Repair ship *Medusa* (AR-2), completed in 1924, with five older destroyers and a destroyer converted into a fast minelayer. The outboard destroyer has had her torpedo tubes and boats removed. *Medusa*, with her heavy equipment and trained craftsmen, was an essential part of the "fleet train," the collection of slow tenders, repair ships, tankers, ammunition ships, and cargo ships that would create and support advanced bases as the fleet moved across the Pacific in wartime. —*Navy Department, National Archives*

Langley, the Navy's first aircraft carrier. By the time this photograph was taken, she was no longer an experimental carrier but an operational one. Her funnels could be tilted to the horizontal to clear her flight deck of any obstructions, and she had no "island" to generate eddies that could buffet the lightweight aircraft first used on board carriers.
—*Navy Department, National Archives*

Saratoga taking her air group on board in 1932. A torpedo plane has just landed. The flight deck plane handlers will push her forward, over the crash barrier, to join the other planes in her squadron (VT-2B) and have her wings folded. Then the barrier will be raised and the next plane will attempt a landing. This photograph clearly illustrates the U.S. Navy practice of landing all the aircraft in a formation in rapid sequence, pushing each plane forward behind a barrier so that the next plane in line can be landed. This practice allowed Navy carriers to launch and recover the maximum number of strikes. —*Navy Department, National Archives*

Saratoga carried a heavy battery of guns as well as her complement of fighters, bombers, and scout aircraft. Shown in this photograph are two of her four twin 8-inch gun turrets and three of her twelve 5-inch antiaircraft guns. When she was converted from a battle cruiser, it was thought that she might carry on as a fast scout if her flight deck were wrecked by bombing early in a battle. After the Japanese attack on Pearl Harbor in December 1941, however, she and sister *Lexington* had their 8-inch guns removed, and no attempt was ever made to use either ship as a cruiser. —*Navy Department, National Archives*

A Vought O2U "Corsair" landing on *Saratoga* in 1929. The carrier has both cross-deck and fore-and-aft arresting gear wires. The cross-deck wires brought the plane to a stop. The fore-and-aft wires kept the plane from swerving from side to side. The O2U has both a tailhook for the cross-deck wires and hooks on her landing gear to engage the fore-and-aft set held off the deck by the "fiddle bridges."—*Navy Department, National Archives*

Lexington passing carrier *Ranger* at sea in 1938. *Lexington* and *Saratoga* were fast ships. On her trials in November 1928, *Lexington* attained a speed of almost 35 knots. *Ranger* did not quite make 30 knots during her trials in April 1934. *Enterprise* and *Yorktown* were designed for higher speeds. The former steamed at over 33.5 knots on her trial runs in March 1938. —*Navy Department, National Archives*

An SU-1, a scout version of the early "Corsair," has careened over *Saratoga's* portside and come to a halt in the ship's after 5-inch antiaircraft gun battery. One sailor is ducking to avoid the plane's still-spinning propeller. Carrier landings were routinely filmed, many in slow motion. Some films still exist, and they reveal the hazards of failing to engage the arresting gear properly. —*Navy Department, National Archives*

A scouting plane from *Lexington* has crash-landed in the water in 1934 but is about to be recovered. Note the inflated floats. Later aircraft, especially monoplanes, were heavier and could not be kept afloat by the inflated bags. —*Navy Department, National Archives*

Ranger in 1937, with her funnels lowered (as they were during flight operations), entering Hampton Roads, Virginia. The palisade forward of her flight deck elevator reduced the buffeting caused by high winds. Significantly smaller than the converted battle cruisers *Saratoga* and *Lexington*, *Ranger* was the first U.S. Navy carrier designed as such. —*Navy Department, National Archives*

An F4B-3 of Fighter Squadron 1 landing on *Saratoga* in 1933. The plane following has been given a wave off and will take another turn in the landing circle before trying to come aboard the carrier. —*Naval Historical Center, courtesy of John Highfill*

From mid-January to mid-February 1936, *Ranger* operated her aircraft in Alaskan waters to see if a carrier could perform her missions in so harsh an environment. Both the Japanese and American navies saw the North Pacific as an area where they might clash, and both exercised there. This photograph shows an aircraft being lowered to the hangar deck on *Ranger*'s unique stern elevator. A doctored version of a similar photograph— without the stern elevator—was made public at the time. The photo was censored for security reasons. —*Navy Department, National Archives*

Enterprise, left, and *Yorktown* completing at the Newport News Shipbuilding and Dry Dock Company in 1937. —*Mariners' Museum, Newport News, Virginia*

First-line carrier aircraft in 1939 flown by squadron leaders from *Enterprise*. Farthest from the camera is an SBC "Helldiver" dive-bomber from Scouting Squadron 6. The other biplane is an F3F fighter from Fighting Squadron 6. In front is a TBD "Devastator" torpedo bomber from Torpedo Squadron 6. The tails of all three are painted a brilliant blue. In 1939, the Navy painted the tails of all aircraft from the same carrier the same color. *Yorktown*'s planes wore red; *Ranger*'s green; *Lexington*'s yellow; and *Saratoga*'s white. —*Navy Department, National Archives*

TBD-1 torpedo bombers lining up before takeoff from *Saratoga* in January 1938. Though not designed as carriers, both *Saratoga* and *Lexington* proved valuable because their great size allowed them to handle increasingly larger and heavier aircraft, such as the TBD. —*Navy Department, National Archives*

Marines load a BG-1 bomber with a 1,000-lb. bomb in February 1937. The introduction of bombers capable of carrying large bombs significant distances dramatically increased the killing power of naval air forces. —*Navy Department, National Archives*

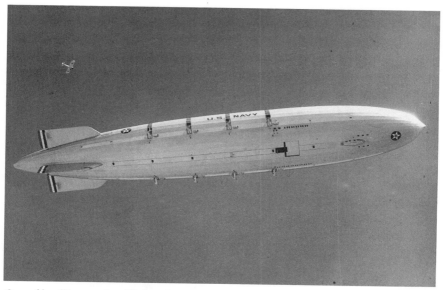

One of her "Sparrowhawk" aircraft approaches the huge airship *Macon* in February 1934. The airship's hangar door is clearly visible. Technological marvels, *Macon* and sister ship *Akron* were intended to be very long-range scouts. —*Navy Department, National Archives*

One of airship *Macon*'s "Sparrowhawk" F9C aircraft is seen in the process of hooking on to her trapeze. Once attached, the airplane would be hoisted up into her hangar. *Macon* and *Akron* normally carried four aircraft apiece for scouting. Though slow, with a maximum speed just over eighty mph, both airships had great range and endurance—over nine thousand miles at sixty mph. —*Navy Department, National Archives*

One of six Consolidated P2Y-1 seaplanes taking off from Naval Air Station Norfolk for a nonstop flight to the Panama Canal Zone in September 1933. Their successful long-distance flight (over two thousand miles in under twenty-six hours) showed that seaplanes could quickly provide air reconnaissance across a whole theater of operations.
—*Navy Department, National Archives*

A Consolidated PBY-2 "Catalina" in 1938. The "B" in her designation meant that she was a potent bomber—able to carry four 1,000-lb. bombs. The development of this aircraft gave patrol seaplane squadrons real offensive power and led to Navy efforts to develop even larger seaplane patrol bombers. The PBY-2 weighed about fourteen tons loaded. The four-engine Consolidated PB2Y "Coronado" of 1940 weighed over twice as much and carried eight 1,000-lb. bombs. —*Navy Department, National Archives*

One of heavy cruiser *Salt Lake City*'s four SOC-1 float-planes has landed in the water and taxied onto the ship's recovery net. The plane's observer has left his rear seat and stands strad-dling the cockpit to hook the cable from the ship's crane to his aircraft. The pilot is using his engine to stay even with the moving ship. Once the cable is attached, the plane will be lifted free of both the water and the recovery net.
—*Navy Department, National Archives*

7
SUBMARINE!

Between the wars, the word *submarine* conjured up images of a stealthy, deadly, silent killer, like a shark in its power, bent on the ruthless pursuit of its victims. But this image was only partly correct. The submarine was a relatively new weapon, based on relatively new technologies. Like the airplane, it had demonstrated great military potential in World War I. Yet, also like the airplane, it still had some way to go before it became one of the dominant weapons in the Navy's arsenal.

World War I had given the submarine a fearsome reputation. Unrestricted submarine warfare—the attack, unannounced, on any and all ships, armed and unarmed—had led to calls at the Washington naval conference in 1921 that submarines be banned outright. That effort did not succeed, and opponents of submarine warfare had to settle for international agreements that forced submarines to operate against merchant shipping as though they were surface raiders. As late as May 1941, for example, the *Tentative Instructions for the Navy of the United States Governing Maritime and Aerial Warfare* banned unrestricted submarine warfare.

To the U.S. Navy's submariners, the successes of Germany's U-boats in World War I was a great surprise because the American submariners had found it impossible to build effective long-range submarines of their own. U.S. Navy doctrine had been to build two sorts of submarines—smaller vessels displacing less than or about one thousand tons submerged for coast defense and larger "fleet submarines" of much greater displacement to operate with the battle fleet at sea. Whole batches of the coast defense type had been laid down, launched, or commissioned by the time the United States declared war on Germany in April 1917, and the great naval authorization of 1916 had given the Navy permission to design and build nine of the larger, "fleet" types.

But the "fleet boats" proved difficult to develop.[1] To meet the battle fleet's needs, they had to have relatively high surface speed (over twenty knots), great range, a powerful torpedo armament, and endurance. Before examining long-range U-boats at the end of World War I, the Navy built three larger (approximately fifteen hundred tons submerged displacement), high-speed (twenty knots) submarines—the T class. They were failures. As Norman Friedman pointed out in his study of the design, "the engines were never successful." As a result, "they could not cruise with the fleet (and its tankers) and they lacked sufficient range to operate independently."[2]

German submarines, some of which were examined carefully by U.S. Navy submariners after the war, and German submarine operations galvanized the small submarine community in the U.S. Navy. German U-boats had superior diesels and impressive endurance, both on the surface and underwater. German U-boat captains had also learned how to take their boats down when there was a need to submerge quickly. The operation of German U-boats had also illustrated the value of projecting submarines *forward*, ahead of the fleet. There, they could scout and strike enemy surface forces as the latter emerged from harbor. In short, encountering clearly superior German technology and German operational practice threw American submariners on their ears. The question was, "How should the U.S. Navy respond?" There was, in this questioning, a parallel with the experience of Navy aviators, who were so impressed with the air forces of Great Britain and France.

Early in 1919, Captain (later Admiral) Thomas C. Hart penned a memo for the Chief of Naval Operations that noted the vulnerability of Japan to the kind of submarine campaign that almost brought Great Britain to her knees toward the end of World War I. Later that year, he made the same basic argument to the class of the Army General Staff College; he carried the identical message to the Naval War College in 1920. Like the proponents of naval aviation, Hart was pushing for a reassessment of the role of *his* new technology—the submarine—in U.S. Navy fighting doctrine.[3]

Hart was not alone. In 1920, the naval architects in the Bureau of Construction and Repair had suggested to the General Board that the Navy consider building a twenty-thousand–ton battle cruiser-like submarine propelled by steam turbines and carrying four 12-inch guns in two armored turrets. The job of this monster was to fight its way through enemy screening formations of cruisers to find the enemy's main body of battleships. Hart and another future admiral by the name of Chester Nimitz (then a lieutenant commander) opposed such extreme designs, but they did want to make sure that the fleet submarines authorized in 1916 took advantage of what had been learned from the captured German U-boats.

In the meantime, U.S. submariners were intent on showing what their existing boats could do. Accordingly, Captain Hart, commanding in tender

Beaver (AS-5), led a group of S-class coast defense submarines from New London, Connecticut, to Manila (via Pearl Harbor and Guam) in the six months from June to December 1921. Prior to that time, submarines assigned to the Philippines had been carried there on Navy cargo ships or colliers. Hart's voyage, which took the first really effective American submarines to the Asiatic Fleet, tested the endurance of the S-class boats. They were found wanting. As Norman Friedman put it, the S-type boats, built for service in the Atlantic, "were the only existing U.S. submarines likely to be useful to a Pacific battlefleet," but their engines were notoriously unreliable.

The problem was an old one for the U.S. Navy: catching up with technology that others had pioneered or pushed ahead faster. But simply copying existing German submarine designs and German equipment would not do. The technologies associated with submarines, including those influencing diesel engines and electric motors, optics, pumps, valves, and torpedoes, were moving ahead. Some means had to be found to foster them in the United States. Otherwise, the scientific and technological foundations of the U.S. submarine force would remain inadequate.

The basic technological problem facing submarines was that of remaining undetected while engaging their targets. As retired Commander W. J. Holmes put it in one of his published stories, "Stealth was the only game we could play, invisibility was our only armor."[4] But stealth was not possible unless a submarine could submerge quickly and *safely*. Submerging quickly, as the Germans had learned the hard way in World War I, meant "riding the vents." That is, U-boats cruised on the surface with the valves to their ballast tanks open. Seawater stayed out, and the sub stayed on the surface because of air pressure holding the water back. By quickly venting the air, a submarine could fill its main ballast tanks and "crash dive."

But diving at too steep an angle could put the submarine below the depth at which its pressure hull could hold out the sea. A submarine could be crushed by water pressure before its crew could level off. The Navy's *S-42*, for example, was just over 225 feet long. That was just about its estimated "crush depth." If the sub's captain took the boat down too fast, or at too steep an angle, it would be destroyed. So designers had to make sure that a quickly submerging submarine stayed under control. If not, its crew would have to "blow ballast"—use compressed air to drive water from the boat's main ballast tanks. That would bring an undamaged submarine to the surface, but once there it would be in danger from enemy antisubmarine forces such as destroyers and patrol bombers. If the sub's skipper flooded its tanks to escape them, his crew would face the danger of diving too deep yet again.

Keeping a submarine under control was not the only problem its crew faced. An equal danger was that the submarine's air intake and exhaust valves for its diesels would not be closed in time as it dived, allowing a fatal cascade of water into the boat's engine room. A submarine had to shift from surface propulsion (diesels) to submerged propulsion (electric motors) in one well timed movement, as the momentum given the sub by its diesels was used to drive the boat below the surface.

Then, while underway on electric power, the submarine's crew had to be alert to any leaks in their craft's battery compartment. The battery spaces of S-class submarines contained 120 lead-acid storage batteries, like those found in automobiles, except that each battery weighed a ton. If any sulfuric acid in those batteries came into contact with seawater, the resulting chemical reaction would produce poisonous chlorine gas. Even while discharging current to run the submarine's motors, such batteries vented small amounts of potentially explosive hydrogen gas, which had to be dispersed so that it would not concentrate at a dangerous level.

Even assuming that a submarine's crew kept their craft effective in an engineering sense, there was no guarantee that a submarine would be effective as a weapon. Its submerged speed was usually only a fraction of its surface speed, and its underwater endurance was usually measured in hours. For *S-42*, it was twenty hours at a speed of five knots. This meant the sub had to approach its target on the surface or submerge in the path of an approaching surface ship. Unfortunately for the submariners, being submerged in the clear waters of the South Pacific might not hide their boat, which could be visible as a shadow to aircraft patrolling overhead. Or, the submarine's raised periscope might produce a wake that a lookout would see, robbing the submarine of the stealth it needed to survive. In addition, until the 1930s, firing a torpedo released a large bubble of air that burst on the surface and revealed a submarine's position. Enemy destroyers or aircraft, seeing the bubble, would head for it at high speed, hoping to detect the submerged submarine before it could slip away.

To make matters even worse, a submarine captain, to quote Commander Harley F. Cope of *S-40*, "personally" fought his own ship. That is, he tracked a target, estimated its course and speed, and then decided when and how many torpedoes to launch against it. In the 1920s, all he had to help him with this problem were some primitive slide-rule-like devices and his periscope. For his defense, he had some useful acoustic equipment, including a fathometer to tell him the depth of water under his boat's keel, and active and passive sonars, which he could use to detect enemy ships and estimate their sizes, speeds, and ranges. But what he really lacked was a responsive, reliable fire control system—a device that would allow him to aim and shoot torpedoes like a soldier would a gun.[5]

In the 1920s, there wasn't a lot of money for submarine development; aviation took precedence. As a result, Navy leaders faced a frustrating dilemma. As historian Ernest Andrade noted many years ago, "naval officers responsible for fleet command and the development of operations doctrine stressed . . . learning by doing, but it was not possible to experiment with new tactical concepts unless experimental vessels . . . were available." Experimental ships, however, cost money, and the Congress did not look favorably on Navy officers who asked for funds that might be wasted on designs that didn't pan out. But if risks were not taken, progress would be slow—too slow. The U.S. Navy could not afford to sit on the sidelines and let other navies get ahead of it in the technologies of undersea warfare.

The two most important decision-making bodies in the field of submarine design were the General Board and a group started by Captain Hart called the Submarine Officers Conference. The latter consisted of all the submarine-qualified officers who could get to the Main Navy building on Constitution Avenue in Washington, D.C. The problem facing both the General Board and the Submarine Officers Conference was that no one was sure just what kind of submarine to build. There was agreement that the S-class boats, the largest of the coast defense submarines, were too small. There was also agreement that a fleet submarine needed to be fast on the surface, with both long range and great endurance. There was even agreement that diesel-engine technology in the United States was inadequate and needed to improve dramatically. Beyond that, consensus broke down, even among the submarine officers who formed the conference.

For example, the first three postwar fleet types (*Barracuda*, *Bass*, and *Bonita*) were over one hundred feet longer than the S-class subs, with over twice the submerged displacement. What did that increase in size buy? First, increased range while cruising on the surface—six thousand nautical miles (nmi.) at 11 knots as against twenty-five hundred nmi. at 6.5 knots. Second, greater speed on the surface (21 vs. 13 knots). Third, two additional torpedo tubes (both in the stern). However, the greater size came at a significant increase in cost. *S-42*, one of the better of the coast defense submarines, had cost almost $2 million; *Barracuda* had cost almost

$5.9 million. Was the increase in fighting power worth the difference in cost? It might have been. Unfortunately, the engines of these three fleet boats were not reliable. They lacked *endurance*.

The next three submarines were called "cruisers," and with some justification. All three (*Argonaut, Narwhal*, and *Nautilus*) were, comparatively speaking, giants—over 370 feet in length and weighing in at approximately four thousand tons submerged displacement. All three were designed for very long-range cruising. Mine layer *Argonaut* had a range of eight thousand nmi. at ten knots. *Narwhal* and *Nautilus* could reach 9,380 nmi. at the same speed. All three mounted two 6-inch guns, and *Argonaut* carried sixty mines along with her complement of sixteen torpedoes (the other two boats carried twenty-four torpedoes each). These submarines were designed to blockade Japan. Given the antagonism to unrestricted submarine warfare that was expressed in international treaties, their 6-inch guns seemed suited for blockade work, in which the submarine would stop a merchant ship with a shot across her bow, force her crew to abandon ship, and then sink her with gunfire.

But all three had grave weaknesses that made building more of them unwise. As Commander John D. Alden, also a historian, observed, "Their great size and huge flat decks made them slow to dive, clumsy to maneuver underwater, and easy to detect both on the surface and submerged." They were also *very* expensive. In 1936, for example, capital investment in *Argonaut* was officially set at approximately $7.9 million; it was about $6.3 million for *Nautilus*. Even the first of the giant "airship aircraft carriers," *Akron*, had cost only about $5.4 million. Moreover, the cruiser submarines took too long to build—three years. What the submarine officers wanted instead was a general purpose submarine, something that was not too large, too expensive, or that took too long to build but that nevertheless had the endurance, range, and firepower to play a significant role in a Pacific war with Japan.

Several separate but related threads came together to lead to an optimal design. The first was the London Naval Treaty of 1930, which limited the U.S. Navy to 52,700 tons of new submarines and set an upper bound on submarine surface (or "standard") displacement of 2,000 tons. The agreement put an end to the large cruiser type and forced the Navy's leaders and submarine officers to think in terms of a tradeoff between the size of an individual submarine and the total number of such submarines that could be built under the cap of 52,700 tons.

The second thread was the development, finally, of reliable, powerful diesel engines in the United States. This development was triggered by a change in railroad technology—the shift from reciprocating steam engines to diesel-electric engines. The whole story is complex, but the outline is clear enough. In the 1920s, there was no domestic market for compact, high power-to-weight ratio diesel engines, but the Navy's Bureau of Engineering did not want to depend on German diesel manufacturers for the surface propulsion plants of U.S. submarines. At the end of the decade, the Chief of the Bureau of Engineering asked Congress for funds—seed money—to subsidize American diesel manufacturers so that they would not have to risk their own funds in developing reliable, effective diesels. Congress did not oblige.

But Charles Kettering, head of research for General Motors, had been studying diesel technology, and he had persuaded Alfred P. Sloan, GM's head, to purchase a firm that had pioneered lightweight, efficient diesels for small boats. There was just a chance that such engines, properly scaled up, could revolutionize railroad engine propulsion, and GM saw a market that it could enter and perhaps dominate quickly. The Fairbanks Morse Company was also convinced that lightweight, reliable diesels would sell to the railroads. In 1932, Congress entered the picture by instructing the Navy to limit its diesel engine procurement to American manufacturers. Soon thereafter, the president of the Burlington Railroad agreed to adopt new GM diesels for an innovative class of high-speed passenger trains. As a result, the outlook for diesel engine production had changed dramatically by the time the Navy solicited bids for submarine diesels in 1932 and 1933.[6]

The third thread was the development, by the Navy's Bureau of Ordnance, of the torpedo data computer, a fire control device for torpedoes. Though not perfected until the late 1930s, this device clearly promised to transform the attack problem for U.S. submarine skippers. Preparing a torpedo attack in an S-class submarine, for example, taxed not only the captain's skill at estimating target course, range, and speed, but also the physical dexterity of a good part of his crew. As the wife of one officer noted:

> The scene was reminiscent of the craze for seeing how many people could fit into a phone booth. The control room, 16 [and a half] feet fore and aft and 20 feet port to starboard, bristled with machinery, and a good chunk of it was taken up by the radio room. Battle Stations Submerged required that the approach officer, diving officer, assistant approach officer, plotting officer, chief of the boat, bow planesman, stern planesman, helmsman, quartermaster, trim manifold man, blow manifold man, telephone talker, messenger, and controllerman be present—14 in all, one-third of those aboard.[7]

The new fire control computer promised to eliminate this awkward assembly and allow the captain of a submarine to engage multiple targets quickly and effectively.

The fourth—and final—thread in this story was the development of welding to the point where a welded ship or submarine hull was both lighter and stronger than a riveted hull of the same type. The improvements in welding meant even more for submarines than for surface ships because submerged submarines tended to lose small amounts of oil through riveted joints, and sometimes that oil was visible at the surface as a slick, giving away the submarine's location.

Together, these four developments—treaty limits, engines, analog computers, and welding—gave the Navy's submarine designers and operators the chance to have the fleet submarine that they had wanted ever since 1919. The result was a series of ever better designs, beginning with the *Perch* (SS-176) and her five sisters, authorized in 1934, and culminating with *Gar* (SS-206) and five more of her class, authorized in 1938. These submarines were about three hundred feet long and displaced about fifteen hundred tons on the surface and nearly twenty-four hundred tons submerged. At twenty knots, they met the submariners' requirement for relatively high surface speed, and the latest of them had a range on the surface of eleven thousand nmi. at ten knots. Beginning with *Salmon* (SS-182), they all could remain submerged for forty-eight hours at two knots. Torpedo armament got heavier with each class until the optimal was reached in *Tambor* (SS-203), authorized in 1938: six torpedo tubes in the bow, four in the stern, and twenty-four torpedoes.

Along the way, the Navy's few but talented submarine designers in the Bureau of Construction and Repair found ways to eliminate the bubble that had accompanied the firing of a torpedo. They also developed storage battery cells that were much more resistant to damage from depth charging. The need for specialized mine laying submarines was eliminated when engineers in the Bureau of Ordnance designed a mine that could be discharged from a submarine's torpedo tube.

The only departure from this path of development came in January 1939, when the General Board approved the design of a new small submarine that displaced only eight hundred tons on the surface and could cruise for approximately seven thousand nmi. on the surface at ten knots. Only two of these smaller submarines, *Mackerel* (SS-204) and *Marlin* (SS-205), were built. At the time, it was not clear that American shipbuilders could fabricate enough of the fleet boats for a war in the Pacific, and so officers such as Rear Admiral Hart thought it would be wise for the Navy to build a smaller, less expensive type. But *Mackerel* and *Marlin* lacked the range required for effective operation against Japanese shipping. Fortunately, the Navy had underestimated the ability of the shipbuilding industry—especially the yards on the Great Lakes—to respond to wartime demand. Wartime production turned out to be more than adequate.

The improved fleet boats, designed for service as scouts for the battle fleet and as bushwhackers of enemy warships, had, as Norman Friedman noted, "exactly [the characteristics] required to attack Japanese shipping." Once equipped with radar, and steered toward Japanese shipping by signals intelligence, the fleet boats devastated Japan's lifeline—her merchant marine—just as Admiral Hart had predicted when he spoke as a captain in 1919. But that future was still uncertain when the Board approved the small submarine.

What made it so uncertain was the problem of affirming submarine attack tactics before World War II. Though submarines had become more deadly, the development of reliable sound ranging equipment (sonar) in the 1930s for destroyers appeared to significantly reduce their ability to escape from attack by surface ships. American submarines had been equipped with both passive listening devices and active sound ranging equipment since World War I, but surface ships were not given effective sound ranging sets until the late 1930s. When they did get them, they began finding submerged submarines.

The problem facing the attacking submarine before World War II was simple. It had to stay hidden until it attacked, and then it had to avoid detection or survive an attack by surface escorts. But it had to close with its target to be certain of a hit. In 1937, the newest fleet boats scored hits on target ships only about one-fourth of the time *unless* they got in close—to within 750 yards or less of their targets. But any warship worth attacking, such as an aircraft carrier or a battleship, would most likely be steaming at high speed and be shielded by a curtain of escorts. It would maneuver to keep attacking submarines at a distance, or, if it slowed down to enter port, its escorts would use active sound ranging gear to spot any lurking submarines. How could a submarine get close enough to sink such quarry?[8]

One way was to close with the target on the surface at night, when the submarine's low profile would make it difficult for escorts lacking radar to see it. On May 10, 1934, during Fleet Problem XV, an S-class submarine cruising on the surface slipped into a darkened formation of "enemy" fleet auxiliaries.

When challenged by blinker light, the captain of the submarine had one of his sailors respond with a flashlight, signaling that his vessel was a yacht and asking the darkened ships to illuminate. When they did, the sub's captain "attacked" the nearest auxiliary and then submerged. In the seventy-five seconds it took the submarine to reach periscope depth, no escort got close, and the submarine escaped undetected.

Was this audacious maneuver taken as a model for future attacks? No. The report of the commander in chief noted that "the simulation of submarine night attacks is considered very dangerous in peacetime operations and the effectiveness of such attacks in war is considered very doubtful." The fear of losing a submarine to collision was strong. Indeed, in Fleet Problem X (1930), submarines had been required to operate on the surface at night, showing running lights. This restriction proved "most disappointing to their personnel." In Fleet Problem XIII (1932), staged in the clear waters near Hawaii, submarines stalking surface ship formations in daytime were spotted again and again by aircraft, even when the submarines were submerged. In response, sub skippers resorted to sound approaches, where they would stay deep and use their underwater listening gear to approach their targets. *S-44* used this technique in an exercise in 1935, staying at a depth of one hundred feet and slipping under a screen of destroyers in a rain squall to attack two slow moving targets by using just its passive sound detection gear.

Submarines were also employed as scouts, to locate enemy formations and to warn the commanders of friendly forces of the approach of enemy units. Unfortunately, when they surfaced to make their scouting reports, their locations could be determined by radio direction finding equipment that picked up their transmissions. As one exercise report noted, "No radio transmission of any nature can be made without imparting some information to an alert enemy." The development of a periscope-mounted radio antenna meant that submarines did not have to surface to make a sighting report, but submarine captains still felt vulnerable to detection and attack.[9]

This sense of vulnerability came through loud and clear in a pre–World War II submarine adventure story written by a retired submariner, Commander W. J. Holmes. In the fictional story Holmes has a division of American submarines conduct a watch outside a potential enemy's base. Their mission is to alert the U.S. fleet if the enemy fleet suddenly emerges, ready for battle. In his words, "It was monotonous work. . . . Around and around the periscope an officer continuously walked, scrutinizing the surface of the sea and the sky above. The hours dragged by . . . but still each minute was fraught with danger. Every time the periscope showed a feather, there was the possibility that it would be sighted by a patrolling plane." Unfortunately for the crew, "the nights were no less wearing than the days. We lay on the surface and charged batteries; five black hulls . . . poised for a crash dive. . . . Safety depended on seeing the enemy before he saw us. . . . Each morning we prayed for the dawn that would see us safely below the surface. Each evening we prayed for the darkness that would permit us to come up and breathe fresh air again." This fictional account presaged the experience of S-class submarines trying to defend the Philippines after December 7, 1941.[10]

In an emergency, of course, a damaged sub could surface and shoot it out with its pursuers, counting on the boat's low silhouette to give it an initial advantage in a gun battle. S-7 reportedly held the record for both accuracy and speed in long-range battle practice with a 4-inch deck gun. Off Chefoo, China, S-7 surfaced from periscope depth, fired sixteen rounds accurately at a moving target two-and-one-half miles distant, then dove again to periscope depth. S-7's crew did it all in three minutes, twenty-three seconds. Because it took time for the S-type submarines to submerge, the craft's captain began flooding its ballast tanks at the twelfth shot of S-7's deck gun. One has to wonder how accurate those last four shots were, as the gun crew felt their boat subsiding beneath them.

A surfaced shoot-out with aircraft or surface ships was not part of prewar submarine doctrine. Submarines were supposed to stalk their quarry submerged, approach quietly, and then stay as silent as possible while avoiding the attacks of surface escorts. This cautious doctrine, coupled with faulty torpedoes, reduced the combat effectiveness of even the newer U.S. submarines at the start of World War II. Yet even the obsolete S-type boats—plagued by old, inefficient diesels, fuel tanks that leaked oil, foul living conditions, and cranky diving controls—went to war against Japan from bases as far apart as Australia and Alaska.[11]

The story of submarine development cannot be separated from that of submarine mishaps. The reason why senior fleet officers were so hesitant to use submarines aggressively in fleet exercises was because they did not want to sacrifice sub crews to collisions with surface ships. This was not just a problem for American naval leaders. The Royal Navy, which had a larger submarine force, had lost two submarines to accidents in 1921, one in 1922, still another in 1924, and yet a fifth that foundered in the harbor at Devonport in 1926. Submarines could vanish after a dive or disappear after colliding with a merchant ship or a warship. Submerging, like flying, was inherently a dangerous business.

The U.S. Navy had its own list of submarine tragedies, including F-4 lost off Honolulu in 1915 (twenty-one dead), F-1 sunk off San Pedro in 1917 (nineteen dead), and *S-5* foundered off the New Jersey coast in 1920 (but all her crew—fortunately—was saved). But the loss of *S-51* on September 25, 1925, run down by a merchant ship off the coast of Rhode Island, and with only three survivors, was almost more than the Navy could bear. Recall that September 1925 had already been a tragic month. Airship *Shenandoah* had crashed in Ohio on September 3. The three airmen trying to fly from the West Coast to Hawaii had been lost at sea on September 1—and then miraculously found nine days later. Navy officers were not in the mood for more tragedies. In the case of *S-51*, there was no way to bring back the lives of its thirty-four dead, but there was a chance that the boat could be salvaged because it lay "only" 132 feet below the surface, and a successful salvage would preserve some of the Navy's hard-won reputation as a technically sophisticated military arm.

Initial efforts to raise the sunken submarine with large derricks were unsuccessful, and at the beginning of October, the Navy Department decided to undertake the salvage using its own resources. Thus began an epic effort that set Navy divers and salvage engineers against the worst that a wrecked hulk and the North Atlantic's continental shelf could deal out to them. Work on the bottom began in mid-October 1925 and was halted in early December because of inclement weather. It resumed in April 1926, and the battered hulk of *S-51* was finally towed in to the New York Navy Yard very late in the evening of July 7, 1926.

Over five months, Navy divers made more than five hundred dives to the sunken submarine. In many cases, the divers, encased in helmets and heavy diving suits, entered *S-51*; other divers took even greater risks by tunneling *under* the bottomed submarine. The story of their efforts, and of their shipmates manning the ships supporting them, is a heroic one, and it was captured in riveting prose by salvage officer Commander Edward Ellsberg in his *On the Bottom*, published in 1929.[12]

To better lead the immediate salvage effort, Ellsberg qualified as a diver. His description of his first dive (in April 1926) on *S-51* was graphic:

> I began to descend. The bright light quickly faded to a deeper blue as I sank, the air roared through my helmet. Down, down, it seemed a long way. . . . Would I never reach the bottom? The pressure increased. I began to breathe more rapidly, the air started to feel different, heavy. Then gradually there took shape, dimly outlined against a dark formless background, the stern of the *S-51* below me, peacefully resting. As it loomed up, magnified considerably in the water, it looked perfectly huge.

Once on the submarine's deck, Ellsberg suffered the disorientation that often plagued beginning hard-hat divers:

> My head began to feel very light, queer. I braced my feet a little apart, tried to steady myself. Never in my life had I ever fainted but now my head felt dizzy, my heart strange. I felt that it would only be a matter of seconds before I collapsed. . . . My knees felt weak, my head swam. But there passed across my mind the thought that there were twelve new divers like myself . . . ; none had yet been down. It would set them a fine example to have their officer ask to be hauled up on his first dive!

Forcing himself to concentrate on the task at hand, Ellsberg recovered. He and his crew of intrepid divers were trying to fasten large pontoons to the submarine. The plan was to flood the pontoons, attach them to *S-51*, and then raise the sub by pumping out the water in the pontoons. But attaching the pontoons proved to be an arduous and perilous task. Using high-pressure hoses, Navy divers had to tunnel through the mud beneath *S-51* so that steel cables, attached to the pontoons, could be threaded under the sunken sub:

> Francis Smith was in the tunnel, burrowing his way along. Imagine his situation. In ice cold water, utter blackness, total solitude, he was buried one hundred and thirty-five feet below the surface of the sea. No sight, no sound, no sense of direction except the feel of the iron hull of the *S-51* against his back, as he lay stretched out flat in a narrow hole, scarcely larger than his body, not big enough for him to turn around in.

Suddenly, the tunnel caved in behind Smith. Ellsberg immediately sent down another diver to help. On the telephone line to Smith, all Ellsberg could hear was the diver's "labored breathing as he struggled in the darkness." When the rescue diver reached the tunnel's entrance, however, he had good news. Smith was coming out. As Ellsberg recounted, "Smith had managed to pass the nozzle [of the hose] back between his legs, and guiding it with his feet, he had washed his way out backward through the cave-in!" Then Smith went back to work—in the same tunnel.

Ellsberg's praise of Smith is eloquent: "No deed ever performed in the heat of battle . . . can compare with Francis Smith's bravery, when in the silent depths of the ocean beneath the hulk of the *S-51*, he washed his way out of what well might have been his grave, then deliberately turned round, went back into the black hole from which he had by the grace of God escaped, and worked his way deeper and deeper into it."

But there was more arduous adventure to come. Assuming that the divers could run steel cables under the submarine, could the crews of the salvage ships properly attach those cables to the chains hanging under the pontoons that had been towed out to the salvage site? It was May 1926, and the raising of *S-51* had become such a media event that getting it off the bottom *soon* had become an obsession for the salvage team. Attaching the first pontoon's chains to the cables initially went smoothly, but then the weather suddenly took a turn for the worse, endangering the whole effort. As Ellsberg related:

> The sea was rough, the wind already bad, and increasing. The [salvage ship] was rolling heavily, and the pontoon alongside was rising and falling violently as the waves rolled by. . . . Two three ton chains, ninety feet long, hung vertically through the hawsepipes of that pontoon down towards the submarine, and from the lower ends of those chains our reeving lines ran under the submarine.

The ninety-foot chains had to be unshackled from the reeving lines. To do that, the hook from the salvage ship's boom had to be attached to each chain in turn, and then each chain had to be pulled up through the pontoon to the deck of the salvage ship, where sailors would disconnect the chains from the cables stretching under *S-51*. Would the worsening weather allow the salvage team to do its work? Ellsberg gambled: "The seas were breaking over us, the pontoon was one moment awash, the next leaping over our heads threatening to crash down on our deck. But I thought of the fight [the divers] had put up to get those lines [under the submarine]. I could not cast their work away without a struggle." Ellsberg asked Lieutenant Henry Hartley, captain of salvage ship *Falcon* (ASR-2), "Will you try it, captain?" In Ellsberg's words, "Back came the sailor's answer, the old, old call of the seaman unafraid: 'Aye, aye, sir!'"

> [Petty Officer William Badders] poised on the rail, leaped to the top of the pontoon as it dropped away in the trough of the sea. . . . A wire strap was flung to Badders; he caught it, slipped it through the end of one chain. On the next roll, as the hanging [hook] shot down on the pontoon and paused a second, he dragged it to the chain link, caught the hook in the strap, leaped clear. The chain rose with a jerk ten feet out of the hawsepipe. . . . Badders rode the pontoon.

When both chains had been lifted to *Falcon*'s deck, Badders "then leaped back on the *Falcon*, thoroughly soaked." Staying assigned to *Falcon*, he was to win a Medal of Honor for his dives to *Squalus* in 1939.

S-51 was, after such great efforts, raised and then, suspended among the salvage pontoons, towed under New York's Hell Gate Bridge to the Navy Yard. As Ellsberg recalled, "Both sides of the East River were lined with huge crowds as we passed; no cheers, but half-masted flags and bare-headed throngs greeted the *S-51* as the silent procession steamed slowly along." The whole effort had been what we now call a media event. Thousands visited the Navy yard to view the battered and slashed *S-51* in dry dock.

Ellsberg and his superior, Captain (later Admiral) Ernest J. King, won the plaudits of the newspapers, and much of the drama of the struggle to raise *S-51* was captured on newsreel film. But it was Ellsberg's *On the Bottom* that captured the imagination of a generation of boys, as it told the "story of victory over the sea, wrought by the quiet courage of men who could . . . fight on till they had wrested from the ocean the tomb of their shipmates."

The salvage of *S-51*, and later (in 1927) the failure of the Navy to rescue six survivors of the sunken *S-4*, inspired Lieutenant (later Rear Admiral) Charles B. Momsen to work seriously on the development of means to rescue submariners who survived a sinking. His work led directly to the famous "Momsen lung," what came to be called the McCann Submarine Rescue Chamber, and special helium-oxygen air mixtures for divers working at depths of two hundred feet and below. This work led to the rescue of thirty-three members of the crew of *Squalus* (SS-192), which had accidentally sunk off Portsmouth, New Hampshire, in May 1939.[13]

Once the survivors had been rescued, *Squalus*, resting on the bottom 240 feet down, was raised in much the same manner as *S-51*, and—despite much progress in the technique of floating sunken submarines—with almost as much nail-biting drama. As Momsen put it, "At the end of fifty days work, . . . the first lift was attempted. We raised the stern successfully. . . . The bow came up like a mad tornado, out of control. Pontoons were smashed, hoses cut and I might add hearts were broken. . . . The second try was successful." Newsreel cameramen filmed both tries, and "Momsen" became something of a household name.[14]

Given the dangers of taking a submarine down and taking her into battle, it makes sense to wonder how navies were able to recruit men for these tasks. The wife of a commanding officer of an S boat based in the Philippines recalled,

"Asiatic pigboat sailors had all the feisty pride of a cadre of hard-living, tough professionals who, by the very fact that they'd been able to survive S-boat existence, considered themselves superior."[15] Submariners, both enlisted men and officers, were an elite. The living conditions on the older subs were, as Commander Harley F. Cope put it, "awful," but the submarine service offered sailors and officers alike the chance to be independent, and to experience the closest thing to familiarity that anyone found in the traditional, formal Navy. There wasn't any choice. Officers and enlisted men were thrown together in an enforced intimacy. There was no room to hide, and no physical obstacle—a desk or a stateroom door—between the leader and the led. But author A. J. Hill may have put it best: "Of all the ties that bound submariners together, however, danger was probably the strongest. The sea is notoriously unforgiving, but it reserves its harshest penalties for those who venture beneath its surface. A mistake that might be embarrassing or even humorous on a surface ship was often fatal—instantly fatal—in a submarine and not just for the sailor who made it, but for every one of his shipmates too."

This emphasis on technical competence *among all the members of a sub's crew* made the submarine service special, and it made submariners resourceful. In May 1921, for example, *R-14*, based at Pearl Harbor, lost all mechanical and electrical power while cruising on the surface at sea. Her crew was able to raise her periscope, use it as a mast, and sail to Honolulu. Similarly, the captain and crew of *S-5*, which sank in 180 feet of water off the coast of New Jersey in September 1920 when the boat's intake for her diesels was not properly closed, kept their heads, and saved themselves by raising her stern above the water, laboriously punching a small hole through the sub's pressure hull, and then attracting the attention of a passing merchant ship with a jury-rigged "flag." The crew was an inch away from death, but no one lost his head.[16]

Once such extraordinary sailors got hold of really effective submarines and torpedoes, and once they were ordered to adopt unrestricted submarine warfare against Japan's merchant marine after Japan's attack on Pearl Harbor in December 1941, they brought the Japanese economy to its knees.[17]

8
RUNNING THE NAVY

The objective of any warring nation is victory, immediate and complete. . . . In all plans for preparedness and policies to be pursued in the event of war it must never be overlooked that while efficiency in war is desirable, effectiveness is mandatory.

> From the foreword to the
> *Industrial Mobilization Plan*, 1933
> revision of the 1931 *Plan* prepared
> by the War Department

If Congress believes that civilian control is a "great evil," that the policy which has prevailed from the foundation of our Government should be reversed, and that the Navy should be removed from civilian control, let it . . . create a general staff on the German model. . . . That would be the frank and open way to do it, rather than put some [admiral] in control of the Navy, with a nominal secretary as his clerk, messenger boy, and rubber stamp.

> Secretary of the Navy Josephus
> Daniels, in testimony to the
> Senate Committee on Naval
> Affairs, May 17, 1920

With the experience of the war behind me, I would decline to be honored with an appointment as Chief of Naval Operations . . . unless I felt that I could, by law, honestly and efficiently perform the duties which I believe that officer owes his country."

> Capt. William V. Pratt, in a letter
> to the Senate Committee on Naval
> Affairs, May 17, 1920

In earlier chapters we have discussed the composition of the Navy, the work of sailors and officers, the development of aircraft and submarines, and life aboard ship. This chapter is about a topic not usually given much attention—how the Navy was led and managed.[1] Not every element of Navy management will be covered. Previous chapters have already devoted space to the selection of officers, to material management, and to the Navy's heavy investment in industrial facilities. Though each of these topics is worth covering in more detail, this chapter will instead focus on organizing the Navy Department, the fleet, and development and procurement so that the peacetime Navy could build a war-winning fleet when the time came.

The organization of the Navy Department reflected the federal structure of government in the United States and was based on a fear of overcentralization. By law, the Secretary of the Navy was head of the department, responsible directly to the president and indirectly to the Congress. The authority and responsibilities of the Chief of Naval Operations, the most senior officer in the Navy, were spelled out in *Navy Regulations*. He was "charged with the operations of the fleet, and with the preparation and readiness of plans for its use in war." However, the same set of regulations specified that "the business of the Department of the Navy shall be distributed in such manner as the Secretary of the Navy shall judge to be expedient and proper" among the Navy's bureaus, the oldest of which dated back to 1842. After 1921, there were eight of them—Yards and Docks (the civil engineers), Navigation (controlling training and officer assignments), Ordnance, Construction and Repair (the naval architects), Engineering (propulsion and electrical matters), Medicine and Surgery, Supplies and Accounts, and Aeronautics. Their roles changed little between 1921 and 1939. Headed by rear admirals, the bureaus were not directly accountable to the Chief of Naval Operations or to the Commander-in-Chief, United States Fleet, but to the Secretary of the Navy.

By 1921, the issue of who ran the Navy had already been given a thorough and acrimonious airing in public and before members of the Congress. So-called reformist admirals such as Bradley Fiske had supported the creation of the Office of the Chief of Naval Operations (OPNAV, as it is still known) in 1915 to coordinate the activities of the shore support organizations (mainly the bureaus) with those of the fleet. But Congress had not given OPNAV (and its leader, the CNO) authority over the bureaus. Instead, the bureaus continued to report directly to the Secretary of the Navy. That official therefore had a whole boatload of "principal advisors": the Chief of Naval Operations, the heads of the eight bureaus, the chairman of the General Board, the judge advocate general (for legal matters), at times a budget officer who was not the CNO, and the major general commandant of the Marine Corps. The potential for confusion stemming from divided leadership was great.

Peacetime CNOs therefore had no choice but to use their personal relationships with secretaries of the Navy and the bureau chiefs to try to achieve their goals. They were largely successful. Admiral Robert E. Coontz established a bureau chief's council in 1919 to review disagreements among the bureau chiefs and between his small staff and the heads of the bureaus. Coontz also persuaded Navy Secretary Edwin Denby to appoint him the Navy's first budget officer in 1921, and with Denby's support, he abolished the Atlantic and Pacific fleets in 1922 and "reorganized the sea forces into four major commands: the Battle Fleet, the Scouting Fleet, the Control Force, and the Fleet Base Force." Coontz was succeeded by several capable officers, especially Admiral William V. Pratt (1931–33), who had changed his mind about being CNO, and Admiral William H. Standley (1933–37).[2]

By 1937, the authority of the Chief of Naval Operations had increased to the point where his office (OPNAV) was at the center of a number of key management processes. In an address to the Army Industrial College in 1937, Rear Admiral James O. Richardson, assistant Chief of Naval Operations, explained how this worked:

> While the Chief of Naval Operations has no direct control over the personnel or the expenditures . . . for the Naval Establishment (all the money that is spent by the Navy is appropriated directly to the control of the bureaus), by the Annual Operating Force Plan, Aeronautical Organization and Shore Establishment Operating Plan flowing from the decisions in the Annual Estimate of the Situation he practically determines the personnel requirements; and by virtue of his responsibility for the readiness of the Fleet and his duty of coordinating all effort to this end he largely influences the expenditures of appropriations without interfering with detailed duties of the Material Bureaus.[3]

Republican Carl Vinson, since 1931 the chairman of the Naval Affairs Committee of the House of Representatives, did not find this arrangement satisfactory. In 1933, he proposed placing all of the bureau chiefs under a "chief of naval material" equal in rank to the Chief of Naval Operations. A special board headed by Assistant Secretary of the Navy Henry L. Roosevelt rejected this idea, as did President Franklin D. Roosevelt. But Vinson continued to hold hearings on the matter through the 1930s, as well as on the issue of the proper way to select officers for promotion. With the support of Republican Melvin Maas, the ranking Republican on the House Naval Affairs Committee, a Vinson bill to rationalize the selection process became law in 1938, and in 1939 Representative Vinson again proposed—unsuccessfully as before—that the structure of OPNAV be changed to make the bureaus responsive to the Chief of Naval Operations.[4]

The chief obstacle to Vinson's proposals was his own political party's leader. President Roosevelt enjoyed being involved in Navy decision making. His Secretary of the Navy, Claude A. Swanson, was ill during a good deal of his six years in that post (1933–39), and the president never hesitated to deal directly with successive chiefs of Naval Operations. Admiral William D. Leahy, Chief of Naval Operations from January 1937 to August 1939—who had known Roosevelt when the latter was assistant Secretary of the Navy during World War I—described his president's management style carefully: the president "had little confidence in some of his executive departments, and therefore took detailed action with his own hands.... This permitted President Roosevelt to be completely familiar with the details of all his written orders and other official communications." Put another way, Roosevelt understood that exerting his influence within the Navy was easier *without* the rational management structure that Carl Vinson proposed creating.[5]

The issue of how the fleet should be organized was left largely to the Navy's senior officers. By Navy General Order No. 211 of 1930, the main body of the United States Fleet was divided into four "forces": (a) the Battle Force, composed of most of the battleships and aircraft carriers and screened by light cruisers and destroyers; (b) the Scouting Force, consisting mainly of the new heavy cruisers and squadrons of seaplane patrol bombers; (c) the Submarine Force, most of whose short-range submarines were based in San Diego, the Panama Canal Zone, and Hawaii; and (d) the Base Force, composed of what was then called the "fleet train"—the auxiliaries directly supporting the fleet, such as tankers, oceangoing tugs, hospital ships, and minesweepers. This collection of "forces" was similar to the structure established in 1922.

In 1930, there was also the Special Service Squadron to police the Caribbean and the Naval Transportation Service, which operated transports *Henderson* (AP-1) and *Chaumont* (AP-5) and the fleet's cargo and ammunition ships, such as *Vega* (AK-17) and *Nitro* (AE-2). Though destroyers routinely refueled from carriers, battleships, and cruisers while under way, there was no underway replenishment of ammunition and other supplies from ammunition and cargo ships until 1944.

When CNO Coontz had merged the Atlantic and Pacific fleets in 1922, he had also created what were called "type commands." The senior officers who served as type commanders were responsible for "standard shipboard organization, training requirements, inspection standards, personnel complements, matériel allowances, and many other administrative matters for their particular ship types." Coontz had established the type commands to, first, standardize training, equipment, and shipboard supplies across the fleet. What this meant was that a sailor trained as a gunner's mate, boatswain's mate, or "water tender" (tending boilers) could move from a ship of one type (a destroyer, say) to another ship of the same type and fit quickly and effectively into the second ship's crew. As the General Board put it, the responsibility of the type commanders was to preserve "uniformity of doctrine, training, methods of upkeep, etc."

The second function of the type command was to serve as a bridge between the tactical units that together formed the forces of the fleet and the bureaus ashore. A type commander and his subordinates were analogous to the operating room staff of a surgeon. When the surgeon needs a scalpel, it is placed in his hand. Similarly, when the captain of a Navy ship needed a training syllabus for the gunners on his type of ship, the type commander's staff made sure a bureau provided it. Equipment, supplies, and manuals flowed from bureaus such as Ordnance and Steam Engineering toward the ships under the supervision of the type commanders. In practice, type and tactical commanders were often the same officers, reducing the chances of friction between the two chains of command.

The third function was to make sure that individual combat ships could compete fairly in the annual contests in gunnery, engineering, and communications. Competitions in these three areas of shipboard operations were required by regulation. High marks—designated by a large letter *E* painted on the side of a ship's turret or funnel—were a source of pride, promotions, and—for enlisted men—financial rewards. The often intense pressure to win inevitably led even the most professional sailors and officers to contemplate actions that would give them the jump on competing ships' crews. At the least, the highly visible competitions could not succeed unless those engaged in them believed that the contests were fair. The type commanders and their staffs saw to it that they were.[6]

In 1934, the Fleet Commander, Admiral Joseph M. Reeves, recommended to the General Board that the members of the board ask the Secretary of the Navy to authorize one or more additional senior type commands for aviation. Reeves noted that there was only one aviation type commander in the fleet—Commander, Aircraft, United States Fleet. He also argued that this one officer and his small staff could not cope with the increasing diversity of aircraft at sea with the fleet—which included carrier air groups, battleship and cruiser floatplanes, and growing numbers of long-range flying boats. Each type of aircraft required a different tactical doctrine, training, and—to use the words of the General Board—"methods of upkeep." His argument appeared logical enough. A second aviation type commander—a rear admiral—could lift a major administrative burden from the vice admiral who was both the tactical and the type commander.

Creating a second aviation type commander would also create another senior flag officer's position for an aviator. That mattered to Reeves because, in the event of war, the Navy's aviation component would expand dramatically as merchant ships were converted to carriers and hundreds, even thousands, of new aircraft joined the fleet. As early as 1925, the Bureau of Aeronautics believed that the Navy would need four new rear admirals—in addition to the Chief of the Bureau of Aeronautics—if once war were declared. Reeves was trying to create an additional path to flag rank so that naval aviation would not lack senior officers once wartime expansion began.

Reeves put his case this way: "The present organization of the Fleet is neither suitable nor adequate for the accomplishment of its primary war mission. . . . In all Fleet Problems which simulate actual war conditions, the Battle Force and Scouting Force inevitably and naturally disappear. . . . The organization of the Fleet should be an organization which best contributes to these two essential steps of training and preparation of the Fleet for war." Put another way, the only senior admirals required—other than the Commander-in-Chief—were type commanders. In peacetime, admirals other than the Fleet Commander-in-Chief would hold "combat" command only temporarily, when they led large task forces.

Reeves's proposal generated an intense controversy among senior line officers that lasted several years. There were two reasons for this. First, by law, Congress limited the number of admirals' positions. If the Navy acted on Reeves's recommendation, then some other two-star position would have to be eliminated. The second reason had to do with training. The members of the General Board and the Chief of Naval Operations, Admiral William H. Standley, argued that change would only be disruptive—that effective training depended on having a stable organization, and that continually drawing off type commanders to command task forces temporarily would keep them from performing their duties as type commanders. As Admiral Standley put it, "It was never intended that 'U.S. Fleet Type Commanders' should be 'Tactical Commanders.'"

On the other side of the debate, agreeing with Reeves, were surface line officers such as Admiral Arthur J. Hepburn, who had succeeded Reeves as Fleet Commander, and Vice Admiral Clarence S. Kempff, who was Commander, Battleships, Battle Force in 1936. As Kempff noted in a letter to Hepburn, "In war the Force Commanders would be done away with and their supporting battle plans with them. The Fleet would operate under *task forces evolved to meet practical situations* and any supporting battle plans would be produced by appropriate commanders to meet *existing conditions*."[7]

This dispute, out of sight of the public and the press, was about an honest difference over how best to prepare the fleet's leaders for war. For Reeves, the fleet could not be prepared if its leaders were not accustomed to organizing by *task*, or mission. For Standley, the fleet would not be ready for a fight if its leaders had not been trained to command large naval forces spread over great distances. It was one thing to command a task force; it was another to hold a fleet command. The two leaders and their supporters disagreed about the nature of the anticipated war with Japan and how best to prepare future commanders to lead the fleet against their Japanese counterparts.

Because of his role in the development of carrier strike forces, Reeves was acutely aware of the ways in which changes in technology and doctrine could alter the balance of forces in war. He was very sensitive, for example, to the importance of naval aviation and signals intelligence. Dramatic improvements in both areas meant that the fleet had to be able to shift from a peacetime to a wartime footing quickly, perhaps without warning. He wanted future fleet commanders to have the adroitness of mind to match the aggressive doctrine of combat that new technology made mandatory.

Standley was also concerned about uncertainty in wartime, but he was even more concerned about training and, particularly, efficiency—wringing the most from every dollar that Congress appropriated. Put another way, he wanted to keep command issues from clouding his focus on what were essentially resource issues. What good would it do to have a cluster of senior officers who could improvise in wartime if they lacked a modern fleet?

One way to express this difference between these two very competent admirals is to say that Reeves had both feet in the fleet and its operational problems, while Standley had one foot in Washington and the other at sea. Standley's task was to foster a more modern force and push it forward. It was easier for him to do that if he and the rest of OPNAV did not have to wrestle with the consequences of constant changes in the fleet's command structure. In the debate with Reeves, Standley's view prevailed—at least until 1941, when the older structure—of Battle Force, Scouting Force, and Base Force—was abandoned, as Reeves and those who supported him anticipated that it would be.

Far more public were the efforts made to provide the fleet with ships and aircraft. Agreeing to naval arms limitations made sense only if the United States could restore its naval strength if the "treaty system" collapsed. But restoring a navy was not an easy thing to do, even then. Before World War II, aircraft could be built—though not developed—quickly, and so could smaller craft, such as patrol boats, small destroyers, and submarines. Merchant ships could be converted to naval auxiliaries, and passenger ships could be converted into troopships. Larger warships, such as battleships and aircraft carriers, however, took years to build, which meant that mobilizing the Navy for war would require careful planning to reduce the time it would take to enlarge the fleet.

As the nation's "first line of defense," the Navy's responsibility to prepare for war was unique. As Chief of Naval Operations Standley told the House Committee on Appropriations in January 1934, the Navy's official policy was "to build and maintain a fleet of all classes of fighting ships of the maximum war efficiency as permitted by treaty provisions; to replace over-age ships under continuing programs." The official policy also was "to maintain detailed plans for rapid acquisition and conversion of merchant vessels to naval use in time of emergency." This meant that the Navy had to sustain a sizeable mobilization base even in peacetime.

To do that, the Navy's bureaus (especially Ordnance, Construction and Repair, Engineering, Aeronautics, and Yards and Docks) supported their own development and industrial establishments *and* purchased ships and aircraft from the private firms whose cooperation would be essential in time of war. Shipbuilding, especially, had to be cultivated in peacetime because it could not be turned on like a light switch in an emergency. The effort to do something like that during World War I had not been successful from either the Navy's point of view or that of the Congress.

Moreover, after World War I, many of the private firms that had produced ships and aircraft for the military services had found themselves with expanded facilities and surplus stocks but no buyers. They quickly dumped excess industrial capacity, were bought out, or went under. Of the seven aircraft makers who supplied the Navy with aircraft in 1918, for instance, only two were still in business in 1921. Two major shipbuilders, Bath Iron Works and William Cramp and Sons, declared bankruptcy in the 1920s. Newport News Shipbuilding and Dry Dock Company, which had built battleships *West Virginia* (BB-48) and *Maryland* (BB-46), stayed alive financially only by building heavy machinery such as water turbines for hydroelectric power plants.

In the 1920s, the Navy still built and tested its own guns, manufactured its own powder, and relied on the Naval Aircraft Factory in Philadelphia to modify existing airplanes and produce experimental types. It managed a substantial industrial base that private firms would not provide because there was so little profit to be made doing it. But the Navy was critically dependent on private firms for many items, such as submarine periscopes, even in peacetime. In wartime, moreover, private firms would be the primary producers of ships, aircraft, and war supplies. Steps had to be taken to make sure those producers existed and were prepared for increased production.

How could the engineering and production talent in these firms be kept active and available when Navy procurement was limited? One way was through government subsidies—payments for services rendered. Congress supported the aviation industry in 1925 by shifting air mail delivery from the U.S. Post Office to private carriers operating under contract. Complementing the Air Mail Act of 1925 was the Air Commerce Act of 1926, which authorized the Department of Commerce to set up radio beacons for air navigation and finance the construction and equipping of radio stations at commercial airfields. (It made little sense to subsidize airmail delivery if the pilots couldn't find their way.) In 1928, Congress authorized payments for overseas mail delivery to commercial shipping companies, granting the latter the kind of support already extended to fledgling airlines. The goal was similar: to make sure there was equipment (in this case ships) available for conversion in the event of war.

A second way was for the federal government to conduct its own research and development. The Naval Appropriations Act of 1915 had authorized the creation of what came to be called the National Advisory Committee for Aeronautics (NACA). The NACA built and operated special facilities at Langley Field near Hampton, Virginia, including a wind tunnel and a shop for developing instruments that could measure the physical loads on aircraft structures tested in the wind tunnel. In 1926, the NACA began holding annual conferences on aircraft technology and design, inviting both government and industry engineers to share the results of their work and suggest new studies that the NACA could undertake. In 1927, the NACA began testing full-size aircraft at the mouth of its new twenty-foot-diameter wind tunnel. The tests led to the development of a drag-reducing cowling for radial, air-cooled engines, and to data on the drag caused by fixed landing gear.[8]

A similar focus on advances in science and technology led the Secretary of the Navy to create the Naval Research Laboratory (NRL) in 1922 and place it under the authority of the Chief of the Bureau of Engineering. The Naval Research Laboratory staff pioneered what came to be called radar. In a 1933 memo to the Chief of the Bureau of Ordnance sent through the Chief of the Bureau of Engineering, the director of the laboratory noted that "new developments in radio at this Laboratory have suggested the idea of building a single 'beam' transmitter and receiver." This was potentially revolutionary. The bane of the fleet was night fighting, which the fleet problems had shown gave the advantage to the attacker. The fleet problems also demonstrated an imperative need for an air search radar, so that aircraft carriers could not be ambushed by surprise. Radar promised to make these problems manageable.

William S. Parsons, a young lieutenant (later admiral) then serving at NRL as liaison officer with his parent bureau (Ordnance), tried very hard to interest officers in both BuOrd and the Bureau of Engineering in this development. It was Parsons who had drafted the memo for NRL's director in the first place. As he recalled in 1949, "In the fall of 1933 certain parts of the navy . . . were aware of the possibility that radar could be developed for search and fire control." Why, then, did it take nearly four more years to test a developmental 200-megahertz radar set on destroyer *Leary* (DD-158) and another two years to have two different prototype sets installed on battleships *New York* and *Texas*? The answer was a lack of vacuum tubes with sufficient power output. As the Chief of the Bureau of Engineering observed in October 1933, progress in "micro ray work" was a function of vacuum tube development, and he recommended a "development contract with a suitable commercial company." But commercial firms such as RCA and General Electric had no apparent need for microwave transmitters and receivers, and so they declined to apply their own research staffs to this work. Only small infusions of money by the Bureau of Aeronautics (BuAer) kept the radar work at NRL going. BuAer wanted a transmitter that could accurately measure a plane's altitude, and microwave technology was something that BuAer's chief, Rear Admiral Ernest J. King, was willing to support.[9]

A third way of supporting what was called the "mobilization base" was to allow the Army and Navy to enter into negotiated contracts for what were called "educational" orders. This technique was particularly suited to military aviation, where dramatic changes in technology often made active aircraft quickly obsolete. Congress granted the military services the authority to negotiate such contracts in the Air Corps Act of 1926. Prior to that time, the services had been compelled to issue invitations to qualified private vendors to bid for the production of aircraft. Existing law had required the government to provide the requirements (including weight, speed, maximum altitude, and bomb load) that the airplanes would have to meet. Interested vendors would respond to the requirements with a design and a price for a certain number of aircraft. Vendor responses would come to the government as sealed bids. The lowest qualified bid won.

The problem with this process was that it hampered progress in aviation technology. New technology, such as the development of high horsepower-to-weight engines and variable-pitch propellers, cost money to develop—money that smaller aircraft manufacturers lacked but desperately needed. Then, as now, manufacturers recouped the cost of their own development and design work by selling large numbers of airplanes. Volume paid for development. But aircraft technology was progressing so fast that the services did not want to purchase large numbers of any particular model airplane, even assuming that Congress would authorize them to do so. Consequently, as aviation historian I. B. Holley Jr., noted, "The seemingly attractive military market was confined more or less to a dozen manufacturers specializing in military types, and even within this group, four firms received the bulk of the business."[10] The others could not hope to win orders that would compensate them for their own research and development.

The services, however, remained concerned about the small size of the aircraft industry compared to overall American industrial capacity, and they wanted to increase the number of private firms developing and building airplanes.

The Army and Navy saw competition among private firms as an effective means of stimulating innovation, and so the more firms there were the better. But smaller companies did not have the workers or the capital to compete head-to-head with the more established enterprises. To both promote innovation and enlarge the manufacturing base, the Air Corps Act of 1926 allowed the Army and Navy to negotiate limited production contracts with those aircraft manufacturers that seemed to have innovative designs. It was a significant break with past government contracting practice.

The Air Corps Act of 1926 also authorized the Army and Navy to procure large numbers of aircraft—one thousand for the Navy and eighteen hundred for the Army—over the next five years. This was the fourth technique for preparing for war—guaranteeing relatively high levels of production for an industry that was militarily necessary but not self-supporting economically. This provision of the act, unfortunately, had one drawback. Congress had not wanted the services to let contracts for the immediate production of all the aircraft authorized by the legislation. Contracts were supposed to be spaced out equally over five years to avoid creating a "bulge" of aircraft that would become obsolete all at once. Because existing aircraft were growing obsolete rapidly, however, Army and Navy aviation officers feared that what appeared to be a good-faith effort on the part of Congress to *increase* aviation forces would in fact not do so. New aircraft would not come into service as fast as obsolete aircraft were retired. The price of avoiding a "bulge" appeared to be accepting a harmful "ceiling" on the numbers of aircraft in service.

The Vinson-Trammell Act of 1934 (Naval Parity Act) had authorized an increase in the number of naval aircraft to 1,910. That increase had come just in time to allow the Navy's Bureau of Aeronautics to procure the aircraft for the new carrier *Ranger* and for the new heavy cruisers that were being commissioned. As in the case of ships, Congress looked carefully at how the new aircraft were acquired. Commander Ralph D. Weyerbacher, a Supply Corps officer assigned to Bureau of Aeronautics when Vinson-Trammell became law, explained the Bureau's acquisition process in detail to members of Congress:

> An informal design competition is held. A proposal stating the Navy's requirements is sent to the industry. Proposals . . . received from interested contractors . . . are classified in accordance with engineering merit only. Contracts are then negotiated with the winners . . . having the highest engineering merits. . . . The contracts usually provide for an option for an experimental squadron.

> After the experimental airplanes have been delivered, there is an additional
> competition in flight of the finished product. . . . The winner in this flight com-
> petition is selected for production. . . .
>
> In negotiating a contract . . . we know from past experience the number of
> man hours of labor that is required; we know the average hourly wage, and the
> price of the material used, and from this we can build up an estimated price.

Members of Congress wondered whether this was the most effective way
to spend public funds. It was definitely not the way that ships were procured.

Admiral Ernest J. King, Chief of the Bureau of Aeronautics, agreed. As he
noted, the bureau was acquiring experimental aircraft "all the time. We try to
build, so to speak, two at a time of each type, so as to get two different contractors and their ideas, . . . and how they are going to put a plane together, and
get those in direct competition in actual planes." A member of Congress wondered whether this wasn't inefficient. King acknowledged that it was. As he
observed, "The construction of planes is not reduced to standard practices or
forms or whatnot, and I doubt if it ever will be. Each time we buy a plane from
a different contractor we have to have a different lot of spare parts. That means
additional expense, storage, distribution, and everything connected with it."

But didn't that mean the Navy's inventory of aircraft was constantly changing? And didn't it therefore follow that maintaining the Navy's air force was very
expensive? Again, King agreed: "We apply [new equipment] as fast as we can, and
in most cases the application can be made to planes in service, to improve their
efficiency." King also noted that the bureau aggressively pursued technology:

> We encourage designs and ideas from any source whatsoever, but when it comes
> to reducing such designs to practice, we must make inquiry as to whether such
> a person or firm has adequate means on hand or in sight . . . to produce such a
> plane. . . . If not, and that is frequently the case, then it becomes a question of
> whether design rights are procured, and the designs then put into the hands of
> people who are competent eventually to produce the production planes.

By saying this, King created a problem for the Navy in the eyes of many
members of Congress. Why, they asked, didn't the Navy buy the rights to innovative aircraft or components and then have them mass-produced at much
lower cost by the winners of competitive production contracts? Why continue
the "experimental orders" allowed by the 1926 law? King responded by shifting to an analogy: A "comparable situation would be for the Navy to buy

designs for a Buick automobile and that the lowest bidder to manufacture it in quantity would be the Chrysler Corporation. I think we could all understand the difficulties that would arise in that case." His words traced the path that the Navy had to take to simultaneously encourage innovation in aircraft development and placate members of Congress who believed that the Navy's procedures for developing and buying aircraft were inherently wasteful.[11]

Congress was equally sensitive about shipbuilding. Navy policy toward the ship construction industry rested on two foundation blocks. The first was the need to award construction contracts to Navy yards such as those at Philadelphia, New York, and Norfolk, Virginia, in order to use their work as a "yardstick" against which to measure the ship construction bids submitted by private yards such as Newport News Shipbuilding and Dry Dock Company, Bethlehem Shipbuilding, and New York Shipbuilding. The second foundation block was the Navy's desire to *expand* the base of qualified shipbuilders so that warships such as destroyers and submarines could be produced in volume during an emergency.

Congress supported this policy. At the same time, however, the law governing contracting tended to lead to the shrinkage of the shipbuilding industry that served the Navy. Contracting for a type of ship was different than contracting for aircraft. The Navy released a preliminary design, prospective *qualified* private bidders responded with sealed bids, and then the lowest bidder was awarded the contract. Because there was no analog to the Air Corps Act of 1926 in ship construction, this process tended to favor the larger firms. They had the trained workers and the facilities already in place for designing and constructing individual ships. How could the Navy legally avoid a situation in which the larger shipbuilders won the bulk of the contracts?

The answer was, again, the Vinson-Trammell Act of 1934. The law allowed the Navy to build to treaty limits, but it did not specify that all the building had to be done at once. The Navy was permitted to increase the number of new ships gradually, at its own pace, until the treaty limit was reached, no later than 1942. This allowed the Navy's Bureau of Construction and Repair to spread the work around. In 1934, for example, the first year to which Vinson-Trammell applied, the Navy awarded the following ship construction contracts: one light cruiser to Newport News Shipbuilding and Dry Dock Company, four destroyers to Bethlehem Steel's shipbuilding division, two destroyers to Federal Shipbuilding in New Jersey (a subsidiary of U.S. Steel), two submarines to Electric Boat in Connecticut, and a light cruiser to New York Shipbuilding. The Navy's own building yards (at New York; Philadelphia; Boston; Mare Island, California; Puget Sound, Washington; Portsmouth, New Hampshire; and Norfolk, Virginia) also built warships. In 1934, these yards were authorized to construct one heavy cruiser, one light cruiser, three submarines, and eight destroyers.

Industry representatives accepted this division of labor between the public and private yards because their firms were already busy working on the new construction authorized by the National Industrial Recovery Act of 1933. Newport News, for example, had already begun work on aircraft carriers *Yorktown* (CV-5) and *Enterprise* (CV-6), and the Bethlehem yard at Quincy, Massachusetts, was beginning construction of two heavy cruisers (later named *Quincy* (CA-39) and *Vincennes* (CA-44). Federal, Electric Boat, New York Shipbuilding, and even a revived Bath Iron Works had also been given portions of the new ship construction program in 1933, and there was only so much work that any one yard could take on.

The Navy continued this policy of "spreading the work" throughout the 1930s. In 1938, after Congress had authorized the Navy to expand beyond the limits set in 1934, the Navy Department awarded one battleship contract (for BB-58, *Indiana*) to Newport News, another (BB-59, *Massachusetts*) to Bethlehem-Quincy, and a third (BB-57, *South Dakota*) to New York Shipbuilding. The Norfolk Navy Yard was authorized to construct BB-60 (later *Alabama*), while the Navy yard at New York got BB-61 (*Iowa*) and the government yard at Philadelphia was given BB-62 (*New Jersey*). Bath Iron Works and Federal Shipbuilding each bid successfully for two destroyers, while Electric Boat was awarded three submarine construction contracts. Government yards began work on a submarine tender (AS-11), three submarines, four destroyers, two minesweepers, four small seaplane tenders, and a minelayer.

During the period 1930 through 1939, forty-five of ninety destroyers begun during the decade were built in private yards. For submarines, the ratio was twenty-one of thirty-seven; for light and heavy cruisers, the ratio was twelve of twenty-one. In short, the Navy's bureaus concerned with ship construction saw to it that both private and public yards were given adequate work. That is, they were given practice in the construction of new ships and new shipbuilding technologies, especially welding.

The Bureau of Engineering also cooperated with commercial boiler and turbine manufacturers in developing higher temperature and pressure steam plants. The four-stack, flush deck destroyers of World War I, for example, had boilers that produced steam at 265 pounds per square inch (psi) pressure.

Farragut (DD-348), the first of the post–World War I destroyers, had boilers that produced steam at 400 psi. *Somers* (DD-381), commissioned in 1937, had a steam plant that worked at 600 psi. Both the Navy and commercial shipping companies wanted lighter, more economical power plants for their ships. The firms making that equipment responded by boosting the energy output per pound of machinery.[12]

Another critical element of the Navy's preparation for war was not, officially, part of the Navy at all. In 1936, Congress passed the Merchant Marine Act. One purpose of the law was to provide American shipping firms with operating subsidies so that they could compete with foreign shippers that offered lower rates over certain transport paths considered essential for national defense. A second goal was to subsidize the construction of merchant ships and tankers that could be converted into Navy auxiliaries. The first chairman of the Maritime Commission was Joseph P. Kennedy, who left early in 1938 to serve as the American ambassador in London. His post was then filled by retired Rear Admiral Emory S. Land, who had headed the Navy's Bureau of Construction and Repair from the spring of 1933 until four years later, when he retired from the Navy to take a place on the board of the Maritime Commission.

Land, a cousin of aviator Charles A. Lindbergh and a protégé of the Navy's highly esteemed naval architect David W. Taylor, was a competent executive who had served as one of the Navy's pioneer submarine designers and then shifted fields to work for Rear Admiral Moffett in the Bureau of Aeronautics. Land, a graduate of the Naval Academy and the Massachusetts Institute of Technology, learned to fly while working for Moffett and then, as head of Construction and Repair, persuaded Congress in 1936 to fund the Navy's large-model-hull test tank at Carderock, Maryland (which he named after Admiral Taylor).

Land was also something of a confidant of President Roosevelt, and with the president's knowledge he hired a number of retired Navy officers for the Maritime Commission's staff, and sent all specifications for subsidized ships to the Navy Department for the latter's approval. As historian Frederic Lane noted:

Under [Land's] leadership the Commission and its staff set to work to get modern freighters built for the American merchant marine without waiting for applications from the industry for construction subsidies. The Commission, not the private companies, took the initiative.... The Commission drew plans for modern fast cargo ships, invited bids from shipyards, played newcomers against old-timers to beat down prices, and then awarded contracts—all without any assurance of being able to sell the ships to operators.

It was an extraordinary achievement that would prove essential to victory in World War II.[13]

Finally, the Navy could build on its civil engineering successes of World War I. The Bureau of Yards and Docks, led by the Navy's civil engineers, was "charged with the design and construction of the public works and public utilities of the Navy, wherever located," and their projects had been both massive and successful in 1917–18. In under two years, "the expenditures for public works of all kinds carried out under the supervision of the Bureau . . . were more than the total expenditure that had been made at all navy yards and naval stations during the preceding 125 years." Put another way, a century of neglect had been compensated for almost overnight.

At the New York Navy Yard, for example, one slip for building battleships had been modernized and enlarged, and another built from scratch. At the Philadelphia yard, two nine-hundred-foot battle cruiser building slips had been constructed; new battleship building slips were also built at Norfolk and Mare Island, California. The industrial facilities at the naval gun factory in the Washington Navy Yard were also dramatically enlarged, and some of the buildings are still standing. The Navy even subsidized the increase of shipbuilding capacity at selected commercial shipyards. All this construction gave Yards and Docks engineers critical experience in designing facilities and working with commercial firms to get them built. Officers in the bureau knew what industry could do, and they relied on that knowledge—and their industry contacts—during World War II.

Yards and Docks had also constructed an aircraft factory near the Philadelphia Navy Yard during World War I. Navy Secretary Daniels had stated that the purpose of the facility was "to supply a part, at least, of its own [aircraft] needs . . . and keep the navy in the forefront with the latest developments in aircraft." Rear Admiral Moffett had defended the factory in 1923 by arguing that "the Naval Aircraft Factory bears the same relation to the Naval Air Service that Navy Yards bear to the Fleet." He had, however, moved the factory's role from that of production of quantities of aircraft to production of experimental aircraft and of items that private firms could not make profitably.

But the proper role of the Philadelphia facility remained a matter of controversy. In 1935, Rear Admiral King, Moffett's successor, was defending the Naval Aircraft Factory against congressional critics with these words: "I think that it is not at all a bad thing for the Government to manufacture 10 percent of its planes and engines for the reason that it will give a great many people, in and out of the service, confidence in the Navy Department's capacity to judge of what prices are being asked by private contractors. In other words, we will have a 'yardstick.'" In plain terms, the Congress could allow the Navy its means of evaluating the cost proposals of private firms or it could bear the consequences. Did the Congress want to strip the Navy of one of its more important industrial plants and give the work to private industry, or did it want to hear the Navy say that costs of aircraft could not be held down because the Navy lacked a "yardstick" against which to measure them? The members had to decide. If they wanted cost controls, then the aircraft factory and the Navy yards had to stay.[14]

And so it went, year in and year out. The Navy's officers had to manage their own industrial facilities, their own research establishments, and their own supply services. They also had to contract with private industry for items ranging from "consumables" such as food to complex systems such as battleships—and they had to do it under exacting legal constraints and the eagle eyes of members of Congress. Much of the Navy's industrial activity, as well as its ongoing contractual relations with private industry, was not visible outside the Navy beyond a small circle composed of members of Congress, industry commentators, leaders of such professional societies as the Society of Naval Architects and Marine Engineers, and industry lobbyists. But this work was critical to maintaining the foundation of naval expansion in wartime, and that expansion was essential to victory in World War II.

This chapter has focused on what many historical studies ignore—the workings of a complex military organization in *peacetime*. The number of *bureaucratic* issues that the Navy had to grapple with were many, and this chapter has highlighted only three: (a) balancing the need for organizational effectiveness, achieved by making the CNO the Navy's real leader, with the need to maintain accountability to the people's representatives in Congress; (b) balancing the need for regular training against the need to prepare the fleet's leading officers for wartime command; and (c) balancing the Navy's desire to support its industrial base against the laws that the Congress had written and the regulations that the Navy's leaders had prepared in order to make the relationship between the Navy and industry open to public scrutiny.

Note that the key word in each case is "balance." Achieving, day in and day out, a succession of lawful but common sense balances is what good public officials do. Unfortunately, the need for qualified officials, both civilian and military, and an awareness of their role, often goes unappreciated because what these public servants do is usually not in the public's eye. This chapter has attempted to rectify that oversight by showing how important these "balance" issues were in the interwar years. Members of the Congress and the Navy's leaders invested their time and their energy in such matters because they knew that the solutions they hammered out would matter not only in peacetime but especially if war came.

S-22 at Portsmouth, New Hampshire, in 1929, after being fitted with an experimental escape hatch forward of her 4-inch deck gun. The several dozen S-type submarines differed among themselves in size, appearance, and performance. They were the mainstay of the Navy's submarine force until the late 1930s. —*Navy Department, National Archives*

Submarine V-4, the minelaying *Argonaut* (later SM-1), in a dock with the smaller O-2 in 1928. *Argonaut* was authorized in 1924 and launched in 1927. She was commissioned a month after this photograph was taken. She was 381 feet in length, and her submerged displacement was 4,080 tons. O-2, commissioned in 1918, was 172 feet long and displaced 629 tons submerged. *Argonaut's* forward 6-inch gun is partially covered in canvas in this photograph.
—*Navy Department, National Archives*

K-5 (SS-36), a small coast defense submarine commissioned in 1914. She has three "Y" tubes of a passive sonar above her bow and an "SC" trainable T-shaped passive underwater sound detector farther back. In World War I, the Navy developed a range of passive sonars. But in 1923, when *K-5* was decommissioned, the Navy switched to active, "pinging" sonars. —*Navy Department, National Archives*

Submarines alongside a tender in 1939. Pictured are *Stingray* (186), *Plunger* (179), *Salmon* (182), *Perch* (176), and one other. Note their dark color, designed to make them less visible to airplanes when they were submerged at periscope depth. Though smaller than the larger B type and cruiser submarines, these "pigboats" had the armament and the endurance to make them effective in a Pacific war. —*U.S. Naval Institute Photo Archive*

This may well be Petty Officer William Badders, wrestling with the salvage pontoons that were used to raise the sunken *S-51*. Cdr. Edward Ellsberg captured the courage and determination of sailors such as Badders in his stirring *On the Bottom*. Submarine sailors might die as the result of peacetime accidents, but the Navy would not abandon them if it could help it. —*U.S. Naval Institute Photo Archive*

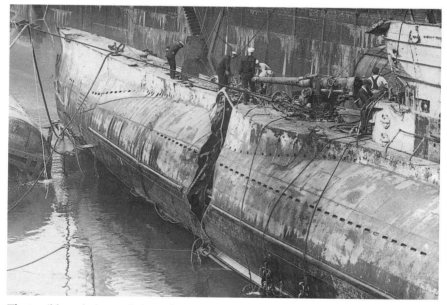

The terrible gash that sank *S-51*. She rests here in a dry dock at the Brooklyn Navy Yard, festooned with the many lines that were tied to her in the course of the long struggle to bring her to the surface. —*U.S. Naval Institute Photo Archive*

Bass (SS-164), one of the first of the post-World War I fleet submarines, in the early 1930s, alongside another of her class. The mast at her bow elevated her radio aerials so she could report sightings of a hostile fleet to U.S. forces. *Bass* was built larger than the flush-decked, four-stack destroyers built during World War I so that she would have the endurance to scout for the fleet. Behind the two subs are an ocean-going tug and a small minesweeper. —*Alex Blendl*

The flagship of the United States Fleet, battleship *Pennsylvania*, steams under the Golden Gate Bridge into San Francisco Bay for a formal fleet review by President Franklin D. Roosevelt in July 1939. *Pennsylvania* carried four seaplanes instead of the usual three. The fourth was reserved for the fleet's commander in chief, Adm. Claude E. Bloch, whose four-star flag flies from *Pennsylvania*'s mainmast. —*San Francisco Maritime National Historical Park*

Battleships being turned and berthed at Pearl Harbor. Two Maryland class are in place. A third is being nudged into its spot alongside another by three tugs. The Army spent large sums before and just after World War I to turn Oahu into a major fortress. Certain that the island was secure, the Navy gradually expanded its base facilities in Pearl Harbor and dredged it so that even the largest ships could berth there.
—*Navy Department, National Archives*

Gunners on *West Virginia* with one of their 15-by-15-feet short-range battle practice targets in 1930. The size and design of the target varied with the contest. Long-range firing by the 16-inch guns was done against long target rafts sporting several hundred yards of wooden battens fastened to large vertical frames. The 5-inch guns practiced against smaller canvas targets like this one, which is draped along the side of a 16-inch gun turret so that the gun crew can be captured in a celebratory photograph. —*West Virginia State Archives*

Carriers *Lexington* and *Saratoga* in the Bay of Panama, off the Pacific entrance to the Panama Canal, in 1934. The ships with the four smokestacks are Omaha-class light cruisers. —*Navy Department, National Archives*

Fleet flagship *Pennsylvania* anchored at San Diego in June 1932. A portion of the North Island Naval Air Station forms the background. The main buildings at North Island were designed with a classic Spanish motif. The airfield is in the distance. The seaplane ramp and main hangar are just behind the battleship. When not at sea, carrier squadrons were based here, and North Island formed the backdrop for such popular movies as *Hell Divers*.
—*Navy Department, National Archives*

A specially built raft used for battleship target practice. The rafts were 140 feet long and carried 40-foot-high frames on which were mounted long horizontal strips of wood loosely wired together. Battleships also practiced gunnery by offset shooting—deliberately setting their heaviest guns to fire in the wake of a battleship steaming on a parallel course. —*Navy Department, National Archives*

This is one of the Navy's images of itself in the 1930s: signalmen on the bridge of battleship *New Mexico* with sister ship *Idaho* in the background. The signalman closest to the camera is rapidly pulling signal flags from their locker and attaching them to the signal halyard. The photograph combines tradition (from the work and the sailors' uniforms), the serenity of a Pacific sea and sky, and the symbolic strength inherent in the battle line. —*Navy Department, National Archives*

9
EFFECT OF THE MARINES ON THE NAVY

Under no circumstances shall any Marine enlisted man be employed as a servant.

U.S. Navy Regulations, 1920

"Good-by," I said.
"Maybe you need a little help."
I shook myself like a wet dog. "I need a company of marines . . ."

Raymond Chandler,
Farewell My Lovely

The Marine Corps has a unique place in American history. It is a hallowed organization. Its saints are common soldiers, most not far beyond adolescence. Some were just boys when they waged the terrible battles that took their lives or shook what humanity they had to its roots. Students of their struggles (some of the better of them Marines themselves) have produced fascinating, thoughtful histories of their campaigns, and the Corps itself (especially its many veterans) has kept charge of an extraordinarily potent myth.

By comparison, this chapter will take its lead from a point Vice Admiral George C. Dyer made in 1966: "Since most of the books devoting any large amount of space to . . . amphibious doctrine have been sponsored by the Marine Corps or written by Marines, it is perhaps natural that the work and contributions . . . of various other parts of the Department of the Navy . . . have not been stressed." In this chapter we will attempt to cover those contributions. We will also suggest, however, that the implications of the amphibious doctrine developed by the Marine Corps in the 1930s did not gain the attention within the Navy that they deserved. That was partly because of timing; amphibious doctrine came along rather late in the interwar period. But it was also because the Navy just did not realize how important an effective, *standing* amphibious force was to war at sea.

The Marine Corps remade itself in the years between World War I and World War II. For example, *U.S. Navy Regulations, 1920* defined the duties of the Marine Corps as follows:

(a) To furnish organizations for duty afloat . . .

(b) To garrison the different navy yards and naval stations . . .

(c) To furnish the first line of the mobile defenses of naval bases and stations beyond the continental limits of the United States.

(d) To man such naval defenses . . . as may be erected for the defense of naval bases and naval stations beyond the continental limits of the United States.

(e) To furnish such garrisons and expeditionary forces for duties beyond the seas as may be necessary in time of peace.

Yet in 1921, Major Earl H. Ellis convinced the commandant of the Marine Corps to accept a different statement of the mission of the Corps:

> In order to impose our will upon Japan, it will be necessary for us to project our fleet and land forces across the Pacific and wage war in Japanese waters. To effect this requires that we have sufficient bases to support the fleet, both during its projecting and afterwards. As the matter stands at present, we cannot count upon the use of any bases west of Hawaii except those which we may seize from the enemy after the opening of hostilities.

The history of the Marine Corps in the 1920s and 1930s is therefore a history of an organization changing itself. And, as the Marines changed, the Navy had to follow. The Marines became an amphibious force *within* the Navy, and, in so doing, began a process of changing the Navy, too. The dramatic implications of this change from within weren't obvious at the time. It took a war to get naval officers to realize that large-scale, successful amphibious warfare gave the Navy and the nation a new and powerful strategic tool.

In 1921, Marines (and sailors, too) were prepared to foray ashore for raids, or to rescue endangered American citizens, or to establish a base for the Navy in wartime (as Marines had done at Guantanamo Bay in the Spanish-American War). But Ellis grasped that what came to be called "amphibious warfare" was much more than the occasional raid. It was the use of forces from the sea to achieve decisive results in major land campaigns. The British had tried just such a move at Gallipoli in 1915—and had failed. Ellis and his colleagues in the Marine Corps had to demonstrate that a major amphibious campaign could succeed.

British forces had a long history of using the sea as a means of moving troops to attack or harass a land-based enemy army at a weak point. In the eighteenth and nineteenth centuries, navies had much greater strategic mobility than armies, and Britain's Royal Navy could use that mobility to gain a tactical advantage for England's small army that offset its relatively modest size. Someone once said that the Royal Navy could therefore be likened to a cannon that fired a "shell" called the British army. The failed amphibious campaign against Turkish forces at Gallipoli in World War I discredited this simile. The Marines set out, in the 1920s and 1930s, to restore it—for the United States.

Others have told the story of how this was done in detail. The studies of Gallipoli and related campaigns led to a series of exercises with the fleet and even with the Army in the 1920s. Marines conducted a mock amphibious assault on the Panama Canal in 1923, and tests of amphibious equipment and tactics on Culebra Island, Puerto Rico, the following year. A major Army, Navy, and Marine Corps exercise was staged on Oahu, Hawaii, in 1925. The goal was to determine whether the assaults that were part of the "Orange" trans-Pacific war plan were feasible.

The assessment of the results of these exercises led directly to a new statement of tactical Marine Corps doctrine: the *Tentative Manual for Landing Operations* of 1934. The *Tentative Manual* overcame the division between sea and shore that had so bedeviled the British at Gallipoli by abolishing it:

> A landing operation against opposition is, in effect, an assault on an organized or unorganized defensive position modified by substituting initially ships' gunfire for that of light, medium, and heavy field artillery, and frequently, carrier-based aviation for land-based air units until the latter can be operated from shore.

This doctrine was revolutionary. It did not just say that the Navy would move the Marines (or the Army) from place to place in order to surprise an enemy. It also did not say that fleet gunfire and air operations would be used temporarily to back up a raid. Instead, it said that the reason why the British failed was because they did not treat the fleet as a source of organic support for the land forces. Put another way, the Marine Corps developed a doctrine that required the Marine Corps "tail" to wag the Navy "dog" instead of the other way around.

According to Vice Admiral Dyer, none of this would have happened without the support of senior Navy officers, especially Admiral Robert E. Coontz, Chief of Naval Operations and then Commander-in-Chief of the U. S. Fleet. In 1925, for example, Coontz recognized that landing operations placed a special burden on the Navy—that of designing special landing craft, providing gunfire support on a continuing basis for Marines assaulting a hostile shore, and systematically training officers to handle the boats carrying Marine infantry to a defended beach.[1]

This new set of *naval* requirements generated conflict between the Navy and the Marines on two levels. The first was over the details of the Orange plan for war against Japan. As Edward S. Miller revealed in his detailed study of pre–World War II Pacific war planning, the Marines immediately took Navy plans for attacks on Japanese-held islands and began drawing from them their force and tactical requirements. How many Marines would be needed for the assaults? What support would they require from the Navy? Who would defend an island after the Marines captured it? Marine planners worked backward from the operational goals set by their Navy counterparts in the Office of the Chief of Naval Operations.

The numbers they came up with stunned Navy commanders. In 1935, for example, Marine planners considering assaults on the Marshall Islands wanted half the Navy's battleships for artillery support and all the active carriers to gain air superiority over the Marshalls themselves. But how could the Navy assign such forces to an amphibious campaign when they knew the Imperial Fleet would be thundering down on what was left of the U.S. Fleet, eager for *the* decisive battle at sea? In front of the General Board in 1938, Marine officers argued for more land-based aircraft for their assault forces, even if getting those aircraft meant taking them from what the naval aviators thought was their minimum requirement. Marines also asked for dedicated ships to move their own aviation units forward with their assault forces. The Navy balked at such requests, even when Army war planners offered new long-range aircraft such as the B-17 to shield amphibious operations from attack by Japanese naval forces.

As Miller found, "The navy remained adamant that the carriers must roam free." But as Miller also discovered, trying to resolve the seeming impasse that divided Navy and Marine Corps planners led to some breakthroughs. First, planners abandoned the idea that they should capture most islands in a cluster. If it were necessary to take and hold a base in the Marshalls, then one or two islands would do. American aviation could keep the Japanese from reinforcing the rest. Second, the island stepping-stones to Japanese home waters would have to be selected from among those that land-based aviation could reach. Instead of using bombers such as the B-17 to shield amphibious assaults, the Navy's carriers would shield the bomber bases with its carriers, and the bombers would pummel Japanese island bases and defenses.[2]

The second level of conflict between the Marines and the Navy focused on particulars. In landing exercises on Oahu in 1932, the participants discovered a number of obstacles to conducting a successful amphibious assault. Ships' boats, for example, were inadequate landing craft for heavily armed Marines who expected to land in the face of enemy defenses. Even the fifty-foot motor launches carried by battleships had problems putting Marines ashore in any kind of surf and pulling off again.

This prompted both the Navy and the Marines to search for new forms of landing craft. The Navy pursued and tested its own designs as well as commercial offerings that might be adapted to mass production. Exercises with prototypes showed that the problem of developing suitable landing craft was not a minor one. As historian Leo J. Daugherty III found, the Marines realized that they needed landing craft for personnel, "lighters" for vehicles and tanks, and amphibious vehicles that could "swim" ashore on their own. The Marines also needed specially designed amphibious transports. The Navy only had one—*Henderson*, built during World War I—and that was clearly not enough.

To make sure that the Marines got their landing craft, Secretary of the Navy Claude Swanson established the senior Continuing Board for the Development of Landing Boats for Training in Landing Operations in January 1937. Admiral Arthur J. Hepburn, the Fleet Commander, set up the Fleet Development Board to oversee the testing of the landing craft that were bought commercially or produced to a Navy design. For the next three years, Navy and Marine Corps officers tried to find landing craft that met their requirements. Seeing Japanese forces use such craft effectively near Shanghai in 1937 provoked the Marine Corps to put extra pressure on the Navy, but the process of finding suitable landing craft was not successful until 1940, when the Navy procured numbers of the soon-to-be-famous Higgins Boats.

In later years, Andrew J. Higgins, who had created the firm that produced the best landing craft of the crop of commercial boats that the Navy tested, claimed that first the Bureau of Construction and Repair and then its successor, the Bureau of Ships, had deliberately tried to avoid buying his shallow-water craft. That may be; the evidence is mixed. But two points should be kept in mind. First, the Navy paid for and staged a series of increasingly sophisticated fleet landing exercises from 1935 through 1941. These exercises tested equipment (including landing craft and radios), doctrine (for fire support from planes and ships), and tactics (whether night landings were safer than those in daylight, for example).[3]

Second, Navy officers did not lose sight of the need to support the Marines. The decisions of Admiral Coontz have already been mentioned. Another, later, case was when Admiral Edward C. Kalbfus brought the "Alligator" amphibious tractor to the attention of his Marine colleagues. The tractor, based on a commercially produced vehicle designed to navigate the Florida Everglades, was the third piece of the puzzle of getting the Marines ashore.

Supporting them once they got there also posed problems for the Navy. At first glance, battleships seemed ideal gunfire support ships. Their 14- and 16-inch guns appeared powerful enough to smash almost any land defenses. However, for Navy battleships to provide amphibious operations with effective gunfire support, they had to have shells that were *not* armor piercing.

The armor-piercing shells, designed to break through dense armor plate, were mostly metal. For example, the 14-inch, 50-caliber armor-piercing shell fired by *Tennessee* in the 1920s had an explosive filler that weighed only 29.5 pounds. The shell weighed a total of 1,400 pounds. The filler was only 2.1 percent of the projectile's weight. The heavier 1,500-pound shell developed by the Bureau of Ordnance in the 1930s had an explosive charge that weighed only 22.5 pounds, or 1.5 percent of the projectile's total weight.

The heavy, dense shells were designed to crash through an enemy's thick armor plates and *then* explode. Explosive force was traded off to increase the chance that the shell would break through armor. The "high capacity" or "bombardment" shells, by contrast, were of lighter construction overall, were fused to burst on impact, and carried a heavier bursting charge. The Mk. 9 for the 14-inch, 50-caliber gun weighed 1,410 pounds and carried an explosive filler weighing 105 pounds. About 7.5 percent of the shell's total weight, and much more of its internal volume, was devoted to its explosive charge.

Assuming that the bombardment shells worked as intended, battleships could strike effectively at those targets ashore that their guns could reach. Ship-to-shore gunfire was tested in all the fleet landing exercises from 1935 until the last of the prewar maneuvers in the spring of 1941. The lessons learned were significant. The need for special bombardment ammunition became very clear very quickly. So, too, were the effects of the various shells: from the larger, heavier ones down to the 5-inch and 4-inch ones fired by destroyers. Gunfire was controlled effectively from the air and from fire control parties ashore. In addition, as one report noted, "fire can be rapidly and effectively shifted at any time, to any target, subject to the limitation [i.e., range] of the particular projectile."

Most important, however, was the lesson learned about coordination: the actions of planes, ships firing at land targets, transports, and assault boats could be conducted successfully "on a strict time schedule." That meant the challenge of Gallipoli had been overcome—Marines could assault a *defended* beach. Unfortunately, there was no funding to conduct full-scale tests. Ships didn't fire what the Army considered an adequate barrage (equal to sixteen 75-mm shells per minute in a one hundred yard square for three consecutive minutes) until 1938. Moreover, the ships—especially the battleships—engaged in fire support exercises tended *not* to be first line units. Even in 1939, the battleships firing at shore targets were *Texas, New York,* and *Wyoming,* and the last of these had been partially disarmed in accordance with the provisions of the London Naval Treaty of 1930.[4]

There was another issue that the landing exercises didn't resolve: What should be the mix of armor-piercing and bombardment shells in a battleship's magazines? *Tennessee* carried a maximum of twelve hundred 14-inch shells, or one hundred for each of her twelve big guns. That may sound like a lot, but it is not—not in a heavy engagement, whether against enemy defenses on land or against enemy ships at sea. In peacetime, however, there was not enough money to pay for a battleship to empty her magazines by continuous firing, so no one knew just what the rate of sustained fire would be in a fleet engagement, and therefore there was no telling just what the mix of shells (armor-piercing and bombardment) should be in a battleship's magazine. It also wasn't clear how much replenishment the battleships would need if they spent several days pounding a defended beach before a Marine assault.

In World War II, when money was no longer a problem, Fleet Commander Admiral Ernest J. King ordered *Idaho* (BB-42) to find out. As Norman Friedman learned, *Idaho* "actually fired off 100 rounds per gun of her two forward turrets on the morning of 10 October 1942." Of the 156 salvos fired, in only twenty were all six guns in the two forward turrets fired together. As Friedman learned, "more often (forty-seven times) five of the six could fire together. . . . On average the interval between salvoes was 1 minute 24 seconds. However, a 5-gun salvo was fired only forty-nine seconds after the previous salvo, and salvoes sixty to eighty, mostly 5-gun salvoes, were fired at an average interval of sixty-seven seconds." That is, it took just over a minute to level the guns, open the breeches, ram home shell and powder bags separately, close the breeches, elevate the guns, and get off the next salvo.

This exercise proved that battleships could indeed sustain high rates of fire, and it would not take long for them to empty their magazines. How, then, should they be loaded for an amphibious operation? If Japanese battleships came out to fight and ships such as *Idaho* carried mostly non-armor-piercing shells, the whole operation—never mind how the Marines were doing ashore— would be in grave danger. But if the battleships did not carry enough bombardment shells, then the Marine assault might be defeated. Or, if it succeeded, the cost in casualties might be so terrible that there would not be enough Marines left for further attacks. Remember that there were only 14,500 Marines in 1934 and just over 17,000 five years later. Individual Marines were (and remained) a scarce resource until war began.

The distribution of shells between armor-piercing and bombardment would not matter as much if fresh supplies were always at hand, but nothing like that could be guaranteed the fleet in the 1930s, and that is one reason the chiefs of Naval Operations in that decade wanted many more auxiliaries (tankers, tenders, supply ships, and so forth) in the fleet. It is also why gunfire exercises in support of operations ashore did not reveal all the problems that would arise in World War II. There just wasn't money to pay for such an expenditure of shells.[5]

By 1939, however, progress was being made in all the areas identified by the Marines in 1935 except one—the development of a unique amphibious command ship. The reason for this lapse (which would be corrected in World War II) was that the naval part of an amphibious operation was placed under the command of a naval officer. It was assumed that the Marine Corps commander would assume command of his ground and air forces after the former had secured enough of a foothold ashore to support his command staff and their equipment. Not well understood was the need to have a joint command that would stay together for the duration of the amphibious operation on a ship dedicated to that mission. The danger—and the Marines were aware of it in the 1930s—was that the Navy ships and aircraft supporting them would pull out and head for the enemy if scouts detected the approach of the Imperial Japanese Navy.

This fear of being left without support was one reason why Marine Corps leaders pressed so emphatically and persistently for their own air force. In the fall of 1932, for example, Marine aviation consisted of eight squadrons (eighty-eight aircraft). Most (forty-eight) were observation planes, assigned the task of spotting gunfire and finding the enemy. Only twenty-two were fighters. The rest were utility aircraft and transports. But all were active. Elements of the two fighting squadrons and twelve observation aircraft had flown off carriers *Lexington* (CV-2) and *Saratoga* (CV-3) in the summer of 1931. Many of the remaining observation planes and most of the eight transports had deployed to Nicaragua or Haiti to support Marine ground units. By the summer of 1938, there were 143 active aircraft in eleven squadrons, but, as in 1932, only two of the eleven squadrons were composed of fighters. Moreover, the only regular overseas deployment was to St. Thomas in the Virgin Islands.

One problem facing Marine Corps aviation was how to get to the fight. As early as 1928, the Marines had asked for a small carrier or at least a specialized aircraft transport. Their leaders were quite aware that the Navy was, because of treaty restrictions, short of aircraft carriers, but the Marines did not want to stage an assault without their own aircraft in support. For its part, the Navy did not want to see any of its scarce and essential carrier tonnage corralled by the Marines. This conflict continued into the early part of 1940, with the Chief of the Bureau of Aeronautics, Rear Admiral John H. Towers, rejecting a proposal for a special seagoing tender for Marine Corps combat aircraft.

However, the exposure of Marine pilots and their ground crews to Navy procedures had some positive effects. In 1968, retired Marine Brigadier General Edward C. Dyer, who served with one of the Marine detachments sent to a carrier, recalled that his experience was

> a rude awakening. . . . There was no monkey business whatsoever. In the first place we were handed a doctrine, a book, a guide, that told us how the squadron should be organized. . . . The organization and operation of the squadron was definitely controlled. . . . All of our material was requisitioned and accounted for. We were required to follow a training syllabus. We had so many hours of gunnery, so many hours of navigation, so many hours of radio practice, so many hours of formation flying, so many hours of night flying, and we jolly well had to do it.

They were part of the Navy, and the Navy was a "fighting machine."[6]

The development of the Fleet Marine Force was an innovation equal to that of naval aviation in importance. Though that force started small—one regiment of infantry and supporting artillery—it advanced in both size and sophistication in much the same way as naval aviation advanced. Marine Corps officers studied the problems of amphibious operations, then drafted tentative doctrine covering such operations, and finally tested that doctrine in a series of exercises. Lessons learned in the exercises were plowed back into the doctrine and also used as the basis for decisions about the development of small landing craft and the purchase (after 1938) of amphibious tractors. This was basically the same cycle of thought, tests, and more thought that had proved so useful in naval aviation. Progress for the Marines, unfortunately, was constrained by a lack of funds to a degree that had not hampered naval aviation.

For example, in the same hearing before the General Board in 1938 when the Marine Corps representatives had asked for more aircraft, they noted that the difference between success and failure in storming a defended beach was the length of time that shells or bombs would *not* strike the defenders as the Marine landing craft approached. Clearly, the Navy's barrage had to stay ahead of the Marines if its shells were not to strike the Marines themselves. But the Marines wanted as much *close, organic* support as possible, and they thought they could get it only from their own air units; they therefore wanted a dedicated carrier. That's what they had learned from the limited number of exercises that a scarcity of funds had allowed, and that was just one piece of the larger tapestry of amphibious operations that they were weaving with the Navy.

The Navy, sadly, was slow to see this tapestry. The first concern of naval officers was to restore and modernize the fleet, especially the combat ships. The General Board, charged with advising the Secretary of the Navy on ship designs, reviewed most of the designs in the 1930s that would play such a major role in World War II—even including smaller ships such as minesweepers and net layers. Little attention, however, was devoted to amphibious transports, and none was given to the military potential of a permanent amphibious command ship.

As late as the spring of 1940, the board was reviewing two small but fast (sixteen knot) transports (APA-1 and APA-11) being designed specifically by the Maritime Commission for the Marines. The Marines had a set of requirements based on the lessons learned from the fleet landing exercises. They knew how much space they needed on these ships for gasoline, ammunition, vehicles, and combat troops. They knew how large the cargo hatches on the ships needed to be and how much deck space they needed on each ship so that they could assemble their men before transferring them to their landing craft. The Marines were happy to see the Maritime Commission designing the first purpose-built amphibious transports in a generation.

But the Navy bureau representatives admitted to the members of the General Board that they had not yet figured out how to get Marines off the decks of these transports and into their landing craft quickly and safely. They accepted the Marine Corps doctrine that Marine units had to be transferred from specialized transports to landing craft while beyond the range of short-range enemy defenses, but no one knew how to do this quickly while preserving the organization of the Marine assault units.

Navy officers testifying before the General Board also complained that smaller transports were less cost-efficient than larger ones, and they admitted that they had voluntarily passed the responsibility for carefully designing such ships to the Maritime Commission. Missing from the discussion was the careful attention to detail that the bureaus usually gave to issues of ship design. Also missing was an appreciation of the scale of construction that would be required in the event of a war in the Pacific. The OPNAV war planners were more or less on target with their estimates of the resources required for a Pacific amphibious campaign. The bureaus weren't nearly ready to support them in 1940, despite the reports of a series of useful fleet landing exercises.[7]

Nonetheless, amphibious warfare changed the Navy profoundly. In 1939, for example, the Navy had only one amphibious transport designed as such— *Henderson*. By the end of 1944, the Navy had over eighty—and that doesn't count the *attack* transports (APAs, of which there were nearly two hundred) or the plethora of other, related ships that formed the Navy's huge amphibious force. Most of these ships were conversions of Maritime Commission designs, which demonstrates the importance of the Maritime Commission to the Navy. But the Navy also paid for the construction of thousands of large (the LST, or landing ship tank) and small (the thirty-six-foot Higgins Boat was just one of many) landing craft during the war—an armada that was, in effect, a navy of its own.

The Marines had chosen to affirm the commitment to the Navy that their most famous prewar commandant, Major General John A. Lejeune, had expressed in an essay in the *Naval Institute Proceedings* in October 1925. In that paper, Lejeune had argued that the Marine Corps "must ever be associated with the Navy, understanding the life at sea, the requirements and methods of naval warfare, and [be] imbued with the *esprit* of the naval service." Despite very real disputes between Navy and Marine Corps officers over funding and just how the fleet would sustain the Marines during amphibious operations, the prewar Marines did not entertain the idea that they would ever abandon their naval roots.

To do so would have meant amalgamation with the Army, and that was an option Marine Corps officers chose not to consider, despite the problems being a part of the Navy caused them.

In the National Archives there is a photograph of a Marine enlisted radio operator on a bridge wing of battleship *Maryland* (BB-46) during the assault on Tarawa in November 1943. He was trying without success to sustain communication with assault troops pinned down by Japanese gunfire. *Maryland* did not have a communications division dedicated to and equipped properly for the assault, and individual Marines paid a terrible price for that lapse. Yet the need for such an organization with its own equipment had been made apparent by the prewar exercises. It is true, as Jeter Isely and Philip Crowl pointed out in their *The U.S. Marines and Amphibious War*, that "at the war's beginning, United States forces had at their disposal a body of tactical principles forming a basic amphibious doctrine which the test of warfare proved to be sound." But it's also true that the Marines, *by accepting the limits of the Navy's budget and the process by which the Navy developed innovations,* found themselves playing a deadly version of catch-up ball once war began.[8]

10
THE LURE OF THE EAST

"China": Around in your ricksha at day break, remorseful and bitter with hate. Back to your ship or your barracks, going on duty at eight. And so the night travel is ended, and all the nights are the same—some more hellish than others, but none of the nights are tame. A lure that is soft and luxuriant, a bidding to the state of the feast. This is the spell of the Orient—the lure of the far, Far East.

"The Philippines": The Philippines are a bunch of trouble gathered on the western horizon of civilization. They are bounded on the north by rocks and destruction, on the east by typhoons and monsoons, on the south by canaballs [*sic*] and earthquakes. On the west by hoveloons [*sic*] and smugglers. The principal imports are American gobs and amunition [*sic*]. The principal exports are rice and war bullets.

> From souvenir photographs sold to
> American sailors by A-Fung Studio,
> Chefoo, China, in the 1930s.
> Courtesy of Chief Warrant Officer
> George N. Gaboury.

We drag at the oars with aching arms, and suddenly a puff of wind . . . laden with strange odours of blossoms, of aromatic wood, comes out of the still night—the first sigh of the East on my face. That I can never forget. It was impalpable and enslaving, like a charm, like a whispered promise of mysterious delight.

> Joseph Conrad, "Youth" from
> *Joseph Conrad, Tales of Land and Sea*

In the late nineteenth century, the United States government extended its authority across the Pacific, claiming or conquering islands (Guam, Hawaii, and Samoa, among others), wresting a whole archipelago (the Philippines) from Spain, forcing Japan to accept foreign trade (and confront

Western ideas), and gaining the right of "extraterritoriality" for its citizens and its military in China. This series of acquisitions, diplomatic initiatives, and conquests forced the United States Navy to consider waging war in waters nearly a third of the way around the globe. But having a permanent military and diplomatic presence in the Far East also compelled the Navy to place some of its forces in cultures that were incredibly alien to officers and sailors alike.

The result was a series of encounters—some full of adventure and wonder, others characterized by fear and violence. The China Station, or, as others called it, "the Asiatic Station"—the words themselves conjured up a host of images for Navy and Marine Corps personnel in the early decades of the twentieth century. One the one hand, adventure beckoned. On the other, the Asiatic Fleet wasn't on the cutting edge of technology or tactics by the 1930s. By then, it was not a place to make a career. So why go to the Far East at all? Retired Marine Corps Lieutenant General Victor H. Krulak, who went there himself, answered that question by observing that it was a chance to live a "high-hearted" and "unfettered" life "in the most improbable and exotic frontier this world has ever seen."[1] The question for us, looking back, is whether service across the Pacific, serving in the Asiatic Fleet on the China Coast, the Yangtze River, or in the Philippines, had much effect on the Navy, and on the way that the Navy planned to fight the coming war with Japan. Our chapter on the Marine Corps noted that a major change in Marine responsibilities and fighting doctrine led inevitably to major changes in the Navy. But the China Station was just a place, like Panama or the Caribbean. Could it leave a mark on the Navy deeper than any of the other outposts sailors and Marines defended? That's the question we will return to at the end of this chapter.

If American gunboats on China's great river do not seem strange, turn the situation around. Imagine Chinese gunboats plying the Mississippi in 1920. Visualize an international settlement, dominating trade in cotton and grain, in New Orleans until the outbreak of World War II. Consider a United States where Chinese and other foreigners could move about without being under the control of American laws. Add to all that a United States torn by warring, looting factions, and a population suffering from malnutrition and cursed by widespread illiteracy, and you have some idea of just how bizarre the situation in China was—a great civilization, the only one from antiquity to survive more or less intact to the modern age, actually in danger of complete ruin.

Making the situation even more bizarre was the peculiar nature of American involvement in China. On the one hand, official American policy after 1900 was to promote the "open door" to Chinese trade and Chinese minds. On the other, the United States was committed to maintaining China's territorial integrity. The "door" was to be kept open to give American firms access to Chinese products and markets and American missionaries access to Chinese converts, the many sick, and the school children needing an education. At the same time, the government of the United States did not want a China ruled by Bolsheviks or anti-Western extremists. The "door" wasn't open to them, or to others who vehemently opposed the Western colonial powers. As historian William R. Braisted put it in assessing the results of the Washington naval conference, "The treaties and resolutions adopted during the three months of discussions promised China improvements in the future rather than a redress for the past."

The complex and often frustrating story of China's encounter with the West in the 1920s and '30s has been told elsewhere, and in great detail, by authors as diverse as Barbara Tuchman and Andre Malraux. Our point is that American involvement in the Far East had two sides—one that stressed self-determination and progress for the people of the region and another that asserted the right of the government of the United States to shape affairs in the far Pacific. On the one hand, the locals were to be trusted. On the other, they were regarded as essentially inferior. The effort to balance these two incompatible points of view was like walking a very shaky tightrope, and the military forces of the United States inevitably struggled to keep any semblance of balance.

Marine Lieutenant Colonel John W. Thomason caught the conflict very well in one of his stories about Marines in the United States legation guard in Peking. A Marine sergeant and an American missionary doctor had fallen in love. To find a moment together, they

> walked north to the Moat of the Forbidden City . . . and eastward along it to the massive Tien An Gateway . . . No wind came to ruffle the springing lotus leaves, and small white herons stalked, contemplative, against the farther bank, or stood dreaming, lean heads cradled between their wings. Over the Moat, the corner towers of the Violet Town glowed like jewels in the level light; splendor of golden tile and emerald, turquoise-blue and vermilion, and pale tracery of marble balustrade, all mirrored most perfect in the quiet water.

As the two lovers touched shoulders, the doctor spoke first: "There was always a garden here. . . . When old Kublai built the palace Marco Polo wrote about, they walked in the spring along these lakes, like we walk now."

Her Marine did not—could not—catch her drift: "They sat too long in their dam' gardens. . . . They lost liaison with the outside. And they were pushovers for the first hard guys that came along and wanted in. If a man can take a thing, he rates it. If he can hold it, he rates it." As Thomason observed, "All afternoon they had fenced," finding no common language. As so it would be with Americans in the Orient.[2]

The Asiatic Fleet was a fleet in name only. Its commander was as much diplomat as admiral, and to give him rank equal to that of his peers from nations such as Great Britain, he had to have four (temporary) stars. He did not have much force on call. In April 1935, for example, the Asiatic Fleet based in the Philippines consisted of one modern heavy cruiser (*Augusta*), one converted yacht (*Isabel*, PY-10), three destroyer divisions composed of thirteen older destroyers, one submarine division (six S-class submarines), three gunboats, two minesweepers, one small seaplane tender with one squadron of planes, and four supporting auxiliaries.

The force had waxed and waned in size as internecine violence within China boiled over or slacked off. In late 1929, for example, Admiral Charles B. McVay Jr., Commander, Asiatic Fleet, had sent a division of destroyers to augment the gunboats "that cruised the China Coast and often served as station ships at Tientsin, Shanghai, and Canton." Thin as it was, the Navy's presence—often made manifest by one old gunboat—extended from the Philippines to the South China coast, up the Yangtze, and then up the coast to Tsingtao, Chefoo, and Taku.

In China proper in 1935, there were also seven old and new gunboats on the Yangtze River and one new gunboat of the South China Patrol. The Marines had about a battalion of troops in Peking, as the Legation Guard, and they shared the duty of guarding American interests and citizens with the Army's Fifteenth Infantry Regiment in Tientsin. The Fourth Regiment of Marines guarded the international settlement at Shanghai and played a very important role in its defense. Still, this was not much with which to face down the forces of an increasingly belligerent Japanese government or antagonistic Chinese nationalists.

Yet the standing of American forces in the Far East at the time was very high. They exercised a surprising amount of influence. Some of that was due to the growing wealth of the United States—at least in the 1920s—and the amount of money her sailors and Marines could spend in local bars and businesses. But some of it was due to the willingness of American missionaries and aid societies to nurse the sick, build and staff schools, and fight the opium trade. Perhaps the very ambivalence of the American government's policy, coupled with the legendary openness of Americans, was the key to the influence of American arms. It also wasn't insignificant that the Marines, the soldiers, and the sailors could shoot.

The Army's main forces in the Far East were in the Philippines, where the Army's coast artillery units manned the formidable defenses guarding Manila Bay from an attack by sea. But the Army and Navy differed in their assessments of the utility of their forces in the Philippines. Once the Washington naval conference had forbidden major modernization of the Army's defenses, Army war planners assumed that Japanese forces could isolate and conquer the islands. In the 1920s, Navy planners thought that a reinforced Asiatic Fleet might do enough damage to the Imperial Japanese Navy to make stubborn resistance worthwhile. A kind of compromise was worked out. The Army agreed to hold Manila Bay for six months in the event of war with Japan while the Navy focused on reaching the besieged defenders with a relief force before the clock ran out on them. As it happened, only the Army kept its side of the bargain.

The do-it-by-the-book approach that characterized the Navy could weaken in the Far East. It depended on where you were. Relations could be informal, especially on gunboats and submarines. A new member of the crew of *S-39* was made to feel at home right away:

> When he first reported on board, he'd missed out on supper . . . and guessed he'd better shut up and forget it. But right away someone asked the hungry 20-year-old, "Had any chow?" and, when he shook his head, went back to the galley and fixed him some. When he finished and went topside, [another sailor] asked, "Got any money?" Pay records were always a couple of months behind, so [he] shook his head again and was told, "We'll lend you some." Then [another sailor] said, "Know anything about Manila?" For the third time [he] had to say no. "Don't go there alone at first," the gunner's mate advised. . . . "I'm going now—I'll show you around if you want."[3]

Retired Rear Admiral Kemp Tolley, in his delightful history *Yangtze Patrol*, recounted a similar example from a 1920 inspection of the old gunboat *Monocacy*. The inspection "revealed a few deficiencies. The boilers couldn't keep a full head of steam for more than three minutes with the engines running full speed. . . .

The radio set wouldn't operate . . . The ice machine was out of whack. Main engines and throttles had leaky valves. One air pump had a broken piston and the other an unserviceable valve rod." And much, much more. However, as Tolley pointed out, "No genuine Old River Rat would be downhearted over such trivia; the inspection report wound up with the opinion that the morale of the crew was excellent."

And why not? In China, at times the purchasing power of an American enlisted sailor's pay was equal to that of a senior Chinese official or military officer. Even when the income difference wasn't all that great, China was a place to hide. In 1921, Lieutenant Commander Glenn F. Howell confided to his diary the reasons one young sailor under his command had eagerly sought duty in the Orient. The sailor's father had died when he was one; his mother handed him over to an orphanage near Pittsburgh when he was two. The boy had tried to run away when he was six, and then again when he was eight. He had nothing of his own except a cheap orphanage uniform; he was semiliterate. Worst of all was "adopting day," when the orphans were paraded in front of adults looking for children to take home. He was not one of those selected. An older boy who had "escaped" promised to take care of him, and the kid was out on his own at age fifteen. After two years, he had a decent job as a bellhop in a hotel. But his mother found him and demanded that he help support her. He fled Pittsburgh for Manila and then China—and for the self-respect that his standing among his shipmates gave him.

Another enlisted man, Radioman Third Class Richard Harralson, found in 1939 that "Shanghai was everything they said it was. There were cabarets, theaters, a racetrack, jai alai, restaurants, bars, and girls. The exchange rate at the time was 17 to 1." Compared to Manila, which Harralson enjoyed, Shanghai was exotic. World War II had already broken out in Europe, and Shanghai was filling up with refugees, many of them desperate for cash. He recalled the taxi dancers in the cabarets: "There were so many of them. There were the Chinese girls, the White Russians, Germans, Jewish girls, and other Europeans." It was a young sailor's dream come true. "Once situated at a table you would survey the girls. Having decided on a lovely prospect you would invite her to dance. If everything went okay you asked her to your table. When the party broke up you would buy her so many yards of dance tickets and drape them around her neck."[4]

There were also many Chinese desperate for work—so desperate, in fact, that they became an essential part of many a Yangtze River gunboat's crew. Richard McKenna described how this occurred in *The Sand Pebbles*:

First the sampans would cluster around the slop chute and the Chinese in them would scream at each other and fight with dip nets for the garbage. So the cooks would give one sampan the garbage contract and people from that sampan would come aboard to collect it. Very quickly, that extended to scraping plates at the mess tables and then to washing them, and in a week or two every sailor-mess cook would have his Chinese helper who did all the work.

The system of having but not hiring on-board Chinese workers and servants was supplemented by contract labor, but there was a catch to it.

Certain big, dirty jobs, such as chipping and painting sides and peak tanks for the deckforce or cleaning bilges and boilers for the engineers, would be saved until the ship came to China. Labor contractors, paid by the [ship's] welfare fund, would bring hundreds of coolies aboard and do the jobs in a few days. A few deck and bilge coolies, the quick and handy ones, would stay on to do routine dirty work. . . .

Within a month they would be all over the ship, humble, crouching in corners, ready to do any dirty, irksome thing that sailors did not like to do, and do it cheerfully and well. They were like water seeking its level, patient, not pressing . . .

They had little choice.[5]

By the early 1920s, most of the ships and submarines of the Asiatic Fleet migrated with the climate—winter in Manila and Philippine waters; summer in Tsingtao and Chefoo on the Shantung Peninsula, "the garden spot of China." One officer wrote of the "Asiatic submarine year" as having three parts: "the torpedo year in China, the gunnery year in and about Manila, and overhaul at Cavite and Olongapo." The submarine and destroyer tenders would wallow north from Manila with their broods in May, stopping in Chinese ports such as Hong Kong and Shanghai. The journey was a long one (about two thousand miles) and therefore arduous for the submarine sailors, but it held out the promise of a kind of working vacation.[6]

Tsingtao had been a leased German base in 1914 when Japanese forces, honoring their government's alliance with Great Britain, had assaulted and taken it. Returned to nominal Chinese control once the Washington Naval Treaty went into effect, "Tsingtao took on the unique character of a typically German city architecturally, controlled by the Japanese financially, and administered by the Chinese apparently." But it was a haven for American Navy families, with clean, affordable accommodations and fresh strawberries and plenty of safe space for wives and children. And Americans were not the only ones who enjoyed its resort atmosphere. The British also enjoyed the light summer monsoon breezes that flowed over the Shantung peninsula in their leasehold in Wei-hai-wei.

The destroyers went to Chefoo, which lacked the amenities of Tsingtao— and even essentials, such as plumbing. Chefoo, "a thoroughly Chinese town," in the words of William R. Braisted, who was there as a child, was celebrated by a verse sung to the tune of "The Monkeys Have No Tails in Zamboanga":

> Oh we'll live a thousand years in Old Chefoo
>
> We'll live a thousand years in Old Chefoo
>
> The smells are not like roses
>
> So we'll powder up our noses
>
> And we'll live a thousand years in Old Chefoo[7]

The tune to this (and many other, mostly unprintable) verses, can be found in John Ford's 1945 movie *They Were Expendable*, which, in its first moments, portrays sailors supposedly in Manila just before World War II singing "The Monkeys Have No Tails in Zamboanga."

Practice with a ship's main guns was not all that the ships and submarines conducted when they returned to the Philippines. For example, Captain (later Fleet Admiral) Nimitz of *Augusta* wanted as many of his sailors and Marines as possible to practice their small-arms shooting. He'd been a gunboat sailor as a very young officer, and he took seriously the responsibilities of Asiatic Fleet ships to provide armed and drilled landing forces. As later recounted by Vice Admiral. Lloyd Mustin, Nimitz landed his Marines at a rifle range in Subic Bay while *Augusta* conducted drills at sea. When the ship returned, "The remainder of the landing force came ashore and was billeted ... at the rifle range for two weeks."

The ship's officers and Marines received an unpleasant surprise:

> We had a great many seasoned sailors in that landing force, third and fourth enlistment men, who had never fired a service weapon. . . . So we really had a substantial exercise in basic instruction to get behind us for this rather numerous group of men, on the order of 220 Navy in the landing force and 60 Marines, . . . out of a ship's company of about 650.

With the Navy and Marine officers taking the lead and running the range, all the sailors qualified as "marksman," and "many of them qualified higher." Mustin, who enjoyed shooting, was in his element, and *Augusta*'s sailors "just turned in a score such as had never been seen before in the small-arms competition and won the trophy."[8]

The shooting competition was not just another means of sharpening a crew's spirit. Sailors were expected to serve, as required, in armed landing parties alongside the small numbers of Marines that cruisers such as *Augusta* or *Houston* carried. Sailors serving on the Yangtze, by contrast, were almost always involved in some form of shooting—or at least the threat of it. Banditry on the river was common, and to deter it Navy sailors often served as armed guards on commercial river steamers flying the American flag. If the rhythm of the ships based in the Philippines was that of a slow, stately rumba, then the Yangtze sailors lived in a world of jazz, always improvising.

Bandits were not the only major problem. At times, sailors found themselves caught in the struggles between warring Chinese factions. When Chiang Kaishek's Nationalist Army moved north against warlords near Nanking in early 1927, the danger to American citizens and the American consulate there became so great that destroyers *Noa* (DD-343) and *William B. Preston* (DD-344) were sent upriver from Shanghai. The situation was ticklish. The American consul did not want to retreat to the ships; to do so would be to lose face. But Nationalist troops were not only out to break the local warlords, they were also fed up with the special status of foreign nationals. The sailors were there to protect the consul and other Americans, but they had to be careful how it was done.

The result was incredibly perilous for the Americans. Though Nationalist officers had assured them that the American, British, and Japanese consulates would not be harmed, all three were attacked, and the Americans retreated to a Standard Oil-owned house on a rise where Navy signalmen on the roof could communicate with the destroyers anchored in the river. *Noa* signalman John D. Wilson "took up his post on 21 March until the final evacuation," handling, while under constant sniper fire, "practically all communications between the foreigners ashore and the ships in the river," until two signalmen from *Preston* joined him three days later. "Chief Quartermaster Charles W. Horn did most of the signaling on the *Noa* and was continually exposed to sniping."[9]

The signalmen kept a log of their communications. In his *Yangtze Patrol*, Rear Adm. Kemp Tolley quoted their stark messages from March 24, 1927:

> To British cruiser *Emerald* at 26 minutes after twelve noon: "American consul is getting in touch with Cantonese officials. No immediate danger. Do not open fire until requested . . ."

> To *Emerald* and the two American destroyers at 2:52: "Commence firing."
> One minute later, from signalman Wilson: "Do not fire."
> Then, on the heels of that message: "We are being attacked. Open fire. SOS SOS SOS." [Note in log: "During this period all hell broke loose."]

Lieutenant Commander Roy C. Smith, *Noa*'s captain, said, "Well, I'll either get a court martial or a medal out of this," and ordered his 4-inch and machine guns to fire. HMS *Emerald* and *William B. Preston* joined in. The Chinese soldiers besieging the party of diplomats, missionaries and sailors (including women and children) fled. Sailors on nearby Japanese destroyers, denied permission to fire their own guns, nevertheless "gave vent to a thunderous '*Banzai!*'" in support of their fellow extraterritorials. It was bizarre. But it was also dangerous as all hell.

Situations of this sort were repeated time and again on the Yangtze, where the gunboats matched the rhythm of their movements to the giant river's annual ebb and flood. The danger that haunted the gunboat skippers, however, wasn't the real risk of being shot at. Instead, it was the rapids. Even with expert Chinese river pilots, moving upstream or downstream through the gorges was a nail-biting experience. Lieutenant Commander Howell of *Palos* (PR-1) described attacking a rapid above Ichang in July 1921:

> You sneak your ship upon it with safety valves popping. Now you are in the very edge of it. Then you go full speed and smash into it. There is a grand smother of foam; the water pours over your fo'c'sle; the ship buries her nose; she vibrates all over; the firemen stoke furiously; her bow edges up into the tongue of the rapid, shaking off the water; there is a tremendous roar; the pilot is at the wheel—old Chinese, serenely edges the ship a little to starboard, a bit to port; you keep your eyes on the beach; inch by inch the ship gains; she stops, steaming frantically at that vicious, overwhelming sweep and rush of water; she is making no headway. This is the critical moment. You give a command. The crew rush forward into the bow. The stern comes up; the bow goes down; very slowly the ship begins to forge ahead again. Of a sudden, as if hidden chains were slipped, the ship lurches ahead, rolling. You are over the rapid; . . . Astern the roar dies to a murmur. You rarely look back.[10]

At other times, the "enemy" was another vessel. Rear Admiral Tolley cited a late 1920s encounter between the very obsolete American *Elcano* (PG-38, commissioned in 1885 as the Spanish *El Cano* and captured at Manila Bay in 1898) and two other ships of the river patrol.

Elcano found herself [anchored] in line abreast, thirty yards outboard of the Japanese HIJMS *Seta*, who in turn was thirty yards outboard of HMS *Scarab*. The latter was closest to the beach—thirty yards from the post office pontoon [at Ichang].

In the afternoon a freshet was reported on the way downriver. A rising river meant the ships would [have] . . . to move. While heaving in the anchor chains, [*Elcano*] took a rank sheer to starboard, bringing her across *Seta*'s bow. The sheer had broken out the newly laid anchors, which commenced to drag. Ringing up full speed, *Elcano* tried to clear *Seta* ahead. She cut the latter's port anchor chain, tore out her windlass, and wound up both *Seta*'s anchor chains in her churning screws.

Both ships then dragged down on *Scarab*, holing her and *Elcano* above the waterline. Like drowning rats clinging to each other for mutual support, all three gunboats next dragged down on the pontoons moored to the shore and there, for the moment, they all managed to hold on. . . . the beset gunboaters could see that if the current hit the starboard (land side) bow of *Scarab*, the whole circus would carry away and sweep downriver, taking with it everything in its path.[11]

Never a dull day. As Lieutenant Howell put it after another tough day fighting both his *Palos* and the Yangtze, "I am now an expert in the art of handling a helpless, drifting ship."[12] Rear Admiral Tolley quoted another young officer as saying "things go on in YangPat [Yangtze Patrol] that would scarcely bear repeating outside this fleet."[13]

Newcomers to the China Station could be surprisingly unaware of what they were getting into. As Rear Admiral Tolley recalled, "An officer ordered to the China station more or less said goodbye to the U.S. Navy. His knowledge of China might well be limited to a dog-eared wardroom copy of the *National Geographic*, and a ballad which alleged that the monkeys had no tails in Zamboanga, which was not in China at all."[14] But this newcomer would soon learn why he was there—to protect American commercial interests, American missionaries (many of whom did not want his protection, and let him know it), and the American government's claim to influence over China's fate.

By comparison, the Philippines were quieter, especially after 1934, when Congress passed an act giving the Philippines commonwealth status and providing for the complete independence of the islands by 1945. Manuel Quezon, who headed the Philippine Nationalist Party and had pressed for independence for the islands his entire public career, argued against the 1933 legislation on the grounds that it gave the United States too much in the way of bases for

American forces. He wanted an independent Philippines, not one trapped in the middle of a confrontation between the United States and Japan. However, the 1934 legislation authorized the creation of a Commonwealth of the Philippines if Philippine voters approved it. They did, in May 1935, and that September Quezon was elected its first president. Independence remained scheduled for 1945.

Most sailors and Marines, whatever their views of American policy in the Far East, took to the Orient because, to cite Tolley, "duty in China was like living in a mild version of the Arabian Nights—something enjoyable, mysterious, and not requiring a great deal of money." In a story entitled "The Sergeant and the Spy," Marine Lieutenant Colonel Thomason gave voice to the fascination some felt for China:

> It was one of those rare evenings with no dust blowing, when the North China air has the tang and sparkle of approaching winter, and is like wine to breathe, and crystal clear, so that the Western Hills, sixteen miles out [from Peking], look near enough to touch. . . . the human motley that uses the street had the appearance of figures in a pageant. There passed him, riding homeward in rickshas, Chinese clerks and merchants from the foreign establishments . . . , elegant in long silk gowns; and fat houseboys; and shaven lamas. A singsong girl, trundling to a discreet appointment, with a white, enameled face, a vermilion mouth, and hair curiously crisped and piled, gave him a slow, direct look, from eyes as hard and bright as jewel jade. A file of polo ponies came along . . . ; and he made way for an enormous Mongol prince, monolithic in brown brocaded silk.[15]

Not bad for a boy off the farm or from some small-town backwater. Not bad at all.

But there was another reason for being in China—to gather intelligence on Japanese operations and weapons. This intelligence was gathered in two ways. The first was passive—listening to Japanese communications. The Navy Department sent small numbers of personnel (most of them enlisted) to man radio listening posts in Peking and Shanghai in the late 1920s. These outposts complemented the stations in Guam, Manila, and Oahu. A staff of cryptologists was set up in Manila in 1932 to support the Commander-in-Chief, Asiatic Fleet, and another permanent group was sent to Pearl Harbor in 1936. Soon thereafter, information provided by the code-breakers was augmented by that obtained from a chain of high-frequency direction finders (HFDFs) stretching from Manila to Dutch Harbor,

Alaska. The direction finders did not intercept Japanese communications. They just tracked the movements of Japanese warships and Japan's commercial shipping. But the movements themselves, supported by other information, revealed the operational rhythms of the Imperial Japanese Fleet.

The second way intelligence was gathered was through direct observation of Japanese military activities, especially starting in 1937, when Japanese troops began conducting amphibious assaults near Shanghai. Working with Chinese forces, Navy officers were able to examine captured or battle-damaged Japanese ordnance, small arms, and even a modern Zero fighter. Their aggressive and successful pursuit of items such as code books and aerial bombsights was most likely the reason why Japanese aircraft bombed and sank gunboat *Panay* (PR-5) near Nanking in December 1937. As the historian Jeffery M. Dorwart noted, the Office of Naval Intelligence "suspected that the Japanese had attacked the ship to block its intelligence work, and persistent requests by the Japanese for permission to raise and salvage the hulk reinforced this impression."[16] It was all part of a deadly cat-and-mouse game played behind diplomatic courtesies.

We began this chapter by asking what influence the China Station had on the rest of the Navy in the 1920s and 1930s. The answer is that it had very little, despite the fact that the Asiatic Fleet is where some officers, such as Admiral. Joseph M. Reeves, had forged a name for themselves in the years before World War I.[17] In the 1920s and '30s, the Philippines and China offered adventure to some and a place to hide out from the regular Navy for others. At the same time, the Far East offered an excellent opportunity to learn how to deal with people whose culture was quite alien. As Rear Admiral Tolley admitted, most Americans "found the Chinese . . . bewildering, frustrating, occasionally insupportably overbearing, and frequently devilishly devious."[18] On their part, the Chinese returned the insult by referring to the foreigners as *fan-quei*, a term of contempt. And why not?

But the chance was there for a number of Americans to find ways to deal with mysterious China, her culture, and her tumultuous uprisings and revolutions. Few (the U.S. Army's Joseph Stillwell was a grand exception) did. The chance was there for the government of the United States to begin laying the diplomatic and economic foundation for a new relationship with China. The foundation didn't survive World War II. There were too few Americans who weren't missionaries or adventurers who knew one of China's major languages and appreciated the country's recent history. There were too few citizens of the

United States who could see the great changes that were about to break on Asia. The way Americans were able to maintain what seems today to be an incredible position of influence in China and the Far East masked the change that was coming—the "thunder out of China" to use the term coined by journalists Theodore H. White and Annalee Jacoby in 1946.[19]

But it would be a mistake to write off the Asiatic Fleet as a minor, even regrettable, piece of the Navy's (and the nation's) past. It was an extension of an adventuring, often exploitative, expansionist past—a logical implication of American government policy that reaches back to the war with Mexico in 1846 and to the expedition of Commodore Perry to Japan and China in 1853 and 1854. The attitudes that fueled that commercial, political, and military expansion weren't consistent except on one point—that Americans would not be kept out of places they wanted to go.

So young Americans in Navy and Marine uniforms showed up where they really weren't wanted, or were at best tolerated. The best of them, like Kemp Tolley, took away an *appreciation* of the Far East and learned at a young age that they were leaders of men like themselves. Others, like Americans scattered all over the world today, became expatriates. They "went Asiatic," to employ a phrase used at the time, and settled in (often with an Asian wife) somewhere where there were other Americans. As Lieutenant Commander Howell noted, "This Orient certainly gets the boys if they don't watch out."[20] Still others—mostly young sailors and Marines—marked their time in the Far East as their "adventure." As Rear Admiral Tolley could see, he and his contemporaries half a world away from the United States "enjoyed a life such as the U.S. Navy will never know again."[21]

CONCLUSION

The Navy emerged from the Washington Conference psychologically bruised and physically curtailed. Never before in their memory had naval men found their views so overwhelmingly rejected by public opinion.

> William R. Braisted, *The United States Navy in the Pacific, 1909–1922*

Strangely, during most of the past 20 years Americans had all but forgotten that they had a Navy. . . . It seemed a luxury, the useless showpiece of a rich democracy, a boast directed at nobody but ourselves. But the Navy itself had not forgotten what seapower means.

> *Life*, October 28, 1940

As the nation had changed in the roller coaster decades of the Roaring Twenties and the Depression Thirties so too had the Navy changed.[1] A whole new Navy was on the horizon. On February 12, 1939, for example, Admiral Claude E. Bloch, Commander-in-Chief, U.S. Fleet, sent a memo to the Chief of Naval Operations, Admiral William D. Leahy, describing the results of using a newly developed radio-controlled target airplane in gunnery exercises off Guantanamo Bay, Cuba. The Bureaus of Ordnance and Aeronautics had developed the radio-controlled target to test the procedures then in use for drilling antiaircraft gunners. Firing at towed cloth "sleeves" had "generally been productive of hitting, which in the instance of certain ships [had] approached certainty."[2] However, antiaircraft batteries on battleships and destroyers had not been successful in knocking down the maneuvering target drones. *Idaho*'s 5-inch, 25-caliber guns, for example, had fired one hundred rounds at a drone and "failed to hit the target." The memo noted, "The procedure to be employed against a maneuvering target is still in the formative stage." That was the equivalent of saying that U.S. warships were terribly vulnerable to attack by fast-moving airplanes.

In five years, by contrast, the deadly accuracy of shipborne antiaircraft guns would drive the Japanese navy to use suicide aircraft.

At the same time, the Navy's patrol seaplanes were providing clear evidence that the airplane was in the process of revolutionizing war at sea. Patrol Wing 1 (PatWing 1), composed of forty-eight PBYs, flew nonstop from San Diego to the Panama Canal on January 10–11, 1939. On the twenty-third of that month, the same aircraft flew to San Juan to participate in Fleet Problem XX. On March 9, PatWing 1 moved first to Norfolk and then, after a layover, went on to Newport, Rhode Island, to exercise with Army aircraft. Two of the four squadrons in PatWing 1 then returned to San Diego via the Caribbean. As Acting Secretary of the Navy Charles Edison noted in his annual report, "Exclusive of distance flown in connection with the fleet problem, Patrol Wing 1 covered a distance of over 10,000 miles on its cruise."[3] Aviation was fast becoming a weapon with dramatic implications for naval strategy.

On July 1, 1939, there were also 105 new ships under construction, including battleships *North Carolina*, *Washington*, *South Dakota*, *Indiana*, *Massachusetts*, *Alabama*, *Iowa*, and *New Jersey*, plus carriers *Wasp* and *Hornet*. Five light cruisers were being built, including the 6-inch gun ship *Helena* (CL-50) and four of the 5-inch gun light cruisers of the Atlanta type. Shipbuilders were also working on twenty submarines and forty-two destroyers, as well as two destroyer tenders, six seaplane tenders, one submarine tender, one minelayer (aptly named *Terror*, CM-5), and other vessels. The Maritime Commission had already delivered the high-speed tanker *Cimarron* (AO-22), and two more like her—*Neosho* (AO-23) and *Platte* (AO-24)—were on the way. These three ships would form the nucleus of the fast-replenishment groups that gave the Navy's carrier task forces such great strategic mobility in World War II.

The new construction was just barely in time. After war broke out in Europe at the beginning of September 1939, President Roosevelt established a "neutrality patrol" in the Atlantic and Caribbean and declared a "limited national emergency," which began the difficult and contentious process of preparing the nation for war. On October 2, a conference of foreign ministers of the American republics approved the "Act of Panama," which created a "neutrality zone" stretching three hundred nautical miles into the Atlantic from the shores of North and South America. On October 5, Chief of Naval Operations Admiral Harold R. Stark created the Hawaiian Detachment of the United States Fleet, setting the stage for the eventual basing of a significant portion of the fleet at Pearl Harbor.

The U.S. Navy, designed and maintained to fight the Imperial Japanese Navy, was about to find itself engaged on two fronts simultaneously. Yet most of its ships—even those being built—were still the products of the so-called treaty system, and the combined effects of treaty limits and constrained budgets had kept the Navy from becoming an effective deterrent to Japanese and German aggression. Pearl Harbor was not close to being an effective fleet base in 1939, and the U.S. Fleet had not developed the means to carry its supply and support organization forward—across the broad Pacific—where it would have to go if its warships, aircraft, and Marines were to execute the Orange war plan against Japan. The Navy's civilian and military leaders had, as historian Braisted observed, waged "a long struggle to build and maintain the Navy at the strength allowed by the naval treaty." But it hadn't been enough.

There was no "balanced fleet" in 1921, but there was a kind of balance to it by 1939, especially considering the new ships then being built. In chapter 1 we argued that the Navy of 1939 was an amalgam of three different sorts of forces and not a military service all of whose ships and aircraft fit together to form a coherent, interlocking structure. Yet there was still great progress in the 1920s and '30s toward the fleet that would overwhelm its opponents in two oceans simultaneously. This progress is clear when one examines the Navy's own official tally, given in its *Ships' Data, U.S. Naval Vessels*.[4]

In 1922, the total displacement of the eighteen "first line" battleships comprised 35 percent of the total displacement of all combat ships. By comparison, the eleven "second line" cruisers (eight large armored cruisers and three others) comprised 9.8 percent of the total. The first line destroyers constituted 23 percent and the first line submarines were 2.6 percent of the total. All the first line warships plus the obsolescent armored cruisers and experimental aircraft carrier *Langley* displaced just under 42 percent of the Navy's total displacement for all "fighting ships." There were a lot of obsolete ships on the Navy list.

By the end of 1937, the last year of the 1930s in which *Ships' Data* was issued, there were fifteen battleships not overage as defined by the Washington and London treaties. The displacements of these fifteen amounted to 38 percent of the total tonnage of all "combatant vessels." So what had changed? Plenty. At the end of 1937, there were seventeen modern heavy cruisers, two recently built light cruisers and ten others from the 1920s, and four aircraft carriers. The heavy cruisers amounted to over 13 percent of the Navy's total "combatant" tonnage. The light cruisers displaced 7.5 percent, and the four carriers over

8 percent. However, there were only forty-eight destroyers and twenty-three submarines that were not over the age limit set by the London treaty. These constituted only 6 percent and 2.8 percent, respectively, of the Navy's total combatant tonnage. Officially overage destroyers and submarines together accounted for over 18 percent of that total. All of the not overage warships combined amounted to about 54 percent of the Navy's total tonnage.

In 1922 the U.S. Navy had a total of 624 "fighting ships," including the types already mentioned plus eighteen minelayers, forty-seven small minesweepers, forty-three submarine chasers (wooden hulled escorts of about seventy-five tons each), and fifty-four war emergency construction Eagle Boats, convoy escorts of five hundred tons apiece. At the end of 1937, the Navy had 424 warships, or 68 percent of the 1922 total. But what we can call the "fighting tonnage" in 1937 was 85 percent of the 1922 figure. That is, the 1937 force was just over two-thirds the 1922 force, *considering only the numbers of combat ships*. But tonnage is a better measure of fighting power because that power tends to scale directly with ship size. And, using the measure of tonnage, the 1937 force—constrained by treaty—was 85 percent that of 1922. It was a smaller force but stronger, ship for ship.

In addition, the newer ships were, on the whole, much more powerful than those they replaced, and by 1937 there was a real naval air force. The 1922 Navy had no first line aircraft carriers or large force of seaplane patrol bombers. The displacement of experimental carrier *Langley* amounted to less than 1 percent of the total displacement of all fighting ships. There was also only one seaplane tender, *Wright* (AV-1). Together, *Langley* and *Wright* constituted less than 2 percent to the total displacement of all the Navy's warships. By the end of 1937, however, the Navy not only had four aircraft carriers, it also fielded two large and nine small seaplane tenders. Together, the carriers and the tenders made up 10.5 percent of the total combatant tonnage. This was a major change, and one that would be accelerated as new carriers and more modern seaplane tenders joined the fleet between 1938 and the end of 1940.

What did *not* change much in the fifteen years between 1922 and 1937 were the fleet's auxiliaries, the ships that sustained the combat vessels. For example, the six destroyer tenders in commission in 1922 were still active in 1937—and the two newest of the eight working destroyer tenders in 1937 had been commissioned in 1924. Of the six submarine tenders serving the fleet at the end of 1937, five were in commission in 1922 and one had been placed in commission in 1926. Of the three active repair ships in 1937, two (*Vestal*, AR-4, and *Prometheus*, AR-3) dated back to 1909 and 1910, respectively, and the third (*Medusa*, AR-2) had been commissioned in 1924. Similarly, the four store ships serving the fleet in 1937 had also been active in 1922, as had the three colliers. All eighteen oilers, or tankers, had been active in 1922, as had all five cargo ships, the two ammunition ships (the appropriately named *Pyro*, AE-1, and *Nitro*, AE-2), the two transports, and the hospital ship *Relief* (AH-1). Put another way, the auxiliary force was allowed to age. Successive chiefs of Naval Operations in the 1930s tried to persuade President Roosevelt to replace many of these aging vessels, but he refused—until he got a 20 percent increase in ship authorizations in 1938.

However, those wanting hard, visual evidence of the change between 1922 and 1937 can visit two surviving battleship memorials. *Texas* (BB-35), designed in 1910, and fleet flagship in the late 1920s, was at the center of the "old" Navy. Completely different is *North Carolina* (BB-55), designed a generation later. True, the comparison is a bit unfair. After all, *Texas* was quite inferior to *West Virginia* (BB-48), which was designed in 1916 and a mainstay of the 1930s battle line. There had been great progress in battleship design between 1910 and 1916, especially in the areas of armor protection and protection against attack by torpedoes. But the difference between *West Virginia* and *North Carolina* was also great.

It was not the fact that the latter had nine improved 16-inch guns to the former's eight. It was, instead, the difference in speed. With a shaft horsepower rating of 31,200, *West Virginia* steamed at twenty-one knots on her trials in 1923. By contrast, the engines of *Washington*, *North Carolina*'s sister ship, produced 121,000 shaft horsepower and drove her through the water at over twenty-seven knots. *West Virginia*'s machinery weighed just over twenty-seven hundred tons, not counting the water that normally filled her boilers. *Washington*'s machinery weighed just over four hundred tons more. Put another way, a 15 percent increase in machinery weight produced almost a 30 percent increase in speed. This was not the result of a "natural" improvement in engine design. It was, instead, the consequence of deliberate improvements financed by the Navy's specialists in steam turbine propulsion.

This change in naval technology was stimulated by strategic imperatives, and the success in improving the technology led to new thinking about how any war against the Japanese navy might be fought. Indeed, one of the members of the General Board went so far as to argue, *in 1935*, that the war against Japan, if it came, would not be decided by a confrontation of battle lines but by engagements between fast carrier task forces, with the new fast battleships escorting the carriers. In 1938, the director of the War Plans Division in the Office of the Chief of Naval Operations argued to the Chief of Naval Operations that the Navy could win a naval war against Japan even if the opposing battle lines never lined up for an engagement. His point was that the struggle would be one of logistics and air operations. Each side would try to protect its carrier force and make sure that its carriers were supported with fuel, new aircraft, and ammunition. Raids conducted by mobile carrier task forces might take the place of a confrontation between fleets. Given the results of fleet exercises, these were reasonable speculations.[4]

The fact that the Navy was caught by surprise at Pearl Harbor, coupled with its near defeat in the battle against German submarines in the Atlantic early in 1942, and its initial losses to the Imperial Japanese Navy around Guadalcanal in the summer and fall of 1942, led many commentators at the time to charge that the Navy was unprepared. Historians examining that period have leveled their criticisms against the prewar Navy, arguing that it was "conservative, complex, and political" and therefore "moored to civilian life." As one put it, "Money is scarce and cruising is costly," and hence the "most pressing engagement" for a peacetime navy is "the battle of the budget." This same historian went on to say that "within the peacetime navy power is diffuse. Decision is a matter of reconciliation and coordination among diverse groups of specialists . . . The impulse at the top is to play safe."[5]

Critics searching for the cause of Pearl Harbor and other disappointments have focused on the 1930s. The 1920s, they suggest, were a time of major developments in aviation. That's when the concept of the carrier as a strike weapon matured, and when the Bureau of Aeronautics, under the politically astute leadership of Rear Admiral Moffett, forged an alliance with the struggling aviation industry that led to the high-wing-loading, more powerful aircraft that were essential to victory in World War II. That's when the Marines and the Navy pioneered and then polished the tactic of dive bombing. That's when airplanes were all over the place—on carriers, hung from airships, folded into watertight hangars on submarines, floating in sheltered lagoons, and mounted on catapults carried by cruisers and battleships. Naval aviation bloomed.

But excellent historians such as Clark Reynolds have said that there was a backlash—that the traditionally minded "gun club" went out of its way to keep naval aviation as a subordinate arm and largely succeeded in the 1930s. The 1930s are therefore seen as a missed opportunity by some historians whose views one dares not dismiss.[6] Are they right? Were the naval catastrophes of the first year of World War II the consequence of institutional lethargy in the decade before the war? Did traditionalism triumph over innovation?

The answer is a qualified "No." The situation was complex—more complex than most citizens knew at the time and more complex than some historians since have been willing to admit. In *Battle Line* we have tried to show that a simple yes or no answer is impossible. The first purpose of the treaty system was to constrain both quantitative and qualitative naval arms competition. That is, the Washington and London naval agreements were designed to hold down the sizes of the major navies and make if difficult for them to take advantage of any breakthroughs in naval warfare technology. One example is the limit on the overall tonnage of aircraft carriers. *This constraint worked.* The number and size of aircraft carriers were less than they might otherwise have been. Other examples include halting battleship construction and constraining the displacement (and hence the military power) of new battleships once the older ones grew "overage" in terms of the Washington treaty. Cruiser armament, sizes, and numbers were also held down, as were those of destroyers and submarines.

The U.S. Navy also suffered because of the concern of some Americans that armaments themselves were less a deterrent to war than an incitement to it. There is a tendency today to dismiss the 1920s and 1930s as a time when American diplomacy and national security were hobbled by a narrow-minded isolationism. But consider this: The Navy was sold as the nation's first line of defense, but defense against whom? Japan? But why couldn't China, with her huge population, defend herself against a belligerent Japan? Was any war with Japan just a struggle between imperialist powers?

Did American cooperation with such nations as Great Britain and Japan in Chinese ports and rivers actually keep China from becoming a nation that could defend itself? And would the Philippines be the cause of war between Japan and the United States if the islands were independent, and not an American colony or commonwealth? Historian Braisted was correct to note that "since Dewey's fateful victory at Manila on May Day 1898, army and naval officers had labored to build American strength in the Far East." But why? Good answers to this question weren't obvious to many Americans.

The United States claimed dominance of the Caribbean after the war with Spain in 1898, and in 1904 President Theodore Roosevelt had used the Navy's new strength as the basis for his Roosevelt Corollary to the Monroe Doctrine. His corollary asserted that the government of the United States could take military action to police the Western Hemisphere, and of course that happened—in Cuba in 1906, in Nicaragua in 1909, and again in Cuba in 1912. The Marines were back in Nicaragua in 1913 and stayed from 1926 to 1933. Both Marines and sailors were in Haiti for twenty years, from 1914 to 1934.

How was American intervention in the Caribbean different from Japan's policies in and around China after Japan's defeat of czarist Russian forces in 1905? That was the question many American citizens asked themselves. As a result, by the 1930s there were two camps: Americans who argued that the United States had major strategic interests in the Far East—interests worth going to war over—and other Americans who denied this. Both groups worked to shape American diplomatic and military policy. The Navy was caught in the middle. The interwar Navy cannot be understood unless this point is kept in mind.

Finally, it wasn't clear—even in the 1930s—where modern technology would go. In an essay published over twenty years ago, retired Navy Captain Charles D. Allen noted that Bureau of Ordnance engineers in the mid-1930s anticipated that a new 6-inch, 47-caliber rapid firing gun they had developed would serve as an effective antiaircraft weapon. Fired to high elevations, the shells would burst and break up dive-bombing attacks before the bombers could begin their dives. The only thing that the new gun needed to be effective was an adequate fire control radar. This weapon in a special mount eventually saw service in the very large light cruisers of the Worcester class, but they were not even launched until two years after World War II had ended, by which time advances in other technologies had made them obsolescent. Captain Allen's point, however, was that no one could see that in 1935 or 1936, just as no one could see that carrier air defenses would improve to the point where aircraft carriers could defend themselves from enemy air attack.[7]

Technology was changing so rapidly that it was dangerous for any navy to freeze its force structure around any weapon, platform, or tactic. In 1940, for example, the official five-year plan for the Navy's force structure showed a fleet organized around seventeen modern fast battleships, six battle cruisers, fifteen fleet aircraft carriers, and five escort carriers. The actual numbers when Japan surrendered in 1945 were ten fast battleships, two battle cruisers, three very large armored deck carriers, twenty-six fleet aircraft carriers, nine light carriers (cruiser conversions), and eighty-five escort carriers. The problem of defending aircraft carriers from attack had been largely solved during the war, and carrier attack aircraft had, because of their great numbers, become potent forces for wiping the seas clean of any opposition.

Those troubled by the Navy's defeat at Pearl Harbor and its subsequent problems are right to scrutinize the period between World War I and World War II. But we believe that this time period in the Navy's history has not been well understood. Captain Edward L. Beach, in his elegant history of the U.S. Navy, eloquently described the Navy's weakness before World War II: "Training was the shibboleth to which we all subscribed." Winning gunnery and engineering competitions "was more important than anything else. Upon it hung prizes and promotion—not to mention that indefinable 'ship's spirit' that denied the impossible. Many were the stratagems devised to improve one's score, including demonstrations that unsatisfactory equipment could be used despite failure by others."[8]

Officers and sailors often placed looking good or scoring well ahead of really *doing well*. As Beach observed, often "depth charge attacks were graded on the excellence of the charts prepared afterward, in which a perfect score was achieved if all the little circles depicting 'lethal radius' touched each other. . . . Ship engineers routinely squirreled away extra fuel in their tanks during noncompetitive periods, so that during engineering competition it could be doled out as necessary to indicate less fuel used than was in fact the case, and thus show operational economy for the judging period." Gunnery competitions also invited special attention: "A gunnery 'E' was once awarded because the ship was given a slight list, by judicious use of fuel, exactly equal to the precalculated elevation required of the guns, which could therefore be fired at a faster rate." Winning such competitions was "the criterion by which careers rose and fell; practice always had to be successful, regardless of what was tested." In 1932–33 the ship with the highest "battle efficiency" scores was *West Virginia*. The ship with the lowest score was fleet flagship *Pennsylvania* (BB-38), as can be seen in table 3.

All the scores were adjusted to take into account differences in the equipment installed in the different ships. The 14-inch guns of *Texas* and *New York*,

Table 3

Ship	Overall Standing	Gunnery Standing	Engineering Standing	Communi-cations Standing	Commanding Officer
West Virginia	1(102.25)	1(100.00)	1(100.00)	1(95.98)	W. S. Anderson
Oklahoma	2(87.369)	5(83.752)	4(90.295)	7(89.16)	H. D. Cooke
California	3(86.189)	4(85.559)	7(82.759)	4(93.74)	W. Brown
Nevada	4(84.261)	6(78.541)	3(92.215)	9(85.85)	W. S. Pye
Maryland	5(84.179)	3(86.289)	9(75.390)	2(95.64)	R. Morris, then L. S. Porterfield
Colorado	6(81.189)	7(66.608)	2(98.061)	3(94.58)	B. B. Wygant
Arizona	7(69.724)	8(56.524)	5(87.649)	8(88.06)	C. S. Kerrick
Texas	8(68.834)	9(54.363)	6(87.415)	6(90.63)	J. C. Townsend
Tennessee	9(55.438)	11(36.931)	8(78.824)	5(93.53)	C. P. Snyder, then W. W. Smyth
Pennsylvania	10(53.953)	10(40.551)	10(75.307)	11(83.05)	W. J. Giles
New York*	—	2(91.986)	—	10(85.50)	G. F. Neal

Note: Battleship *New York* was not eligible for the engineering competition and so didn't place in the overall competition.

Source: Op-22-B, A5-8/BB, 19 August 1933; from: CNO; to: Commander-in-Chief, U.S. Fleet, Commander Battle Force, Commander Battleships, Battle Force, Commander Battleship Division 1, 3, and Commanding Officers all Battleships; subject: Battle Efficiency—Battleships, 1932–33. RG 38, Fleet Training Division, Confidential Correspondence, 1914–1941, Box 125, A5-7 (25)/FS-A16-3(5), 1933, National Archives.

for example, could elevate to only 15 degrees, while those of all the other battleships could elevate to 30 degrees. The difference gave the more modern ships a range advantage that had to be compensated for in the scoring.

Consider the spread of the scores. Gunnery scores ran from 100.00 down to 36.931 (for *Tennessee*). Engineering scores, by contrast, only varied from 100.00 to 75.307, and the scores for communications were bunched between 95.98 and 83.05. What those numbers show is that communications competitions were tight, while the gunnery race produced wide variability. Yet note how close the overall scores often were. The difference between second place (*Oklahoma* [*BB-37*], with 87.369) and fifth place (*Maryland* [BB-46], with 84.179) was only 3.190 points! The difference between fourth and fifth place was just .082 points!

Is it any wonder that officers and senior enlisted men focused on these competitions at the expense of other forms of training (and perhaps thinking as well)? Remember that these scores were sent around to all the battleship captains and then announced to their crews. Everyone knew everyone else's standing in the competitions. This applied to other ship types, too—even to the numerous destroyers, each of which had its own score from the destroyers' own special competitions. Serving in this Navy was like playing baseball, and each ship was like a team. The season was long, the "stats" told everyone everything that mattered, and the competition was fierce and sustained.

Many officers objected to this emphasis on formalized competitions. As Beach recalled, however, they "were usually put down as being too lazy to engage in real competition. The payoff was in results, regardless of usefulness or applicability to improved efficiency, and the fervor was analogous to the hysteria over college football." This was a calamity for the Navy because it kept Navy personnel from gathering the evidence necessary to evaluate their own performance in light of what was likely to happen in wartime. The persistence of this way of doing things also rewarded those best able to play the game and not necessarily those best able to win wars.

It would be easy to write off such bad habits as being caused by poor leadership. But the actual cause was in fact paradoxical. It was one inevitable consequence of the formation of the modern Navy. Frank Uhlig Jr., for many years the editor of the *Naval War College Review*, put it this way:

> The war with Spain . . . , the strategic views expressed by Captain Mahan (one of the most important of which was "do not divide the fleet"), the growing concentration of foreign navies into coherent battle fleets, and the sense that at some time in the future the United States might have to fight one or another of those fleets, meant that the U.S. Navy must also form its ships into a tactically coherent fleet.
>
> Such fleets require that . . . the ships of which they are comprised be as much alike as possible, that those ships sail together and exercise together, and that the formerly independent captains become used to following the tactical commands of the flag officers placed over them.

As we showed in chapter 5, a battle line has to be able to shoot accurately. The record of the Navy's warships in the war with Spain in 1898 had been shockingly bad. Commander William S. Sims, with the direct support of President Theodore Roosevelt, reformed the fleet's gunnery practices. To make sure that gunnery stayed accurate, Sims implemented gunnery competitions. Gunners had been artists; Sims made them professionals:

> Rewards soon followed for excellent shooting in the form of higher pay, and 'E' insignia on uniforms and on ships' funnels and turrets . . . [and] soon extended to engineering efficiency, and then on to other skills.
>
> Then . . . the Navy chose to improve the quality of its senior officers by selecting for promotion to the next grade only those considered best fitted for the responsibilities of that grade. One way of helping a selection board choose who among the officers under review were "best fitted" and who were not was to examine how well the ship each one commanded (or in which each officer under review was the gunnery officer, chief engineer, or whatever) did in competition with all the others of her kind.
>
> This led to the requirement . . . that if people's careers depended on the results of competitions, then the competitions must be governed by rules in order to assure fairness to all. Most people would obey the rules, some would bend or twist them a little, some a lot; after all, some people probably reasoned, ingenuity is a military virtue, so the ingenuity exhibited by twisting the rule a bit should count in one's favor. In any event, one's career was at stake and, if one were not among those promoted, he would soon be among those discarded.
>
> It was these necessary reforms: the creation of a tactically coherent fleet; the improvement in gunnery, engineering, and other skills fostered by competition among like ships; the advancement of those officers believed best fitted at the expense of the others; and the need for rules to ensure fairness . . . , that led to the unhealthy culture, in which success in competition against the other ships in the fleet, rather than readiness for war, became the goal.[9]

Agreed. This inability to keep the real goal in mind—this shift of "what mattered" from the things that really did matter to the things that did not—was not confined to the Navy. It was, *and remains*, one of the most prominent characteristics of modern life. The reason it does is because modern life is bureaucratic, and bureaucracies require uniform performance to standards that make sense and that apply to all competitors equally. At the same time, people in those bureaucracies are always working to get around those standards, or developing ways to substitute personal relationships for formal, impersonal, bureaucratic ones.

This sort of behavior can have very dangerous consequences. As James Hammond noted in his study of the interwar Navy, all that painting to make the ships look good that former enlisted man Allan Bosworth described in his *My Love Affair with the Navy* in fact just made them firetraps once war began. Yet once the old paint had been scraped off, new paint had to be applied to the bare metal surfaces to prevent rust!

To be modern, the Navy had to be bureaucratic. But all bureaucracies suffer from certain kinds of problems, and the Navy was not immune to them. Indeed, some bureaucracies can be so loaded with problems like those Captain Beach described that they cannot shake them off and therefore fail when tested by an emergency. Leaders of such bureaucracies face the task of yanking their organizations out of the bad habits that inevitably arise. One way this was done in the interwar Navy was to compel ships and force commanders to participate in annual fleet problems.

For a time, in the 1920s, the fleet problems were part of a very productive intellectual relationship among the Naval War College, the Bureau of Aeronautics, and the fleet. The fleet problems did not become mere formalities because the War College was always feeding the fleet the results of its highly competitive war games. In turn, the Bureau of Aeronautics was always providing the war gamers at the Naval War College the latest information about existing *and* anticipated aircraft performance. Given the fact that the Navy's finest officers attended the War College at Newport, it became an engine of innovation and change. During the 1920s the War College's war games and studies counteracted the unhealthy consequences of the reforms that Frank Uhlig Jr. so clearly described.

The point is that there were means by which Navy leaders could combat the negative effects of their own bureaucracy's tendency to measure and reward the wrong kinds of performance. At the same time, senior officers had to walk a tightrope between unnecessary attention to "spit and polish" and the pressures to scrap both the weapons (such as the battleship) and traditions inherited from past. In 1897, Admiral George E. Belknap had proclaimed to the members of the Naval War College that "the bedrock of a naval service is organization; its soul, honor; its necessity, subordination; its demand, courage; its inspiration, love of country; its crown, honor."[10] Note that his list says nothing about technology—nothing about the Navy as a "fighting machine." His words could have been spoken in 1797 as well as 1897.

By 1939, the more thoughtful enlisted sailors would have been joined by many officers in tempering Lieutenant Commander Leland P. Lovette's claim that same year that "ceremony is to a marked degree the cement of discipline, and upon discipline the service rests." They *knew*, instead, that the service rested on demonstrated competence, professionalism, and initiative. To them did Rear Admiral Harris Laning, president of the Naval War College, deliver his convocation remarks on July 2, 1930: "While we all believe that a proper navy will tend to prevent war, we must not overlook the fact that such a proper navy is more than mere material. It also must be thoroughly skilled in the conduct of war. . . . With naval armaments limited and equalized by treaty, skill—and skill alone—will be the decisive factor of our naval campaigns in the future."[11]

In August 1935, Admiral Joseph M. Reeves, then-Fleet Commander-in-Chief and a successful innovator, believed that the forces under his command had a long way to go before they could meet the "applicable Standards of Readiness prescribed by the Navy Department."[12] By January 1940, Admiral James O. Richardson, who had been Reeves's chief of staff in 1935, had risen to the fleet commander's position. As Richardson pointed out in his memoirs, the problems that had afflicted the fleet in 1935 had still not been solved by the end of 1939. First, there were not enough officers to command the expanding fleet. As Richardson noted, "Just after I left the Bureau of Navigation, there were 10,597 officers of all grades of the Line, Staff Corps, and warrants on the active list of the Navy. A year later, despite nine months of war in Europe, there were just 10,817—a gain of 220."[13]

There also were not enough enlisted personnel. The Navy Department appropriation for fiscal year 1940 (beginning in July 1939) only provided for a maximum strength of 116,000 enlisted sailors. The real number needed was closer to 200,000. President Roosevelt declared a state of "limited emergency" in September 1939 and "ordered an increase of naval enlisted strength . . . to 145,000," but it was still not high enough to meet the growing fleet's needs. The shortage of enlisted sailors was actually more of a problem than the shortage of surface line officers because, whereas it took only a year to adapt a college graduate to the duties of a junior officer, it took "four to six years to make the ordinary grammar or even high school graduate into a leading petty officer, skilled in diagnosing the ills of an aircraft engine, a radar, a radio, a torpedo, a gun, or a fire control instrument."

Related to the shortage of personnel was their constant rotation. Admiral Richardson called it "a daisy chain of huge proportions." It was driven by the schedules of the Naval Academy, the Navy's schools, and the public schools.

The Academy's midshipmen graduated in June, and places had to be found for the newly commissioned ensigns. The children of enlisted and officer personnel completed their school terms at the end of May and the beginning of June, and so summer was thought the best time for families to move. Funds for Navy schools were allocated across the fiscal year, which began on July 1 and finished the following June 30, so the tempo of Navy education followed the same pattern, starting in July and completing a one-year's course the following June. As Richardson noted, "Each June and July about half of the officers of each ship or aircraft unit were changed. As soon as the new officers and men were aboard, a new year of training of the ship's company started."

This was the rhythm of Navy life. But it had very mixed consequences: "This . . . movement, so conducive to high morale amongst naval personnel, had its disadvantage in that the battle efficiency of the individual ship or aircraft unit and of the Fleet as a whole was at its lowest ebb each June and July and at its highest peak each April or May." Within that annual rhythm, the battle line "left port early Monday morning for the training areas and returned Thursday evening or Friday afternoon for a weekend in port, with inspection on Saturday morning. This regular schedule had a high morale value for the married personnel." This, too, had a negative side, however, because it made training dependent not on a sailor's needs or skills but on the fact that most officers and many senior enlisted were married. In the event of war, the need to get home to see one's family would be quickly discarded, so a valuable peacetime custom—being home for the weekend—did not prepare ships' crews for their wartime routine.

But brighter days were ahead because the *institution* of the Navy was taking the resources available to it and acting accordingly. In December 1939, to take just one example, a special board headed by Rear Admiral Frederick J. Horne (admiral and vice chief of Naval Operations in World War II) reported on the shortage of naval aviators. Aircraft authorizations were growing faster than the Navy was able to train pilots. The solution recommended by Rear Admiral Horne had two parts. The first was to commission reserve pilots as regular line officers in the Navy. The second was to draw more on the Navy's reserve officer training program for pilot trainees. Temporarily overlooked were the naval aviation cadets, whose rank, upon being recalled to duty, was below that of the freshly trained reserve pilots. Just as important, however, was the appointment of John Towers, perhaps the Navy's foremost aviator, as Chief of the Bureau of Aeronautics and rear admiral in March 1939. He proved to be an outstanding administrator in the run-up to war.[14]

Battle Line has followed two related but different paths. The first path has been to let Navy officers and enlisted men speak for themselves, often at length, and sometimes with eloquence. The second path has been to examine the workings of the Navy as a complex, sophisticated institution by analyzing its documentary record. We have taken these two paths because the interwar Navy cannot be understood except through both the eyes of those who served in it and the lens through which researchers can examine it. This has not been an easy thing to do because of the limits of space.

Put another way, the interwar Navy was a matter of details, from engineering to finance, from the chaplains who administered to the spiritual needs of sailors to the physicians who treated them for the medical consequences of their sexual adventures (or misadventures, as the case may be). In November 1937, for example, Admiral Arthur J. Hepburn, Commander-in-Chief of the United States Fleet, sent a memorandum to fleet officers reminding them to notify the commandant of the Twelfth Naval District (San Francisco) when their ships would be passing under the Golden Gate Bridge.[15] The bridge, which had opened that May, had attracted pedestrians who were dropping objects from the bridge's central span onto Navy ships passing under it. Most of the objects dropped were quite small, and weren't meant to hurt anyone, but they picked up quite a bit of speed by the time they landed on the ships below and were both potentially harmful and practically irritating. The bridge authorities could stop this behavior if they were given adequate warning, and so the commander-in-chief sent out his official memo arranging for the bridge authorities to be warned. Such a small thing for a four-star admiral to be concerned with!

But it wasn't the exception. In the 1930s, for example, the captain conning a battleship approaching her berth in Pearl Harbor faced a definite test. Berthing alongside the concrete interrupted quays on the south side of Ford Island was never easy because a ship as large as a battleship approached the quays toward Aiea but could not swing around on her own in the narrow harbor and berth facing back out toward the channel. As a fleet memorandum noted, "The practice has been to berth them in the order of entry, headed in, then, after the completion of this operation, to immediately wind them so that they would be headed out, ready for . . . sortie. This . . . requires the ship to be pulled out from her berth, swung through 180 [degrees] . . . , and then pushed back into her berth."[16] And that meant a lot of work for Pearl Harbor's tugs.

Using the tugs properly called for careful seamanship. The primary job of the tugs was to push a large ship sideways, but this called for careful coordination between the ship and her tugs. Otherwise, one or the other might be damaged. Pulling a large ship with a towline was more difficult than pushing because there was always the danger that some miscommunication would lead to a tug or a towline fouling a battleship's propellers. In one case in 1936 a battleship was approaching her berth with her bow too close to a quay and her stern too far away. To straighten out, her captain ordered her starboard engines to "Back," or turn in reverse. Instead of pulling the bow out, as the captain expected, this action pushed it further in. Pearl Harbor was only forty feet deep. The battleship's draft was just over thirty feet. The water being pushed forward by the starboard screws was actually flowing along the harbor bottom and then exerting force against the bow. This was counter to what happened in deeper harbors, and it took a while for the battleship's captain to grasp that he needed to stop his engines and allow the tugs to guide his ship into its berth.

Details, details. They ate up a sailor's time and energy and kept his focus on the short term. As Admiral Richardson recalled, the commanding officer of an undermanned destroyer—and they were all undermanned in the 1930s—"spent many hours trying to obtain an allocation of additional seamen or firemen from higher authority so that his ship would have its authorized" complement. That officially sanctioned complement "was a 'heaven' far in the future from the day-to-day heavy tasks of the present, which had to be accomplished with the number of officers and men actually on board."[17]

But we should not forget that there were few sights as beautiful as a Caribbean sky on a clear night, or few liberty ports as enticing as Shanghai or as fun as San Francisco in the 1920s and '30s. A young man who stood on the deck of his ship off Maui and drew in the sight of the gentle slope of land above Lahaina Roads in these years was seeing something that few of those his own age would ever see at all. Other young men were finding their adventures in high-performance aircraft, or in new submarines, or even at desks in the Navy's bureaus and in the Naval Research Laboratory.

They might even find their adventure in the peril of storms at sea, when "something formidable and swift . . . seemed to explode all round the ship with an overpowering concussion and a rush of great waters, as if an immense dam had been blown up to windward."[18] As Joseph Conrad knew from experience, this was "the disintegrating power of a great wind. . . . An earthquake, a landslip, an avalanche, overtake a man incidentally, as it were—without passion. A furious gale attacks him like a personal enemy, tries to grasp his limbs, fastens upon his mind, seeks to rout the very spirit out of him." This was the sea, at times alluringly breathtaking and then again quite literally a fearsome monster. A young sailor who performed well if and when his ship was in peril could indeed count himself a man.

Sailors traveled the world, and their adventures ashore stayed with them as extraordinary memories, but what turned the best of them from boys to men, and then from young men to seasoned veterans, was their work—the way they did it, and their triumph over the natural obstacles of storm and fog and over the perversity of complex machines. They and their "treaty fleet" did just what was expected of it in 1941 and 1942 and then, augmented by a tidal wave of weapons created and produced by the world's most powerful economy, fought to victory in the greatest naval war in human history.

THE WASHINGTON AND LONDON NAVAL TREATIES

Part 1: Major Provisions, Washington Naval Treaty (1922)

Quantitative Limits

1. The United States was allowed eighteen battleships and a maximum standard displacement tonnage in all battleships of 525,000 tons. Great Britain was allowed twenty battleships and battle cruisers with a maximum standard displacement of 525,000 tons. Japan was permitted to have ten battleships and a battleship force with a maximum standard displacement of 315,000 tons.

2. Total aircraft carrier tonnage (standard displacement) allowed: 135,000 each for the United States and Great Britain; 81,000 tons for Japan.

3. The maximum standard displacement of cruisers was 10,000 tons. They could not carry guns larger than 8-inch.

Qualitative Limits

1. All new battleships for all navies limited to 35,000 tons standard displacement.

2. No new battleship could be armed with guns larger than 16-inch.

3. For those battleships and battle cruisers retained under the treaty, 3,000 tons could be added "for providing means of defense against air and submarine attack. No alterations permitted in side armor, in caliber, number, or general type of mounting of main armament."

4. With exceptions, no aircraft carrier could be larger than 27,000 tons standard displacement. The United States was allowed to complete *Lexington* and *Saratoga* at 33,000 tons standard displacement each, "provided total tonnage allowance of aircraft carriers is not thereby exceeded." Moreover, "In the case of retained aircraft carriers, 3,000 tons per ship" was "allowed for providing means of defense against air and submarine attack."

5. No carrier could carry guns larger than 8-inch. The maximum number of guns larger than 6-inch a carrier could mount was ten, except for the carriers larger than 27,000 tons, which could only carry eight. The number of antiaircraft guns 5-inch or smaller was not limited.

6. Battleships and carriers were "overage" (legally obsolete and hence replaceable) "20 years after date of completion." New ships to replace those "overage" could be started after seventeen years. This would allow them to enter service just as the ships they replaced were being sent to the scrap yard.

7. "All aircraft-carrier tonnage in existence or building on November 12, 1921, considered experimental, and may be replaced, within the total tonnage limit, without regard to its age." For the U.S. Navy, this covered carrier *Langley*.

General Provisions of the Washington Treaty

1. The treaty's provisions applied from August 17, 1923, and were to remain "in force until December 31, 1936, and in case none of the contracting powers shall have given notice two years before that date of its intention to terminate the treaty, it shall continue in force until the expiration of two years . . ." On December 29, 1934, the Japanese government told the other parties to the Washington Naval Treaty that it would not renew the agreement, and so the treaty ended on December 31, 1936.

2. "The standard displacement of a ship is the displacement of the ship complete, fully manned, engined, and equipped ready for sea, including all armament and ammunition, equipment, outfit, provisions, and fresh water for crew . . . but without fuel or reserve feed water on board."

Part 2: Major Provisions, London Naval Treaty (1930)

Quantitative Limits

1. No new battleship construction between 1931 and 1936.

2. Battleship *Florida* to be scrapped. *Wyoming* to become a training ship.

3. Cruisers were divided into two classes—those carrying "a gun above 6.1-inch caliber" and those with guns "not above 6.1-inch caliber." Maximum standard displacement tonnage of cruisers with guns smaller than 6.1 inch was 10,000 tons, and the United States could possess a maximum of 143,500 tons of cruisers of this second type. There was no limit on the *number* of the

smaller cruisers that the United States could possess. The total "completed tonnage" for all cruisers allowed the United States (180,000 plus 143,500) was "not be to exceeded on December 31, 1936." Great Britain was allowed 146,800 tons of heavy cruisers and 192,200 tons of light cruisers. The numbers for Japan were 108,400 tons and 100,450 tons, respectively.

4. "Not more than 25 percent of the allowed total tonnage in the cruiser category may be fitted with a landing-on platform or deck for aircraft."

5. The United States was allowed to convert three of its 10,000-ton, 8-inch-gun cruisers to light (guns not larger than 6.1-inch) cruiser tonnage. If the United States chose not to take this option, then its sixteenth 8-inch cruiser could not be completed before 1936. The seventeenth "heavy" cruiser could not be completed before 1937, nor the eighteenth before 1938.

6. For ships between 3,000 and 10,000 tons standard displacement, "overage" would come after twenty years *if* the ship were "laid down after December 31, 1919." If construction were begun before January 1, 1920, then the ship would be "overage" after sixteen years.

7. For ships smaller than 3,000 tons, "overage" came after twelve years *if* the ship was "laid down before January 1, 1921" and sixteen years *if* the ship was "laid down after December 31, 1920."

8. Destroyers were defined as having a standard displacement not greater than 1,850 tons and "a gun not above 5.1-inch caliber." The United States was allowed no more than 150,000 tons of such ships by December 31, 1936. Not more than "16 percent of the allowed total tonnage in the destroyer category" could be taken up by ships larger then 1,500 tons standard displacement. Great Britain was also allowed 150,000 tons of destroyers, and Japan was permitted 105,500.

9. The United States was allowed 52,700 tons of submarines.

Qualitative Limits

1. Ships designed originally as battleships, battle cruisers, or cruisers could be given a deck for launching or recovering aircraft without thereby becoming carriers and having their tonnage charged against the carrier tonnage limits.

2. "No submarine" exceeding 2,000 tons standard displacement "or with a gun above 5.1-inch caliber shall be acquired by, or constructed by, or for, any of the . . . high contracting parties."

3. However, each navy could retain or build three submarines no larger than 2,800 tons standard displacement so long as these large submarines did not carry guns larger than 6.1-inch.

4. The "overage" limit on submarines was thirteen years.

5. Certain ships were exempt from the treaty constraints, particularly ships less than 2,000 tons standard displacement that (a) did not mount guns larger than 6.1-inch, (b) did not carry more than four guns larger than 3-inch, (c) steamed at less than 20 knots, and (d) did not launch torpedoes. This provision allowed the United States to build gunboats *Erie* and *Charleston*.

6. Certain U.S. Navy ships were excluded from the tonnage totals applied by the treaty, including minelayers *Aroostook* and *Oglala*, transport *Henderson*, and tenders *Bridgeport*, *Dobbin*, *Melville*, *Whitney*, and *Holland*.

General Provisions

1. The London Naval Treaty "came into force December 31, 1930, and terminated December 31, 1936," except for the prohibition on unrestricted submarine warfare.

Part 3: Major Provisions, London Naval Treaty of 1936 (not signed by Japan)

1. Battleships and battle cruisers would be limited to 35,000 tons and 14-inch guns, but the 14-inch gun limit would be void if Japan refused to renew the Washington Naval Treaty. In that case, the gun size limit would be 16-inch.

2. Aircraft carriers were limited to 23,000 tons standard displacement and could not carry a gun larger than 6.1 inches.

3. Light cruisers (with guns less than 6.1-inch) were limited to 8,000 tons standard displacement.

4. Submarines were limited to 2,000 tons standard displacement and guns no larger than 5.1-inch.

Source: Ships' Data, U.S. Naval Vessels, Jan. 1, 1938 (Washington: GPO, 1938), pp. v–xvii, 277–83.

APPENDIX B
NAVY LEADERS

Year	Commander-in-Chief, U.S. Fleet	Chief of Naval Operations (CNO)	Secretary of the Navy
1920	None (no U.S. Fleet until 1922)	Robert E. Coontz	Josephus Daniels
1921	None	Robert E. Coontz	Edwin Denby (March 1921)
1922	Hilary P. Jones	Robert E. Coontz	Edwin Denby
1923	Hilary P. Jones, then Robert E. Coontz (Aug. 1923)	Robert E. Coontz, then Edward W. Eberle (July)	Edwin Denby
1924	Robert E. Coontz	Edward W. Eberle	Edwin Denby, then Curtis D. Wilbur (March 1924)
1925	Robert E. Coontz, then Samuel S. Robison (Oct. 1925)	Edward W. Eberle	Curtis D. Wilbur
1926	Samuel S. Robison, then Charles F. Hughes (Sept. 1926)	Edward W. Eberle	Curtis D. Wilbur
1927	Charles F. Hughes, then Henry A. Wiley (Nov. 1927)	Edward W. Eberle, then Charles F. Hughes (Nov.)	Curtis D. Wilbur
1928	Henry A. Wiley	Charles F. Hughes	Curtis D. Wilbur
1929	Henry A. Wiley, then William V. Pratt (May 1929)	Charles F. Hughes	Curtis D. Wilbur, then Charles F. Adams (March)
1930	William V. Pratt, then Jehu V. Chase (Sept. 1930)	Charles F. Hughes, then William V. Pratt (Sept.)	Charles F. Adams

Year	Commander-in-Chief, U.S. Fleet	Chief of Naval Operations (CNO)	Secretary of the Navy
1931	Jehu V. Chase, then Frank H. Schofield (Sept. 1931)	William V. Pratt	Charles F. Adams
1932	Frank H. Schofield, then Richard H. Leigh (Aug. 1932)	William V. Pratt	Charles F. Adams
1933	Richard H. Leigh, then David F. Sellers (June 1933)	William V. Pratt, then William H. Standley (June)	Charles F. Adams, then Claude S. Swanson (March)
1934	David F. Sellers, then Joseph M. Reeves (June 1934)	William H. Standley	Claude S. Swanson
1935	Joseph M. Reeves	William H. Standley	Claude S. Swanson
1936	Joseph M. Reeves, then Arthur J. Hepburn (June 1936)	William H. Standley	Claude S. Swanson
1937	Arthur J. Hepburn	William H. Standley, then William D. Leahy (Jan. 1937)	Claude S. Swanson
1938	Arthur J. Hepburn, then Claude E. Bloch (Jan. 1938)	William D. Leahy	Claude S. Swanson
1939	Claude E. Bloch	William D. Leahy, then Harold R. Stark (Aug. 1939)	Claude S. Swanson, then Charles Edison (July)
1940	Claude E. Bloch, then James O. Richardson (Jan. 1940)	Harold R. Stark	Charles Edison, then Frank Knox (July)
1941	James O. Richardson, then Husband E. Kimmel (Feb. 1941)	Harold R. Stark	Frank Knox

APPENDIX C

SUMMARIES OF U.S. NAVY VESSELS: 1922, 1937, AND 1938 AUTHORIZATION

Summary for July 1, 1922

Ship Type	Number Fit for Service	Their Displacement	Under Construction	Their Displacement	Authorized, Not Started
Battleships, first line	18	500,650 tons	9	357,000 tons	–
Battleships, second line	14	215,240	–	–	–
Battle cruisers, first line	–	–	6	261,000	–
Cruisers, 2nd line	11	139,450	–	–	–
Lt. cruisers, first line	–	–	10	75,000	–
Lt. cruisers, 2nd line	12	43,175	–	–	–
Aircraft carrier, 2nd line	1	12,700	–	–	–
Mine layers, 2nd line	4	16,096	–	–	–
Destroyers, first line	278	330,272	3	3,645	12
Destroyers, 2nd line	21	15,582	–	–	–

Ship Type	Number Fit for Service	Their Displacement	Under Construction	Their Displacement	Authorized, Not Started
Light mine layers	14	16,674	–	–	–
Submarines, first line	59	37,120	34	29,575	–
Submarines, 2nd line	27	10,645	–	–	–
Fleet subs, first line	3	3,300 (approx.)	3	3,300 (approx.)	6
Eagle patrol boats	54	27,000	–	–	–
Submarine chasers	43	3,311	–	–	–
Gunboats	9	6,355	1	1,575	–
Yachts	9	9,697	–	–	–
Destroyer tenders	8	87,320	2	21,200	–
Submarine tenders	7	44,443	1	10,000	–
Aircraft tender	1	11,000	–	–	–
Repair ships	2	25,170	1	10,000	–
Store ships	6	66,385	–	–	–
Colliers	10	140,560	–	–	–
Oilers	20	283,026	–	–	–
Ammunition ships	2	21,200	–	–	–
Cargo ships	9	80,670	–	–	–
Transports	3	36,800	–	–	1
Hospital ships	4	35,917	–	–	–
Fleet tugs	40	34,211	–	–	–
Mine sweepers	47	44,650	–	–	–
Misc.	6	48,386	–	–	–

Summary for December 31, 1937

Ship Type	Number Fit for Service	Their Displacement	Under Construction	Their Displacement	Authorized in 1938
Battleships, not overage	15	464,300 tons	2	70,000 tons	230,000 tons (6 ships)
Heavy cruisers, not overage	17	161,200	1	10,000	—
Heavy cruisers, overage	1	7,350	—	—	—
Lt. cruisers, not overage	12	90,500	7	70,000	24,000 tons (4 ships)
Aircraft carriers	4	100,400	2	34,600	40,000 tons (2 ships)
Destroyers, not overage	48	72,880	36	57,200	24,700 tons (13 ships)
Destroyers, overage	158	178,710	—	—	—
Submarines, not overage	22	31,315	15	21,740	12,000 tons (8 subs)
Submarines, overage	63	43,820	—	—	—
Submarines, mine laying	1	2,710	—	—	—
Mine layers	2	8,400	—	—	6,000 tons (1 ship)
Light mine layers, overage	8	9,400	—	—	—
Mine sweepers	27	22,680	—	—	1,400 tons (2 ships)
Eagle boats	17	7,310	—	—	—
Submarine chasers	15	1,125	—	—	—
Gunboats	5	7,680	—	—	—
River gunboats	7	2,940	—	—	—

Ship Type	Number Fit for Service	Their Displacement	Under Construction	Their Displacement	Authorized in 1938
Converted yachts	2	1,620	—	—	—
Destroyer tenders	8	53,425	1	9,450	9,450 tons (1 ship)
Submarine tenders	6	36,120	—	—	9,250 tons (1 ship)
Seaplane tenders	2	19,725	1	8,625	8,625 tons (1 ship)
Seaplane tenders (small)	9	7,560	—	—	6,780 tons (4 ships)
Repair ships	3	21,375	—	—	—
Floating dry docks	1	2,482	—	—	2
Store ships	4	19,940	—	—	—
Colliers	3	19,175	—	—	—
Oilers	18	89,030	—	—	22,650 tons (2 ships)
Ammunition ships	2	14,050	—	—	—
Cargo ships	5	21,140	—	—	—
Transports	2	16,050	—	—	1
Hospital ships	2	13,800	—	—	—
Oceangoing tugs	25	20,020	—	—	1
Submarine rescue ships	6	6,260	—	—	—
Misc.	11	55,570	—	—	—

Source for both tables: Ships' Data, U.S. Naval Vessels (Jan. 1, 1938), pp. 405, 424–25, and "Summary of Vessels—U.S. Navy," Sept. 30, 1939, attached to "Summary of Vessels of the U.S. Navy," a memo from the Bureau of Construction and Repair to the General Board, A9–11–(4) (RP), Record Group 80, National Archives, General Board Records, Subject File 420, Box 55, Folder "1938–1939."

NOTES

Introduction

1. The quotation from *Naval Leadership* (Annapolis: United States Naval Institute, 1929) is from page 154.
2. Secretary Swanson's quote is from the foreword to *Men and Ships of Steel*, by Wayne Francis Palmer (New York: William Morrow, 1935).

Chapter 1. The Three Navies: An Unbalanced Fleet

1. For background on the Washington Naval Treaty, see William R. Braisted, *The United States Navy in the Pacific, 1909–1922* (Austin: University of Texas Press, 1971), especially chaps. 11 and 12. Other excellent books on the interwar period include the following: (a) Stephen Roskill's *Naval Policy between the Wars*, vol. 1 (New York: Walker and Co., 1968) and vol. 2 (Annapolis: Naval Institute Press, 1976); (b) George Baer's *One Hundred Years of Sea Power* (Stanford: Stanford University Press, 1994); (c) Harold and Margaret Sprout's *Toward a New Order of Sea Power* (Princeton: Princeton University Press, 1940); (d) Raymond O'Connor's *Perilous Equilibrium: The United States and the London Naval Conference of 1930* (Lawrence: University of Kansas Press, 1962); and (e) Robert G. Kaufman's *Arms Control during the Pre-Nuclear Era* (New York: Columbia University Press, 1990).
2. For a note on how *Nevada* came to be designed as she was, see Norman Friedman and Thomas Hone, "Innovation and Administration in the Navy Department: The Case of the *Nevada* Design," *Military Affairs* (April 1981), pp. 57–62. See also Norman Friedman's *U.S. Battleships: An Illustrated Design History* (Annapolis: Naval Institute Press, 1985). The story of the Navy's interest in and development of bomb-carrying seaplanes is in chap. 3 of Thomas Hone et al.'s *American and British Aircraft Carrier Development, 1919–1941* (Annapolis: Naval Institute Press, 1999).

3. The best history of Navy planning for a Pacific war before December 7, 1941, is Edward S. Miller's *War Plan Orange: The U.S. Strategy to Defeat Japan, 1897–1945* (Annapolis: Naval Institute Press, 1991). The politics of rebuilding the Navy during the 1930s are covered in detail in Robert H. Levine's *The Politics of American Naval Rearmament, 1930–1938* (New York: Garland Publishing, 1988). An interesting anecdotal history of the interwar Navy is *The Treaty Navy*, by James W. Hammond (Victoria, Canada: Wesley Press, 2001).

4. The sources for the Navy's work in HFDF, communications intelligence, and decipherment are (a) "A Brief History of Communications Intelligence in the United States," by Captain Laurance F. Safford, SRH-149, Record Group 457, National Archives; (b) "Use of Decryptors in Fleet Problems," memo from Op-20-G to Assistant Chief of Naval Operations, 28 October 1931, RG 80, Confidential Correspondence of the Secretary of the Navy, 1927–1939, Box 25, National Archives; (c) "The Silent War against the Japanese Navy," by Captain Duane L. Whitlock, *Naval War College Review* (autumn 1995), pp. 43–52; (d) "Report" of the Commander-in-Chief, U.S. Fleet, 1 June 1934, "Exercise N," p. 54, RG 38 microfilm, National Archives; (e) "Critique of Fleet Problem 16 Held at San Diego, California, 15 June 1935," remarks of Vice Admiral H. V. Butler (p. 1), in "Report" of the Commander-in-Chief, U.S. Fleet, 15 September 1935, also RG 38 microfilm; and (f) "Fleet Problem XX, Comments and Recommendations," from Commanding Officer USS *Ranger* to Commander-in-Chief, U.S. Fleet, 31 March 1939 (CV4.A16–3FPXX), RG 38 microfilm. Record Group 80 in the National Archives, which contains the confidential and secret correspondence of the secretaries of the Navy, is an invaluable source for the historian trying to track the growth of signals intelligence for this period. The secret correspondence files for the years 1927–1939 contain reports from Op-20-G, from the directors of the War Plans Division of the Office of the Chief of Naval Operations, from the commander in chief of the Asiatic Fleet, and the commanding officer of the Marine detachment in Peiping. Boxes 214, 215, and 216 are particularly useful. There is also "Military Study: Communication Intelligence Research Activities," by J. N. Wenger, 30 June 1937, SRH-151, Record Group 457.

5. The quotations from the Secretary of the Navy's *Annual Report* for 1933 are from pages 15 and 16. Admiral Standley's quotation is from "Budget—1936, Annual Estimate of the Situation, including Shore Establishment Projects," in RG 80, Office of the Secretary, Confidential

Correspondence, 1927–1939, File L1–1, "Annual Estimates of the Chief of Naval Operations," pp. 59, 63–64, and 73.

6. The quotation from Stephen Roskill is from page 320 of his *Naval Policy between the Wars*, vol. 2. George Baer's quotation is from his *One Hundred Years of Sea Power*, p. 131.

7. Official data on the Navy's ships is contained in various editions of *Ships' Data, U.S. Naval Vessels*, published in the interwar years by the Navy Department. A well-illustrated layman's guide to the Navy of 1939 is James C. Fahey's *The Ships and Aircraft of the United States Fleet*, reprinted in 1976 by the Naval Institute Press.

8. The Secretary of the Navy's comment on ship complements is from the *Annual Report* for 1939, p. 6. See also page 17 for details.

Chapter 2. The Ship: The Navy as a Fighting Machine

1. The quotations from Rear Admiral Bradley A. Fiske's *The Navy as a Fighting Machine*, originally published in 1916, are from pages 195–97 of the 1988 reprint (Annapolis: Naval Institute Press), which has a new introduction by Captain Wayne P. Hughes Jr.

2. One of the best explanations of triple expansion reciprocating engines is in *Naval Machinery*, Department of Marine Engineering, United States Naval Academy (Annapolis: U.S. Naval Institute, 1946), part 4, chaps. 1 and 4. Earlier versions of *Naval Machinery* were published in 1935 and 1937.

3. The long description of what it was like to be in the presence of such an engine is from *End of an Era*, by David Plowden (New York: W. W. Norton, 1992), p. 11.

4. The data on the 14-inch guns (45-caliber, Mark V, Model 2) from *Texas* are from *Naval Ordnance*, by Officers of the United States Navy (Annapolis: U.S. Naval Institute, 1937), chap. 6, plate 1, after p. 124. Other sources for information on *Texas* are "Historic Structures Report: Battleship *Texas*," Texas Parks and Wildlife Department and Sue W. Moss (Austin: Texas Antiquities Permit HS 44, 1993), and *Battleship Texas*, by Hugh Power (College Station: Texas A&M University Press, 1993). For details of her design, see *U.S. Battleships: An Illustrated Design History*, by Norman Friedman (Annapolis: Naval Institute Press, 1985). For photos of the ship, see "USS *Texas*, BB-35," Warship Pictorial No. 4, by Steve Wiper (Tucson: Classic Warships Publishing, 1999).

5. For information on Navy guns from this period, see *U.S. Naval Weapons*, by Norman Friedman (Annapolis: Naval Institute Press, 1983), especially appendix I-1. Each 16-inch, two-gun turret in *Colorado* (BB-45) weighed 835 tons, and each three-gun turret in museum ship *North Carolina* (BB-55) weighs over fourteen hundred tons.

6. The lecture by Lieutenant Commander Blandy is in *Navy Shipboard Administration*, edited by Captain Harley F. Cope (New York: W. W. Norton, 1944), pp. 142–44.

7. The information on battleship *West Virginia* (BB-48) is from "Recruit's Handbook of the U.S.S. *West Virginia*," 1935, courtesy of Mr. Elsworth Woody, in the collection of battleship *West Virginia*, West Virginia Division of Culture and History, Charleston, West Virginia.

8. Commander Carney's essay is "Material Administration aboard Ship," in *Naval Essays of Service Interest* (Annapolis: U.S. Naval Institute, 1945), pp. 213–14.

9. Furlong's testimony to the Special Subcommittee of the Committee on Naval Affairs, House of Representatives, March 6, 1940, is in *Naval Administration: Selected Documents on Navy Department Organization, 1915–1940* (Washington, D.C.: Navy Department, n.d.), pp. VI-257–58, VI-278–79, and VI-293.

10. Another approach to material administration is in *Principles of Warship Construction and Damage Control*, by Lieutenant Commander G. C. Manning, USN, and Lieutenant Commander T. L. Schumacher, USN, members of the Navy's Construction Corps in the Bureau of Construction and Repair (Annapolis: U.S. Naval Institute, 1935). There were also useful books for young sailors, such as *Handbook for Seaman Gunners* (New York: Navy Mobilization Bureau, 1918), as well as very sophisticated "manuals," such as Rear Admiral David W. Taylor's *The Speed and Power of Ships* (Washington, D.C.: Ransdell Publishers, 1933). See also "The Material Control System," *Shipyard Bulletin* 5, no. 1 (Newport News Shipbuilding and Dry Dock Company, 1933), pp. 3 and 6. Copies of the *Bulletin* are in the collection of the Mariners' Museum.

Chapter 3: The Work of Sailors

1. The memoir of Allan Bosworth is *My Love Affair with the Navy* (New York: W.W. Norton, 1969), p. 95.

2. Ted Mason's memoir is *Battleship Sailor* (Annapolis: Naval Institute Press, 1982), p. 22.

3. Bosworth, *My Love Affair with the Navy*, pp. 96–98.

4. Marcus Goodrich's haunting novel *Delilah* exists in two modern editions. The first was published by Time, Inc., in 1965, and the second by Southern Illinois University Press in 1978. Our excerpt is from the Time, Inc. version, pp. 157–61.

5. Mooring a ship is described in detail in *Modern Seamanship*, by Rear Admiral Austin M. Knight, USN (Ret.), 10th ed. (New York: Van Nostrand, 1941), chap. 10.

6. Richard McKenna's award-winning novel, *The Sand Pebbles*, was published by Harper & Row in 1962 and in paperback by Fawcett that same year. Our quotations are from the Fawcett paperback, pp. 13 and 16.

7. Ibid., 35–36.

8. Ibid., 404–5.

9. The quotation from *Delilah* is from page 105 of the Time, Inc. version.

10. Oree Weller's memories are from his "*Arizona* Survivor," in *Naval History* (winter 1991), p. 29.

11. The quotation from the *Bluejackets' Manual* is from page 216 of the 1940 edition.

12. The account by Captain Joseph Taussig Jr. is from *Air Raid: Pearl Harbor*, by Paul Stillwell (Annapolis: Naval Institute Press, 1981), p. 135.

13. Albert Pelletier's oral history is in the collection of the U.S. Naval Institute. We have taken the first quotation from page 13.

14. The quotation from *Delilah* is from pages 206–7.

15. The quotation from *The Sand Pebbles* is from page 445. The excerpt from *Battleship Sailor* is from page 144.

16. Floyd Beaver's book is *White Hats: Stories of the U.S. Navy before World War II* (Palo Alto, Calif.: Glencannon Press, 1999), and the quotation is from p. 70.

17. The quotation from Allan Bosworth's *My Love Affair with the Navy* is from pages 99–100.

18. Commander Charles Pollow's story is from the *Washington Post*, April 27, 1997, p. A-23.

19. Albert Pelletier's oral history, p. 13.

20. The *Colorado Lookout* excerpts are from the June 21, 1930 edition, in the collection of the Naval Historical Center.

21. Albert Pelletier's oral history, pp. 8–9.

22. An excellent scholarly history is *Manning the New Navy: The Development of a Modern Naval Enlisted Force, 1899–1940* (Westport, Conn.: Greenwood Press, 1978), by Frederick S. Harrod. Richer is Floyd Beaver's *White Hats, Stories of the U.S. Navy before World War II*.

Chapter 4: The World of the Officer

1. The *Recruit's Handbook,* USS *West Virginia* is courtesy of Elsworth Woody, through Debra Basham and Joseph Geiger of the West Virginia Archives and History Center in Charleston, West Virginia. The quotations from *U.S. Navy Regulations, 1920* (Washington: GPO, 1920) are from chap. 1, section 1, article 1, and section 1, article 4; chap. 18, section 3, article 723; and, regarding inspections, chap. 18, section 1, article 690.

2. The quotation by Captain W. J. Holmes is from page 22 of a story entitled "Night Action," in *Open Fire!* by Alec Hudson (Holmes's pen name), published by Macmillan in 1945.

3. The *Watch Officer's Guide* was copyrighted by the U.S. Naval Institute in 1930, 1935, and again in 1941. The quotations in the text are from the 1941 edition, pp. 114–115 and 7–8.

4. Admiral Galantin's memoirs, *Submarine Admiral,* published by the University of Illinois Press (Urbana, 1995), provided the quotations concerning his service on battleship *New York*. See pp. 9, 20, and 11–12.

5. Vice Admiral Lloyd Mustin's oral history is from the collection of the U.S. Naval Institute. The story of his quick-thinking action at the 5-inch gun is from Interview No. 1 (8–8–1972), pp. 40–41. Mustin's memories of Chester Nimitz are from Interview No. 6 (8–31–1972), pp. 5–7. His comments about *Augusta*'s readiness are from Interview No. 7 (9–22–1972), p. 6.

6. Captain William J. Ruhe's memoir is *Slow Dance to Pearl Harbor: A Tin Can Ensign in Prewar America* (Washington, D.C.: Brassey's, 1995), and the incident he recounts is from pages 150–151.

7. *Naval Leadership (With Some Hints to Junior Officers and Others)* was published by the U.S. Naval Institute in 1929. The quotation is from page 163.

8. Richard McKenna's story about fictional cruiser *Bennington* is from his uncompleted novel, *The Sons of Martha,* in *The Left-Handed Monkey Wrench,* edited by Robert Shenk (Annapolis: Naval Institute Press, 1984), pp. 266–68.

9. The quotation by Josephus Daniels regarding selection is from the monumental study by Donald Chisholm, *Waiting for Dead Men's Shoes* (Stanford University Press, 2001), p. 600. Another very worthwhile work, but one which compares how different navies recruited and trained their officers and enlisted sailors, is Ronald H. Spector's *At War, At Sea* (New York: Viking, 2001).

10. W. J. Holmes's description of a competent but passed-over officer is from page 4 of the already cited "Night Action." W. J. Holmes's description of the same officer's ship-handling is from pages 8–9.

11. *On a Destroyer's Bridge* was published by the U.S. Naval Institute (1930). The quotations are from pp. 11, 42, 59, and 102. Those interested in small ship handling will find this slim volume a treasure.

12. The anecdote about Admiral Thomas Hart is from James Leutze's *A Different Kind of Victory* (Annapolis: Naval Institute Press, 1981), p. 130.

13. The long selection from Marcus Goodrich's *Delilah* is from pages 81–82 of the Time paperback edition of the book published in 1965. The words about the captain's covenant with his crew are taken from page 208.

14. Rear Admiral Rufus F. Zogbaum's autobiography (dedicated to his three sons, all of whom fought in World War II) is *From Sail to Saratoga* (Rome: Grottaferrata, n.d.). It makes wonderful reading, especially *if* you know something of the history of the Navy.

15. The quotation from the letter by Louise Pratt is from Gerald Wheeler's *Admiral William Veazie Pratt, U.S. Navy, A Sailor's Life* (Washington: Naval History Division, Navy Department, 1974), pp. 80–81.

16. The career of John Towers is covered with great skill by Clark Reynolds in his *Admiral John H. Towers: The Struggle for Naval Air Supremacy* (Annapolis: Naval Institute Press, 1991).

17. Peter Karsten's *The Naval Aristocracy* was published by the Free Press in 1972. We drew especially on chap. 5, "The Naval Mind," and page 267.

18. Captain Frederick A. Edwards's memory of coaling at sea is from his "Reminiscences" (U.S. Naval Institute, 1992), Interview No. 1, pp. 43–45.

19. Rear Admiral David Taylor's *The Speed and Power of Ships* was first published in 1910 and revised in 1933.

20. *Delilah,* p. 83.

21. *From Annapolis to Scapa Flow: The Autobiography of Edward L. Beach, Sr.* (Annapolis: Naval Institute Press, 2003), p. 264. Captain Edward L. Beach Jr., USN (Ret.) prepared this wonderful account of his father's life in the Navy for publication.

Chapter 5: The Tactics of a Battle Line Engagement

1. For the U.S. Navy's view of the Royal Navy's performance at Jutland, see "The Battle of Jutland," a lecture delivered at the Army War College, May 1925, by Captain Joseph M. Reeves, head of the Department of Tactics at the Naval War College (RG 38, National Archives, Box 10). See also *Report of Tactical Exercises 3-5 October,* Commander-in-Chief, United States Fleet, Oct. 12, 1933 ("Fleet Problem XV, Correspondence Regarding Concept of the Problem," RG 38, National Archives, Microfilm Roll 16, Target 2), p. 12.

2. The quotation from the 1923 *War Instructions* is from p. 90 of *W.P.L. 7, War Instructions, United States Navy,* 1923 (RG 38, Strategic Plans Division, Office of the Chief of Naval Operations, Box 5, National Archives).

3. The circular cruising formation diagram is from *U.S.F. 10, Current Tactical Orders, United States Fleet,* 1934 Cruising Disposition 4L, Diagram Number One (in the Naval Historical Center's World War II Command File, Box 270).

4. Admiral Laning's 1933 revision to *The Naval Battle* is appendix 2 in *An Admiral's Yarn,* his memoir, edited by Mark R. Schulman (Newport, R.I.: Naval War College Press, 1999); the quotation is from p. 429.

5. The typical approach formation diagram is from *U.S.F. 10, Current Tactical Orders, United States Fleet,* 1938, Cruising Disposition 6R, p. 13 (in the Naval Historical Center's World War II Command File, Box 270).

6. The quotation regarding the fleet's actual deployment for battle is from "Tactical Employment of the Fleet," Naval War College Staff Presentation (29 October 1937), p. 11 (RG 38, Box 34, National Archives).

7. The typical battle formation diagram is from *U.S.F. 10, Current Tactical Orders and Doctrine, United States Fleet,* 1941, Diagram Number One (Naval Historical Center, World War II Command File, Box 270).

8. Lieutenant Commander Whiting's comments to the General Board are described in Thomas Wildenberg, "In Support of the Battle Line: Gunnery's Influence on the Development of Carrier Aviation in the U.S. Navy," *Journal of Military History* 65 (July 2001), p. 700.

9. The shift from "top spot" to "air spot" is described in W. J. Jurens, "The Evolution of Battleship Gunnery in the U.S. Navy, 1920–1945," *Warship International* 28, no. 3 (1991), p. 246.

10. The 1934 *War Instructions are F.T.P. 143, War Instructions, United States Navy*, p. 87 (in the Naval Historical Center's World War II Command File, Box 108).

11. The Naval War College's 1922 pamphlet is "Fire Control: I, Turret Guns," by Commander G. J. Rowcliff; the quotation is from pp. 6–7.

12. Information on gunnery practices is from Jurens, "The Evolution of Battleship Gunnery in the U.S. Navy, 1920–1945," p. 246. Also consulted was the August 1972 oral history of Vice Admiral Lloyd M. Mustin in the Naval Institute's collection (vol. 7, pp. 21–24).

13. Admiral Schofield's quotation is from *United States Navy Fleet Problem XIII* (1932), "Report of the Commander-in-Chief United States Fleet," May 23, 1932 ("Fleet Problem XIII, CINCUS Report," May 23, 1932, RG 38, National Archives, Microfilm Roll 14, Target 1), p. 30.

14. The document *Tentative Fleet Dispositions and Battle Plans* was issued and first tested during fiscal year 1930. See "Annual Report of the Commander-in-Chief, U.S. Fleet, for the Period 1 July 1929 to 30 June 1930" (in the Naval Historical Center's World War II Command File, Box 256.

15. Vice Admiral Cole's comment is from *United States Navy Fleet Problem XI* (1930), "Report of the Commander-in-Chief United States Fleet," 14 July 1930 ("Fleet Problem XI, CINCUS Report," July 14, 1930, RG 80, National Archives, Microfilm Roll 13, Target 7), p. 65.

16. The first quotation by Admiral Sellers is from *Fleet Problem XV*, May 1934 ("Fleet Problem XV, Correspondence Regarding Concept of the Problem," RG 38, National Archives, Microfilm Roll 16, Target 2), p. 13.

17. The second quotation by Admiral Sellers is from *Report of Fleet Problem XV*, 1 June 1934 ("Fleet Problem XV, CINCUS Report," June 1, 1934, RG 38, National Archives, Microfilm Roll 16, Target 1), p. 66.

18. Laning, *The Naval Battle*, p. 414.

Chapter 6: Naval Aviation

1. The quotation from Rear Admiral Moffett is from a memo, "Design of Future Aircraft Carriers," that he wrote for the General Board, October 2, 1931. The memo is part of the records of the Navy's General Board, now held by the National Archives. The quotations from the General Board's 1919 memo to the Secretary of the Navy are from "Future Policy Governing Development of Air Service for the United States Navy," General Board Number 499, Serial No. 887, June 23, 1919.

2. There are many studies of the controversy between Army Brigadier General Mitchell and his opponents. See Charles Melhorn, *Two-Block Fox: The Rise of the Aircraft Carrier, 1911–1929* (Annapolis: Naval Institute Press, 1974) and A. F. Hurley, *Billy Mitchell: Crusader for Air Power* (New York: Franklin Watts, 1964). Also see *American and British Aircraft Carrier Development, 1919–1941*, by Thomas C. Hone, Norman Friedman, and Mark D. Mandeles (Annapolis: Naval Institute Press, 1999). The latter also describes the relationships within the U.S. Navy among the Bureau of Aeronautics (BuAer), the Naval War College, and the fleet, as well as the work of Captain Joseph M. Reeves to turn the experimental carrier *Langley* into an operational warship.

3. A brief study of Rear Admiral Moffett as a skilled bureaucrat is Thomas C. Hone, "Navy Air Leadership: RADM W. A. Moffett as Chief of the Bureau of Aeronautics," in *Air Leadership*, ed. by Wayne Thompson (Washington, D.C.: Office of Air Force History, GPO, 1986), pp. 83–118. Historian Thomas Wildenberg has covered the career of Admiral Reeves in his *All the Factors of Victory: Admiral Joseph Mason Reeves and the Origins of Carrier Airpower* (Washington, D.C.: Brassey's, 2003).

4. The work of LSOs and flight deck crews is described in Lieutenant George H. Durand, "Silent Communications in the Old Carrier Navy," *The Hook* 20, no. 4 (winter 1992), pp. 28–33.

5. The actual day-to-day work of carrier operations was captured well in words by Lieutenant Max Miller in his *Daybreak for Our Carrier* (New York: McGraw-Hill, 1944).

6. Progress in Navy aviation is documented in detail in *United States Naval Aviation, 1910–1995*, compiled by Roy A. Grossnick (Washington, D.C.: Naval Historical Center, Department of the Navy, 1997). This is an invaluable resource.

7. The best account and analysis of the crash of *Shenandoah* is in *Up Ship! U.S. Navy Rigid Airships, 1919–1935*, by Douglas H. Robinson and Charles L. Keller (Annapolis: Naval Institute Press, 1982). *Akron* and *Macon* are given their due in *The Airships* Akron *and* Macon: *Flying Aircraft Carriers of the United States Navy*, by Richard K. Smith (Annapolis: Naval Institute Press, 1965). Both books are very well researched, highly readable, and beautifully illustrated. The Navy published an interesting and brief account of its lighter-than-air activities as part of the celebration of the seventy-fifth year of naval aviation: *Kite Balloons to Airships . . . the Navy's Lighter-than-Air Experience*, edited by Roy A. Grossnick (Washington, D.C.: GPO, 1987). A contemporary account of the loss of *Akron* and of airship *J-3* sent to search for her was published in *Our Navy*, "First of May," 1933, pp. 7, 10, and 12. Technical information on *Akron* is in "Some Features of a Modern Airship— U.S.S. *Akron*," by Commander Garland Fulton in *Transactions of the Society of Naval Architects and Marine Engineers* 39 (1931), pp. 135–154.

8. Fletcher Pratt's description of a blimp in flight is from his *The Navy Has Wings* (New York: Harper & Row, 1942), p. 89.

9. The data on aircraft are taken from *United States Navy Aircraft since 1911*, 2nd ed., by Gordon Swanborough and Peter M. Bowers (Annapolis: Naval Institute Press, 1976) and from *U.S. Navy Aircraft, 1921–1941*, by William T. Larkins (New York: Crown, Orion Books, 1988). Both books contain many wonderful illustrations. In addition, Hal Andrews published a series of short but informative articles on Navy aircraft from the interwar years in *Naval Aviation News* in the late 1980s and early 1990s (see bibliography).

10. The information about the 1926 exercises dealing with aviation tactics is taken from "Aircraft Tactics, Development of," a compilation of an incomplete document in File A16–3(4) in the National Archives. The compilation includes a memo from the commander of Aircraft Squadrons, Battle Fleet, to the chief of Naval Operations dated February 15, 1927 (A16–3 [VV] FF2–3), and was supplied to the authors by Captain A. L. Raithel Jr.

11. The development of air-to-air tactics is covered in *The First Team: Pacific Naval Air Combat from Pearl Harbor to Midway*, by John B. Lundstrom (Annapolis: Naval Institute Press, 1984), appendixes 1, 2, and 4.

12. *Naval Aviation*, the 1933 text on the subject used at the Naval Academy, and published by the U.S. Naval Institute, pp. 16–36. See also *That Gallant Ship, U.S.S. Yorktown*, by Robert Cressman (Missoula, Mont.: Pictorial Histories, 1985).

13. The percentages of flying time devoted to training were found in "Table 2, Flying Time—Breakdown, U.S.N.—Aeronautical Organization—H.T.A. (Fiscal Years 1936–1941 Inclusive," in "DCNO Air, Administrative History, vol. XV," Box 70, World War II Command File, Naval Historical Center.

14. The information on changes to carrier doctrine is from *Experimental Carrier Type Tactics*, No. 1–39, relating to USF-74 and USF-77, issued March 1, 1939, by the commander of Aircraft, Battle Force, in Box 309, Classified Operational Archives, Naval Historical Center. The cover memo from Vice Admiral King is A7–3/00-So/FF2–3, February 27, 1939. Carrier aircraft launching and recovery rates are given in part 5, chap. 7 of *Experimental Carrier Type Tactics*. See also "Analysis of Aircraft Carrier Operations—Fiscal Year 1938," from the chief of the Bureau of Aeronautics to the chief of Naval Operations and the commander in chief, U.S. Fleet, Nov. 25, 1938 (Aer-E-342-JWK, CV/VV, CV/A4), RG 80, Office of the Secretary of the Navy, Formerly Secret Correspondence, 1927–39, Box 253, Folder "CV/A4 to CV8/S1-1," National Archives.

15. From *The Golden Age Remembered: U.S. Naval Aviation, 1919–1941*, ed. by E. T. Wooldridge (Annapolis: Naval Institute Press, 1998), p. 219.

16. Robert A. Winston's engaging and highly readable memoir is *Dive Bomber* (New York: Holiday House, 1939; reprinted by the Naval Institute Press—without, unfortunately, the color title page of the original—in 1991), pp. 72–73. The quotations are from the 1991 edition.

17. Winston, *Dive Bomber*, pp. 75–76.

18. Wooldridge, ed., *Golden Age Remembered*, p. 99.

19. Ibid., p. 104.

20. Winston, *Dive Bomber*, pp. 117–18.

21. Wooldridge, ed., *Golden Age Remembered*, pp. 153–54.

22. Ibid., pp. 166–68.

23. Aircraft markings and colors are well illustrated in *The Official Monogram U.S. Navy & Marine Corps Aircraft Color Guide, Vol. 1, 1911–1939*, by Maj. John M. Elliott, USMC (Boylston, Mass.: Monogram Aviation Publications, 1987).

24. Wooldridge, ed., *Golden Age Remembered*, p. 273.

25. The high cost of carrier aviation was made clear to the Secretary of the Navy by the General Board in a memo, "Force Operating Plan Based on Treaty Navy," General Board No. 420 (Serial No. 1552), September 8, 1931, in the Records of the General Board, File 420. This file was in the Navy's Operational Archives, and is now in the collection of the National Archives. The quotation from the Naval Academy's *Naval Aviation* is from page 36.

Chapter 7: Submarine!

1. Pioneering research on U.S. Navy submarine design and policy was published by Ernest Andrade Jr., as "Submarine Policy in the United States Navy, 1919–1941," *Military Affairs* (April 1971), pp. 50–56. John D. Alden published a very carefully researched and written book on submarine development, *The Fleet Submarine in the U.S. Navy* (Annapolis: Naval Institute Press, 1979). Alden's book covers both the submarines and the cadre of naval architects who designed them. We have taken material from pages 15 through 21, a quotation from page 31, and more information from pages 42 through 53.

2. The best source for information about the interplay between the technology of submarine design and submarine tactics is Norman Friedman's *U.S. Submarines through 1945* (Annapolis: Naval Institute Press, 1995). We have quoted from the following pages of Friedman's book: pp. 103–104 (on the T class), p. 133 (on the usefulness of the S class), and p. 163 (on fleet subs as commerce destroyers). But his excellent analysis informs the whole chapter, and his data tables (especially appendices A, C, and D in his book) are invaluable. Friedman is also the source for the information about the twenty-thousand-ton steam-powered submarine battle scout and for an explanation of the development of the torpedo data computer.

3. "Weapons Development, War Planning, and Policy: The U.S. Navy and the Submarine, 1917–1941," by J. E. Talbott, *Naval War College Review* (May–June 1984), p. 56.

4. The quote on stealth as the submarine's armor is from "Battle Stations," by Alec Hudson [W. J. Holmes], in *Open Fire!* (New York: Macmillan, 1945), p. 41.

5. Commander Harley Cope's comment is from his *Serpent of the Seas* (New York: Funk & Wagnalls, 1942), p. 50.

6. Both Friedman and Alden discuss the development of reliable diesel engines, but material on the involvement of the railroads can be found in *My Years with General Motors*, by Alfred P. Sloan Jr. (New York: Doubleday, Anchor Books, 1972), pp. 398–412. Another reference is *Internal Combustion Engines*, 5th ed., by the Officers of the Dept. of Marine Engineering, U.S. Naval Academy (Annapolis: U.S. Naval Institute, 1937). Material on Navy relations with submarine builders is in *Building American Submarines, 1914–1940*, by Gary E. Weir (Washington, D.C.: Naval Historical Center, 1991), esp. pp. 106–110.

7. The description of crowding in *S-39*'s control room is from Bobette Gugliotta's *Pigboat 39* (Lexington: University Press of Kentucky, 1984), p. 92.

8. The comment on the 1937 submarine attacks is from Friedman, *U.S. Submarines through 1945*, p. 165. There is a biography of Admiral Hart: *A Different Kind of Victory*, by James Leutze (Annapolis: Naval Institute Press, 1981). Vice Admiral Emory S. Land, an important submarine designer during World War I, wrote an interesting memoir, *Winning the War with Ships* (New York: Robert M. McBride, 1958).

9. The following were found in the National Archives: (a) The night surface attack by an S-class sub in 1934 is described in *Fleet Problem XV*, Exercises L, M, and N (May 5–10), CINCUS Report, June 1, 1934, pp. 30–31, in Record Group 38, "Records of the Office of the Chief of Naval Operations;" (b) The time for an S-class sub to submerge is from "Assistant Umpire Report, SS-53 (S-48), to Chief Umpire," May 11, 1934, p. 1, in the documentation accompanying the report of Fleet Problem XV; (c) The quotation from Fleet Problem X is from *Fleet Problem X*, CINCUS Report, May 7, 1930, p. 78, in Record Group 80; (d) The note about how visible submerged subs were to aircraft during Fleet Problem XIII in 1932 is from *Fleet Problem XIII*, CINCUS Report, May 23, 1932, p. 22, in Record Group 38; (e) The 1935 attack under a destroyer screen is from *Fleet Problem XVI*, CINCUS Report, September 15, 1935, p. 6, in Record Group 38; (f) The quotation about the information provided by radio intercepts is from "Communications; Fleet Problem XVII," from C-in-C, US Fleet, to CNO, A6-2/FPXVII/3285, June 14, 1936, Document 6788, p. 15, in Record Group 38; (g) Periscope

antennas are mentioned in the microfilmed documents pertaining to Fleet Problem XVIII.

10. The long quotation by W. J. Holmes is from "Battle Stations," pp. 15–16 (in *Open Fire!*, already cited).

11. The long-range battle practice of *S-7* is mentioned in Robert H. Barnes, *United States Submarines* (New Haven, Conn.: H. F. Morse, 1944), p. 59. Information on the operation of S-class submarines during World War II was found in their logs, which are stored in the National Archives.

12. The quotations from *On the Bottom*, by Commander Edward Ellsberg, are from the Literary Guild edition (New York, 1929), pp. 142–143, 175–177, 211–214, 299, and 320. Today, *On the Bottom* would be regarded by many readers as overly dramatic, even melodramatic, but it remains a riveting read.

13. An introduction to submarine salvage is in *Mud, Muscle, and Miracles: Marine Salvage in the United States Navy*, by Captain C. A Bartholomew (Washington, D.C.: Naval Historical Center and Naval Sea Systems Command, 1990), chaps. 1 and 2. The quotation from Commander Momsen on the frustrations of raising *Squalus* is from page 43. Photographs of the four divers awarded the Medal of Honor for work on *Squalus*, one of whom was Chief Petty Officer William Badders, are on page 45. See also "Salvaging U.S.S. *S-51*," by Captain Ernest J. King, *U.S. Naval Institute Proceedings* (February 1927).

14. The story of the sinking of *Squalus*, the rescue of her survivors with the diving chamber, and her salvage has been told by Peter Maas in *The Terrible Hours* (New York: Harper-Collins, 1999). Maas is full of praise for Commander (later Admiral) Charles Momsen, and rightly so. But like many biographers, he neglects others who played important roles in the story he tells. A more balanced account is *Blow All Ballast!* by Nat A. Barrows (New York: Dodd, Mead, 1940), which contains the report of Rear Admiral Cyrus W. Cole, commandant of the Portsmouth Navy Yard.

15. The quotation about the Asiatic S-boat sailors is from Gugliotta, *Pigboat 39*, p. 54.

16. A. J. Hill's account of the sinking of *S-5* is *Under Pressure* (New York: Free Press, 2002). The quotation is from pages 55–56 of this interesting book. Unlike many of the others describing submarine operations between World Wars I and II, this one contains clear photographs of the boat's interior. The story of *R-14* is from page 129 of *Under Pressure*.

17. The law governing submarine attacks was covered in *Tentative Instructions for the Navy of the United States Governing Maritime and Aerial Warfare* (May 1941). Section III described the rules of blockade. Section VI presented the rules governing the stopping and searching of ships. Section XI, covering the treatment of a ship and her crew, noted that Title 34, U.S. Code, listed the rules for prizes of war. The *Tentative Instructions* did not permit unrestricted submarine warfare. An article discussing how and why the U.S. Navy adopted unrestricted submarine warfare against Japan in World War II is J. E. Talbott's "Weapons Development, War Planning, and Policy: The U.S. Navy and the Submarine, 1917–1941," already cited.

Chapter 8: Running the Navy

1. The quotation from the *Industrial Mobilization Plan*, 1933 revision, was published by the Special Congressional Committee Investigating the Munitions Industry (Washington, D.C.: GPO, 1935). Under the terms of the National Defense Act of 1920, the War Department was in charge of leading the process of industrial base planning. The quotation from Secretary Daniels is from "Naval Administration, Selected Documents on Navy Department Organization, 1915–1940," Navy Department, 1944, National Defense University Library, p. III-A-12. Captain Pratt's letter is from page III-B-22 of the same document.

2. Chapter 6 of *United States Navy Regulations, 1920* spells out the structure of the Department of the Navy and describes the authority given the Secretary of the Navy. The authority and responsibility of the bureaus is described in section 393 of that chapter. Chapter 7 outlines the authority of the chief of Naval Operations, but the CNO's relationship to the Secretary of the Navy is described in section 392 of chapter 6. The careers of the chiefs of Naval Operations are covered by various authors in *The Chiefs of Naval Operations*, edited by Robert W. Love Jr. (Annapolis: Naval Institute Press, 1980). The history of war planning in OPNAV is told in detail in *War Plan Orange: The U.S. Strategy to Defeat Japan, 1897–1945*, by Edward S. Miller (Annapolis: Naval Institute Press, 1991). The "Annual Estimates of the Chief of Naval Operations" are in Record Group 80, Confidential Correspondence of the Office of the Secretary of the Navy, 1927–1939, File L1-1, National Archives.

3. Rear Admiral Richardson's remarks to the Army Industrial College in Washington, D.C., on December 9, 1937, are from an address, "Organization of the Navy Department," AIC 94 (12/30/37) 11, p. 4, in General Board Study 446, 1933–1939. The General Board records were in the Navy's Operational Archives and are now in the National Archives. The organization of OPNAV in World War II is covered in some detail in *Administration of the Navy Department in World War II*, by Rear Admiral Julius Augustus Furer (Washington, D.C.: GPO, 1959). See also "The Evolution of the U.S. Fleet, 1933–1941: How the President Mattered," by Thomas C. Hone, in *FDR and the U.S. Navy*, edited by Edward J. Marolda (New York: St. Martin's, 1998), esp. pp. 82–86.

4. The creation and deliberations of the [H. L.] "Roosevelt Board of 1933–34" are contained in the previously cited "Naval Administration, Selected Documents on Navy Department Organization, 1915–1940." Congressman Vinson's later proposals are discussed on page VI-2. There is an interesting discussion of Vinson's 1938 bill in the March 1940 *United States Naval Institute Proceedings*, pp. 409–414.

5. An outstanding study of Franklin Roosevelt as chief executive is James M. Burns's *Roosevelt: The Soldier of Freedom* (New York; Harcourt Brace Jovanovich, 1970). The quotation from Admiral Leahy is from his memoir, *I Was There* (New York: McGraw-Hill, 1950), p. 5. Another insightful memoir of Roosevelt is Joseph Alsop's *FDR, A Centenary Remembrance* (New York: Viking, 1982).

6. Navy fleet organization before World War II is a neglected area. A few details are in Furer, *Administration of the Navy Department in World War II*, esp. pp. 167–178. Another source is Robert G. Albion, *Makers of Naval Policy, 1798–1947*, ed. Rowena Reed (Annapolis: Naval Institute Press, 1980). Terms such as "fleet," "type," and "task force" are defined in chap. 1, sections 1 and 2 of *General Tactical Instructions, U.S. Navy, 1934* (Fleet Tactical Publication 142). The problem with distinguishing type commands from operational commands was that the same officer usually headed both before World War II because of the congressional limit on the number of admirals. For example, the commander, Battleships, Battle Force held a type command. As a line rear admiral, however, he also had tactical command of a division of three battleships. The existence of such "dual hat" commands was both curious and confusing to people outside the Navy.

7. Admiral Joseph Reeves began the argument over fleet organization in the summer of 1934, when he was Commander-in-Chief, U.S. Fleet. The General Board listened to his views in an August 14, 1934, hearing, "Facilities for Enlarged Aviation Program." CNO Standley's views are in a memo he wrote to the General Board, "Fleet Organization and command [*sic*]," October 12, 1936 (Op-12-MG, (SC)P17-1, Serial 352), Record Group 80, General Board records, Subject File 420, Box 55, file folder "Fleet Organization and Command," National Archives. Admiral Hepburn's views are in a memo, "Fleet Organization and Command," Oct. 1, 1936, and Admiral Kempff's position is in his memo "Fleet Organization and Command," September 17, 1936 (emphasis in original). Both are in file folder "Fleet Organization and Command," Box 55, Subject File 420.

8. Admiral Standley's statement of "United States Naval Policy" is on pages 44–45 of the "Hearing before Subcommittee of House Committee on Appropriations on Navy Department Appropriation Bill for 1935" (Washington, D.C.: GPO, 1934). The problems of shipbuilders in the 1920s are contained in the articles in *Historical Transactions, 1893–1943*, part 3, Society of Naval Architects and Marine Engineers (New York, 1945). The early history of the National Advisory Committee for Aeronautics is from *Sixty Years of Aeronautical Research, 1917–1977*, by David A. Anderton (Washington, D.C.: National Aeronautics and Space Administration, 1980). For a survey of Navy preparations for mobilization in the interwar years, see Thomas C. Hone, "Naval Reconstitution, Surge, and Mobilization," *Naval War College Review* (June 1994), pp. 67–85.

9. The initial memo from the director of NRL to the chief of the Bureau of Ordnance via the chief of the Bureau of Engineering is "Fire Control Possibilities of Radio Micro Rays," September 15, 1933 (C-F42-2), in Record Group 74, Confidential Correspondence of the Bureau of Ordnance, 1926–39, Entry 25c, Box 213, Folder 571, National Archives. The 1949 quotation from Rear Admiral William S. Parsons is in *Target Hiroshima: Deak Parsons and the Creation of the Atomic Bomb*, by Al Christman (Annapolis: Naval Institute Press, 1998), p. 51. For a description of the experiments on destroyer *Leary* and battleships *New York* and *Texas*, see *New Eye for the Navy: The Origin of Radar at the Naval Research Laboratory*, by David K. Allison (Washington, D.C.: Naval Research Laboratory, 1981), pp. 101–10. The October 1933 memo that

answered the earlier memo from the director of NRL to the chief of BuOrd is "Fire Control Possibilities of Radio Micro Rays," October 20, 1933, from the Bureau of Engineering to the Bureau of Ordnance (C-S71-8[9-15-W1). It is in the same folder and box as the September 15, 1933 memo from the director of NRL to the chief of BuOrd. Support by the Bureau of Aeronautics for radar research at NRL is documented in Allison, *New Eye for the Navy*, p. 117.

10. I. B. Holley Jr.'s *Buying Aircraft: Materiel Procurement for the Army Air Forces* (Washington, D.C.: Office of the Chief of Military History, Department of the Army, 1964) is a superb study. The quote is from page 22.

11. The testimony by Commander Weyerbacher and Rear Admiral King on how the Bureau of Aeronautics procured "experimental" aircraft is from "Hearing before Subcommittee of House Committee on Appropriations on Navy Department Appropriation Bill for 1935" (Washington, D.C.: GPO, 1934), pp. 415–18. Admiral King's point about having Chrysler make a Buick is from page 460 of the same source.

12. In the mid-1930s, there were five major private shipbuilders: Newport News, Federal, New York Shipbuilding (at Camden, New Jersey), Sun (at Chester, Pennsylvania; a subsidiary of Sun Oil Company), and Bethlehem, which had yards at Quincy, Massachusetts; Sparrows Point, Maryland (near one of its steel mills); and Staten Island, New York. Bethlehem also did repairs in Boston, Brooklyn, Baltimore, and Hoboken, and on the West Coast at San Pedro and San Francisco. For information on which ships were built where and when, consult *Ships' Data, U. S. Naval Vessels*, January 1, 1938, Navy Department (Washington, D.C.: GPO, 1938). A source for the development of high-temperature, high-pressure steam propulsion power plants is Admiral Harold G. Bowen, *Ships, Machinery, and Mossbacks* (Princeton: Princeton University Press, 1954), especially appendices F and G.

13. An excellent source on the Maritime Commission is Frederic C. Lane, with B. D. Coll, G. J. Fischer, and D. B. Tyler, *Ships for Victory: A History of Shipbuilding under the U.S. Maritime Commission in World War II* (Baltimore: Johns Hopkins University Press, 1951). The quotation is from page 12. Vice Admiral Land's memoir is *Winning the War with Ships* (New York: Robert M. McBride, 1958). Land played key roles in submarine and aircraft development, and was more important to the Navy than his memoir lets on.

14. The work of the Bureau of Yards and Docks is described in detail in *Activities of the Bureau of Yards and Docks: World War, 1917–1918* (Washington, D.C.: GPO, 1921). The quotation is from page 17; the figure for public works expenditure is from page 19. The building in specific Navy yards is given on pages 160–61. The program of adding to the capacity of commercial shipyards is described on page 217. There is an excellent study of the Naval Aircraft Factory: *Wings for the Navy*, by William F. Trimble (Annapolis: Naval Institute Press, 1990). The quotations are from pages 13 and 67. Rear Admiral King's "yardstick" quotation is from "Hearing before Subcommittee of House Committee on Appropriations on Navy Department Appropriation Bill for 1936," p. 510.

Chapter 9: The Effect of the Marines on the Navy

1. The quotation from Vice Admiral Dyer is from his essay, "Naval Amphibious Landmarks," published in *U.S. Naval Institute Proceedings* (August 1966), p. 51. *U.S. Navy Regulations, 1920* sets out the duties of the Marine Corps in chap. 16, section 1, p. 174. For the role of Major Ellis, see pages 25–27 of *The U.S. Marines and Amphibious War*, by Jeter A. Isely and Philip A. Crowl (Princeton: Princeton University Press, 1951). For an excellent discussion of the ways the Marines proposed to avoid the mistakes made at Gallipoli, see Norman Friedman, *U.S. Amphibious Ships and Craft: An Illustrated Design History* (Annapolis: Naval Institute Press, 2002), introduction and chap. 2, "Developing the Techniques." The quotation from the *Tentative Manual* is from page 37 of *The U.S. Marines and Amphibious War*. Vice Admiral Dyer quotes Admiral Coontz on page 51 of his *Proceedings* essay.

2. In his *War Plan Orange* (Annapolis: Naval Institute Press, 1991), Edward S. Miller covers Marine Corps assault requirements on pages 199–200. The quote about the Navy not giving its carrier aviation to the Marines is from page 200. Miller's argument that the impasse over how to get enough aviation forward with the Marines is what led to the concept of bypassing most Japanese-held islands is from page 184. The hearing before the General Board, "Procurement of Airplanes for Fleet Marine Force" (September 22, 1938), is from the stenographic record, number 128 for that year.

3. Leo J. Daugherty III's book is *Fighting Techniques of a U.S. Marine* (Osceola, Wis.: MBI Publishing, 2000). His description of what was learned in the exercise in 1931 is from page 37. The creation of the Continuing Board and the Fleet Development Board is described in *Andrew Jackson Higgins and the Boats that Won World War II*, by Jerry E. Strahan (Baton Rouge: Louisiana State University Press, 1994), p. 30. Photos of Japanese soldiers and their landing craft at Shanghai in 1937 are in the Naval Historical Center, Washington Navy Yard, Washington, D.C. (photos NH-77967 and NH-77748). Procurement of the Higgins Boats is described in Strahan, pp. 46–47.

4. Daugherty describes the contribution of Admiral Kalbfus on page 40 of his *Fighting Techniques of a U.S. Marine*. Specifications for the 14-inch shells are taken from *U.S. Navy Projectiles*, U.S. Army, Aberdeen Proving Ground (1943), pp. 150–57. The information on the fleet landing exercises is from "Gunfire Support in Fleet Landing Exercises," by Lieutenant Commander David L. Nutter prepared by direction of Rear Admiral A. W. Johnson, Commanding Atlantic Squadron, Sept. 1939. The folder is "Atlantic Squadron-Chronology," in Box 225 of the U.S. Navy Command File (Fleets), in the Classified Operational Archives, Naval Historical Center. The specific quotations are from "Fleet Landing Exercise No. 1," p. 4; "Fleet Landing Exercise No. 2," p. 4; and "Fleet Landing Exercise No. 4," p. 2.

5. The account of the firing of battleship *Idaho*'s 14-inch guns in October 1942 is taken from Norman Friedman's *U.S. Battleships*, p. 352. An account of the 1936 exercises is in Isely and Crowl, *U.S. Marines and Amphibious War*, pp. 48–51. For a general view of the development of Marine Corps doctrine during this period, see Raymond O'Connor, "U.S. Amphibious Doctrine and Naval Policy in the 20th Century," *Military Affairs* (October 1974), pp. 97–103. There is also Leo J. Daugherty III, "Away All Boats: The Army-Navy Joint Amphibious Maneuvers of 1925," a paper written in 1997 while Daugherty was studying for his PhD.

6. There are several interesting books that deal with Marine Corps aviation between World War I and World War II. The Marine Corps has published *Marine Corps Aviation: The Early Years, 1912–1940*, by Lieutenant Colonel Edward C. Johnson and edited by Graham A. Cosmas

(Washington, D.C.: History Division, USMC, 1977). The quotation from Brigadier General Dyer is from pages 74–76 of this work. See also *U.S. Marine Corps Aviation*, 3rd ed., by Peter B. Mersky (Baltimore: Nautical and Aviation Publishing, 1997). Sources differ on the numbers of Marine aircraft in the 1930s. The figures given in the Secretary of the Navy's *Annual Reports* often don't agree with other sources. We have used *U.S. Marine Corps Aircraft, 1914–1959*, by William T. Larkins, as published with *U.S. Navy Aircraft, 1921–1941* (New York: Crown, Orion Books, 1988). The opposition of Rear Admiral Towers to a special aircraft-carrying ship for the Marines is cited in Clark G. Reynolds, *Admiral John H. Towers: The Struggle for Naval Air Supremacy* (Annapolis: Naval Institute Press, 1991), p. 291. See also *Hearings of the General Board of the Navy*, December 29, 1939, "Seaplane Tenders—Large and Small—and Seaplane Carriers."

7. The General Board hearing where members and witnesses discuss the small fast transports is "Minesweepers AM 57-65, Small Transports," September 26, 1940, vol. 2 of *Hearings of the General Board of the Navy* for 1940, pp. 7–17. See also "Construction Program of Combatant Ships, Fiscal Year 1942," May 8, 1940, in vol. 1 of the General Board hearings for that year.

8. The October 1925 paper by General Lejeune, "The United States Marine Corps," is from *U.S. Naval Institute Proceedings* 51, no. 10, pp. 1858–1870; the quote is from page 1862. The final quotation from *The U.S. Marines and Amphibious War* is on page 582. Authors Isely and Crowl argue that what hurt the Marines in the first two years of World War II was the lack of adequate types and numbers of critical equipment, especially amphibious tractors. See chapter 7. The idea for this chapter came from a chapter in *Developing New Tactics, Operational Concepts, and Organizations: The Interwar Period and Transformation to a Twenty-First Century Military* (Washington, D.C.: Office of Net Assessment, Office of the Secretary of Defense, 2003).

Chapter 10: The Lure of the East

1. The verses "China" and "The Philippines" were donated to the Naval Historical Center in Washington, D.C. The quotation from Conrad's "Youth" is from *Joseph Conrad, Tales of Land and Sea* (New York: Hanover House, 1953), p. 28. The quotation from General Krulak is from Rear

Admiral Kemp Tolley's *Yangtze Patrol* (Annapolis: Naval Institute Press, 1971), p. v. We use the terms "the China Station" and "the Asiatic Station" interchangeably. Professor William R. Braisted of the University of Texas at Austin, who has both lived in China and written extensively about the Marines there before World War II, suggests that "the Asiatic Station" is the more accurate term.

2. Barbara W. Tuchman's study of General Joseph Stilwell is *Stilwell and the American Experience in China, 1911–1945* (New York: Macmillan, 1970). André Malraux's *Man's Fate* was published in the United States in 1934 by Smith & Haas, New York. The quotation by William R. Braisted is from his *The United States Navy in the Pacific, 1909–1922* (Austin: University of Texas Press, 1971), p. 648. The quotation from John W. Thomason's story "The Sergeant Runs Away" was taken from pages 376–77 of *Fix Bayonets! and Other Stories* (Washington, D.C.: Marine Corps Association by arrangement with Charles Scribner's Sons, 1973). For an interesting memoir of the Peking legation Marine guard, see *The Old Corps: A Portrait of the U.S. Marine Corps between the Wars*, by Brig. General Robert H. Williams (Annapolis: Naval Institute Press, 1982), chaps. 4 and 5.

3. The story of the new member of the crew of *S-39* is from *Pigboat 39: An American Sub Goes to War*, by Bobette Gugliotta (Lexington: University Press of Kentucky, 1984), p. 23. The account of mechanical troubles but high morale on *Monocacy* is from Tolley's *Yangtze Patrol*, p. 85. Lieutenant Commander Howell's diary entry is from March 16, 1921, and is contained in *Gunboat on the Yangtze: The Diary of Captain Glenn F. Howell of the USS* Palos, *1920–1921*, edited by Dennis L. Noble (Jefferson, N.C.: McFarland & Co., 2002), pp. 109–110.

4. The quotation from Harralson is in Richard Harralson, "Asian Cruise of USS *Augusta*," *Sea Classics* (March 1998), p. 26.

5. The selection from Richard McKenna's *The Sand Pebbles* is from the Fawcett paperback edition of 1962, pp. 146–47.

6. The quotations about Tsingtao and the "Asiatic submarine year" are from "Notes from the Submarine Divisions Asiatic," by Lieutenant Emil B. Perry, *United States Naval Institute Proceedings* 55, no. 322 (December 1929), pp. 1031 and 1032. The quotation about Tsingtao's "unique character" is also from the same essay, p. 1033.

7. The material on Chefoo is from a letter to Thomas Hone from William R. Braisted, May 28, 2003.

8. The quotations from Vice Admiral Lloyd Mustin's oral history (in the collection of the U.S. Naval Institute) are from Interview No. 6, pp. 4–5.

9. The quotations concerning violence at Nanking in March 1927 are from *Yangtze Patrol*, pp. 156–59.

10. Lieutenant Commander Howell's account of steaming up a rapid is from his diary entry of July 10, 1921, and is on page 134 of *Gunboat on the Yangtze*. Rear Admiral Tolley provides another very interesting account of a different assault on a rapid in *Yangtze Patrol*, pages 229–30. When the Three Gorges Dam is finished below Wushan, the major rapids will be covered, and what Tolley called "breathtaking landscape" will be changed forever.

11. Tolley's account of the three gunboats jamming together is from *Yangtze Patrol*, 189–90.

12. Lieutenant Commander Howell's lament about handling a "helpless, drifting ship" is from his diary, October 8, 1920, from *Gunboat on the Yangtze*, p. 73.

13. The quotation about "things going on" is taken from *Yangtze Patrol*, p. 256.

14. It is also *Yangtze Patrol* (p. 124) that contains Tolley's observation on how often so little of China was known by officers posted there. His reference to *The Arabian Nights* is from page 213 of the same book.

15. The quotation from "The Sergeant and the Spy" is from John W. Thomason's *Fix Bayonets! and Other Stories*, pp. 174–75. A succinct overview of Navy intelligence between the wars is "Gazing at the Sun: The Office of Naval Intelligence and Japanese Naval Innovation, 1918–1941," by Thomas G. Mahnken in *Intelligence and National Security* 11, no. 3 (July 1996), pp. 424–41.

16. The discussion of *Panay*'s intelligence gathering is from Jeffery M. Dorwart's *Conflict of Duty: The U.S. Navy's Intelligence Dilemma, 1919–1945* (Annapolis: Naval Institute Press, 1983), p. 93.

17. The Asiatic Station was no backwater when Lieutenant Joseph Reeves first saw Cavite in 1904. There were two battleships, two monitors, four cruisers, a division of destroyers, and a squadron of gunboats. See

Thomas Wildenberg's *All the Factors of Victory* (Washington, D.C.: Brassey's, 2003), chap. 5.

18. Tolley's quotation is from *Yangtze Patrol*, p. 3.
19. Theodore White and Annalee Jacoby's *Thunder Out of China* (New York: Sloane) was first published in the United States in 1946.
20. Howell's last quote is from *Gunboat on the Yangtze*, p. 111.
21. Tolley's last quotation is from *Yangtze Patrol*, p. vii.

Conclusion

1. The quotation from William R. Braisted's *The United States Navy in the Pacific, 1909–1922* (Austin: University of Texas Press, 1971) is from page 670. The quotation from *Life* magazine is from page 23 of the Oct. 28, 1940, edition. For general histories of the United States in the 1920s and 1930s, see Frederick Lewis Allen's *Only Yesterday* and *Since Yesterday*. Another interesting study of how individuals dealt with the Great Depression is *Hard Times: An Oral History of the Great Depression*, by Studs Terkel (New York: Random House, 1970). The father of the elder of us, who lived as an adult through the Depression, thought that *Hard Times* had indeed captured the spirit of that decade.

2. The memo describing antiaircraft practice is "Radio Controlled Target Airplanes—Exercises with during current quarter, advance partial report," from commander in chief, United States Fleet, to chief of Naval Operations, February 12, 1939 (General Board No. 436, Serial No. 3908), formerly in the Navy's Operational Archives and now in the collection of the National Archives. One of the developers of the drones, Captain Pliny G. Holt, confirmed this account in a talk with Thomas C. Hone. Navy 5-inch antiaircraft batteries were so much better after 1942 because of proximity fuses, the development of which is covered in *U.S. Navy Bureau of Ordnance in World War II*, by Buford Rowland and William B. Boyd (Washington, D.C.: GPO, 1954), pp. 271–76.

3. The exploits of Patrol Wing 1 are documented in the *Annual Report of the Secretary of the Navy, 1939* (Washington, D.C.: GPO, 1939), pp. 13–14. The discussion of the importance of the new tankers is on page 11, and the list of the ships under construction is on page 21.

4. The numbers from *Ships' Data, U.S. Naval Vessels* are from pages 405 and 424–25 of the Jan. 1, 1938, edition. The information on auxiliaries is from pages 164–211. The progress made between the design of battleships 36 and 37 (*Nevada* and *Oklahoma*, the two battleships that followed *Texas* and her sister ship *New York*) and battleships such as *West Virginia* was graphically illustrated during the attack on Pearl Harbor. See Thomas C. Hone, "The Destruction of the Battle Line at Pearl Harbor," *U.S. Naval Institute Proceedings* (December 1977), pp. 50–59. The data on battleship machinery is from Norman Friedman, *U.S. Battleships: An Illustrated Design History* (Annapolis: Naval Institute Press, 1985), appendix D. The source for the claim in 1935 that future battles in the Pacific would be fought by carrier forces is from *Hearings of the General Board*, "Fast Capital Ship," October 29, 1935, p. 237. The *Hearings* are part of the collection of the National Archives. The November 5, 1938, memo from the director of the War Plans Division of OPNAV to the CNO is in General Board File 420-7, para. 5, National Archives.

5. The strong criticism of the prewar Navy is in "The Role of the United States Navy" by historian Waldo Heinrichs, in Dorothy Berg and Shumpei Okamoto, eds., *Pearl Harbor as History* (New York: Columbia University Press, 1973), pp. 197–223. For a critique of Heinrichs, see "Managerial Style in the Interwar Navy: A Reappraisal," by Thomas C. Hone and Mark D. Mandeles, *Naval War College Review* 32, no. 5 (Sept.–Oct. 1980), pp. 88–101.

6. Clark Reynolds's criticisms are in his *The Fast Carriers: The Forging of an Air Navy* (New York: McGraw-Hill, 1968; republished by the Naval Institute Press in 1992). For a discussion of the effectiveness of the Washington and London naval treaties as instruments of arms limitations, see Thomas C. Hone, "The Effectiveness of the 'Washington Treaty' Navy," *Naval War College Review* (Nov.–Dec. 1979), pp. 35–59.

7. The paper by Captain Charles D. Allen is "Forecasting Future Forces," *U.S. Naval Institute Proceedings* (November 1982), pp. 74–80. Those interested in aircraft carrier development should consult Norman Friedman, *U.S. Aircraft Carriers: An Illustrated Design History* (Annapolis: Naval Institute Press, 1983), chaps. 3 and 4.

8. The quotation from Captain Edward L. Beach is from his *The United States Navy: 200 Years* (New York: Henry Holt, 1986), p. xix.

9. The comments of Frank Uhlig Jr. are from a letter to Thomas C. Hone. The letter has no date but was written in response to a paper that the elder of us presented at a conference sponsored by the Center for Naval Analyses in June 2001.

10. Admiral Belknap's quotation is from page 4 of *Naval Customs: Traditions and Usage*, by Lieutenant Commander Leland P. Lovette (Annapolis: U.S. Naval Institute, 1939).

11. Rear Admiral Laning's remarks are from appendix 1 of his memoir, *An Admiral's Yarn*, Naval War College Historical Monograph Series, No. 14, edited by Mark Russell Schulman (Newport, R.I.: Naval War College Press, 1999), p. 400.

12. Admiral Reeves's comment is taken from a memo to Chief of Naval Operations William Standley, "Logistic Readiness for War—U.S. Fleet," paragraph 1, CinC File No. A16-3/(4039), August 17, 1935, in Secretary of the Navy Confidential Correspondence, 1927–39, File L1-i, "Estimate of the Situation," Folder 2 (Box 110), National Archives.

13. The quotations from Admiral Richardson's memoir, *On the Treadmill to Pearl Harbor* (Washington, D.C.: Naval History Division, Department of the Navy, 1973) are from pp. 160, 63, 42, and 43.

14. The excellent biography of Admiral Towers is *Admiral John H. Towers: The Struggle for Naval Air Supremacy*, by Clark G. Reynolds (Annapolis: Naval Institute Press, 1991), especially chap. 11.

15. The memo from Admiral Hepburn is "Fleet Memorandum No. 28M-37," November 2, 1937, P13/L11-1/A2-11/FF1(1), 3937, in Command File, World War II, Box 265, Folder "Memorandum, Fleet (M), 1937," in the Naval Historical Center, Washington, D.C.

16. The description of the use of tugs in Pearl Harbor is from "Fleet Memorandum 15M-40," April 4, 1940, CinC File No. A2-11/FF1(1)/H2/(1264), in the World War II Command File, Box 265, Folder "Memorandum, Fleet (M), 1940," in the Naval Historical Center. The quotation is from page 1.

17. The Richardson quote is from his memoirs, *On the Treadmill to Pearl Harbor*, p. 61.

18. The quote by Joseph Conrad is from "Typhoon," published in *Joseph Conrad: Tales of Land and Sea* (New York: Hanover House, 1953), p. 310.

BIBLIOGRAPHY

Primary Sources

Official Navy documents were the main sources for this book. They include the annual copies of the "Estimate of the Situation" prepared by the Chief of Naval Operations as guidance for the preparation of the Navy's budget. These documents are in Record Group 80, "Confidential Correspondence, Office of the Secretary, 1927–1939," File L1–1, National Archives. Another source was the "Records Relating to United States Navy Fleet Problems I to XXII, 1923–1941," thirty-six rolls of microfilm drawn from Record Groups 38 ("Records of the Office of the Chief of Naval Operations"), 80 ("General Records of the Department of the Navy"), and 313 ("Records of Naval Operating Forces") in the National Archives. When the elder of us examined them, the records of the General Board of the Navy (including both the board's confidential hearings and its studies) were held by the Navy Department's Operational Archives in the Washington Navy Yard. They have since been transferred to the National Archives. The various copies of the "Annual Report of the Commander-in-Chief, U.S. Fleet," are also in Record Group 80 (Subject File 420) in the National Archives, as are the papers of the Aeronautical and Joint Army-Navy boards (Subject File 262) and the records of OP-20G, the Navy's code-breakers (in the Secretary of the Navy's Confidential Correspondence file). The records of the Navy's Bureau of Ordnance are in Record Group 74, National Archives. Other useful records in the National Archives are those of the Fleet Training Division of the Office of the Chief of Naval Operations, also located in Record Group 38. See the source notes for details.

The Navy's official public documents from this period are also a valuable source of information, especially the annual *Report of the Secretary of the Navy*, *United States Navy Regulations* (1920; reprinted, with changes, in 1932), and various copies of the *Navy Directory*, published quarterly or semiannually. Appended to or accompanying the Secretary of the Navy's annual report was a section compiled by the Bureau of Supplies and Accounts. In some years, this detailed financial report was published separately under the title *Naval Expenditures*. The Navy Department also published a number of manuals and instruction booklets, such as "Instructions for the Operation, Care, and Repair of Boilers" (Bureau of Engineering, 1934); "Instructions for Use in Preparation for the Rating of Gunner's Mate 3c" (Bureau of Navigation, 1939); and *Ship and Gunnery Drills* (1927). The "Tentative Instructions for the Navy of the United States Governing Maritime and Aerial Warfare" (Office of the Secretary of the Navy, 1941) put together material that had superseded the earlier "Instructions for the Navy of the United States Governing Maritime Warfare" (1917). Finally, there are the various editions of

Ships' Data, U.S. Naval Vessels, an invaluable source issued at intervals by the Navy Department during this period; and the official *Register of the Commissioned and Warrant Officers of the United States Navy and Marine Corps*, published annually.

Books

Ageton, Arthur A., Commander *The Naval Officer's Guide*. New York: McGraw-Hill, 1943.

Alden, John D. *The Fleet Submarine in the U.S. Navy*. Annapolis: Naval Institute Press, 1979.

Allen, Frederick Lewis. *Since Yesterday: The 1930s in America*. New York: Harper & Row, 1939.

Anderton, David A. *Sixty Years of Aeronautical Research, 1917–1977*. Washington, D.C.: National Aeronautics and Space Administration, 1980.

Baer, George W. *One Hundred Years of Sea Power*. Stanford: Stanford University Press, 1994.

Baldwin, Hanson W. *What the Citizen Should Know about the Navy*. New York: Norton, 1941.

Banning, Kendall. *The Fleet Today*. New York: Funk & Wagnalls, 1940.

Barnes, Robert H. *United States Submarines*. New Haven, Conn.: H. F. Morse, 1944.

Barrows, Nat A. *Blow All Ballast! The Story of the* Squalus. New York: Dodd, Mead, 1940.

Beaver, Floyd. *White Hats: Stories of the U.S. Navy before World War II*. Palo Alto, Calif.: Glencannon Press, 1999.

Bosworth, Allan R. *My Love Affair with the Navy*. New York: W. W. Norton, 1969.

Bowen, Harold G., Admiral *Ships, Machinery, and Mossbacks*. Princeton: Princeton University Press, 1954.

Bradford, James C., ed. *Admirals of the New Steel Navy*. Annapolis: Naval Institute Press, 1990.

Braisted, William Reynolds. *The United States Navy in the Pacific, 1909–1922*. Austin: University of Texas Press, 1971.

Brodie, Bernard. *A Layman's Guide to Naval Strategy*. Princeton: Princeton University Press, 1942.

Buell, Thomas B. *Master of Sea Power: A Biography of Fleet Admiral Ernest J. King*. Boston: Little, Brown, 1980.

Bureau of Engineering, Department of the Navy. *Instructions for the Operation, Care, and Repair of Boilers*. Washington, D.C.: GPO, 1935.

Bureau of Naval Personnel, Department of the Navy. *Naval Ordnance and Gunnery* (NAVPERS 16116-A). Washington, D.C.: GPO, 1946.

Bureau of Navigation, Department of the Navy. *Navy Directory* (1 April and 1 Oct. 1929). Washington, D.C.: GPO, 1929.

———. *Instructions for Use in Preparation for the Rating of Gunner's Mate 3c*. Washington, D.C.: GPO, 1938.

Burns, James MacGregor. *Roosevelt: The Soldier of Freedom*. New York: Harcourt Brace Jovanovich, 1970.

Bywater, Hector C. *The Great Pacific War*. New York: St. Martin's, 1991.

Chisholm, Donald. *Waiting for Dead Men's Shoes: Origins and Development of the U.S. Navy's Officer Personnel System, 1793–1941*. Stanford: Stanford University Press, 2001.

Christman, Al. *Target Hiroshima: Deak Parsons and the Creation of the Atomic Bomb*. Annapolis: Naval Institute Press, 1998.

Coast Artillery Journal. *Tactics and Technique of Coast Artillery*. 1st ed. Washington, D.C.: National Service Publishing, 1931.

Coletta, Paolo E., ed. *American Secretaries of the Navy, 1913–1972*. Vol. 2. Annapolis: Naval Institute Press, 1980.

Connolly, James B. *Navy Men*. New York: John Day, 1939.

Coontz, Robert E., *From the Mississippi to the Sea*. Philadelphia: Dorrance & Co., 1930.

Cope, Harley F., Commander *Serpent of the Seas*. New York: Funk & Wagnalls, 1942.

Cox, Ormond L., Commander, and Commander Miles A. Libbey. *Naval Turbines*. Annapolis: United States Naval Institute, 1924.

Cressman, Robert J. *USS* Ranger: *The Navy's First Flattop from Keel to Mast, 1934–1946*. Washington, D.C.: Brassey's, 2003.

Dorwart, Jeffrey M. *Conflict of Duty: The U.S. Navy's Intelligence Dilemma, 1919–1945*. Annapolis: Naval Institute Press, 1983.

Dyer, George C., Vice Admiral (Ret.). *The Amphibians Came to Conquer: The Story of Admiral Richard Kelly Turner*. Vol. 1. Washington, D.C.: Naval History Division, Department of the Navy, 1969.

Elliott, John M., Major, USMC (Ret.). *The Official Monogram U.S. Navy and Marine Corps Aircraft Color Guide, Vol. 1 (1911–1939)*. Boylston, Mass.: Monogram Aviation, 1987.

Ellsberg, Edward, Commander *On the Bottom*. New York: Literary Guild, 1929.

Evans, David C., and Mark R. Peattie. *Kaigun: Strategy, Tactics, and Technology in the Imperial Japanese Navy, 1887–1941*. Annapolis: Naval Institute Press, 1997.

Ferrell, Henry C., Jr. *Claude A. Swanson of Virginia*. Lexington: University Press of Kentucky, 1985.

Fiske, Bradley A., Rear Admiral *The Navy as a Fighting Machine*. Annapolis: Naval Institute Press, 1988 (originally published in 1916).

Friedman, Norman. *U.S. Destroyers: An Illustrated Design History*. Annapolis: Naval Institute Press, 1982.

———. *U.S. Aircraft Carriers: An Illustrated Design History*. Annapolis: Naval Institute Press, 1983.

———. *U.S. Cruisers: An Illustrated Design History*. Annapolis: Naval Institute Press, 1984.

———. *U.S. Battleships: An Illustrated Design History*. Annapolis: Naval Institute Press, 1985.

———. *U.S. Submarines through 1945: An Illustrated Design History*. Annapolis: Naval Institute Press, 1995.

————. *U.S. Amphibious Ships and Craft: An Illustrated Design History.* Annapolis: Naval Institute Press, 2002.

Frost, Holloway H., Commander *On a Destroyer's Bridge.* Annapolis: United States Naval Institute, 1930.

Fry, John. *USS* Saratoga, *CV-3.* Altglen, Penn.: Schiffer, 1996.

Furer, Julius Augustus, Rear Admiral *Administration of the Navy Department in World War II.* Washington, D.C.: GPO, 1959.

Garzke, William H., Jr., and Robert O. Dulin, Jr. *Battleships: United States Battleships, 1935–1992.* Annapolis: Naval Institute Press, 1995.

Goodrich, Marcus. *Delilah.* New York: Time, Inc., 1965; reprint, Carbondale: Southern Illinois University Press, 1978.

Gruner, George F. *Bluewater Beat: The Two Lives of the Battleship USS* California. Palo Alto, Calif.: Associates of the San Francisco Maritime Museum Library and Glencannon Press, 1996.

Harrod, Frederick S. *Manning the New Navy: The Development of a Modern Naval Enlisted Force, 1899–1940.* Westport, Conn.: Greenwood Press, 1978.

Hone, Thomas C., and Norman Friedman and Mark D. Mandeles. *American and British Aircraft Carrier Development, 1919–1941.* Annapolis: Naval Institute Press, 1999.

Hovgaard, William. *Structural Design of Warships.* Annapolis: United States Naval Institute, 1940.

Hudson, Alec [pseudonym of W. J. Holmes]. *Open Fire!* New York: Macmillan, 1945.

Hughes, Wayne P., Jr. *Fleet Tactics, Theory, and Practice.* Annapolis: Naval Institute Press, 1986.

Isely, Jeter A., and Philip A. Crowl. *The U.S. Marines and Amphibious War.* Princeton: Princeton University Press, 1951.

Knight, Austin M., Rear Admiral (Ret.). *Modern Seamanship.* 10th ed. New York: Van Nostrand, 1941.

Knott, Richard C. *The American Flying Boat.* Annapolis: Naval Institute Press, 1979.

Land, Emory S., Vice Admiral *Winning the War with Ships.* New York: Robert M. McBride, 1958.

Larkins, William T. *U.S. Marine Corps Aircraft, 1914–1959.* New York: Crown, Orion Books, 1988.

————. *U.S. Navy Aircraft, 1921–1941.* New York: Crown, Orion Books, 1988.

————. *Battleship and Cruiser Aircraft of the United States Navy, 1910–1949.* Altglen, Penn.: Schiffer, 1996.

Leutze, James. *A Different Kind of Victory: A Biography of Admiral Thomas C. Hart.* Annapolis: Naval Institute Press, 1981.

Levine, Robert H. *The Politics of American Naval Rearmament, 1930–1938.* New York: Garland, 1988.

Love, Robert W., Jr., ed. *The Chiefs of Naval Operations.* Annapolis: Naval Institute Press, 1980.

Lundstrom, John B. *The First Team: Pacific Naval Air Combat from Pearl Harbor to Midway.* Annapolis: Naval Institute Press, 1984.

Manning, G. C., Lieutenant Commander, and Lieutenant Commander T. L. Schumacher. *Principles of Warship Construction and Damage Control.* Annapolis: United States Naval Institute, 1935.

Marine Engineering Department, U.S. Naval Academy. *Naval Machinery, 1946,* parts 1 and 2. Annapolis: United States Naval Institute, 1946.

Marolda, Edward J., ed. *FDR and the U.S. Navy.* New York: St. Martin's, 1998.

Mason, Theodore C. *Battleship Sailor.* Annapolis: Naval Institute Press, 1982.

McKenna, Richard. *The Sand Pebbles.* Greenwich, Conn.: Fawcett, 1962.

———. *The Left-Handed Monkey Wrench.* Edited by Robert Shenk. Annapolis: Naval Institute Press, 1984.

Melia, Tamara M. *"Damn the Torpedoes": A Short History of U.S. Naval Mine Countermeasures, 1777–1991.* Washington, D.C.: Naval Historical Center, 1991.

Miller, Edward S. *War Plan Orange: The U.S. Strategy to Defeat Japan, 1897–1945.* Annapolis: Naval Institute Press, 1991.

Musicant, Ivan. *Battleship at War: The Epic Story of the USS* Washington. New York: Harcourt Brace Jovanovich, 1986.

Ordnance and Gunnery Department, U.S. Naval Academy. *Naval Ordnance: A Textbook.* Annapolis: United States Naval Institute, 1937.

Navy Department. *Ships' Data, U.S. Naval Vessels, 1938.* Washington, D.C.: GPO, 1938.

Navy Department. *Organization of Naval Aviation.* (Reserve Officer's Manual). Washington, D.C.: GPO, 1932.

Office of the Secretary of the Navy. *Tentative Instructions for the Navy of the United States Governing Maritime and Aerial Warfare.* May 1941. Washington, D.C.: GPO, 1941.

Packard, Wyman H. *A Century of U.S. Intelligence.* Washington, D.C.: Office of Naval Intelligence and Naval Historical Center, 1996.

Palmer, Wayne Francis. *Men and Ships of Steel.* New York: William Morrow, 1935.

Power, Hugh. *Battleship Texas.* College Station: Texas A&M University Press, 1993.

Prados, John. *Combined Fleet Decoded.* New York: Random House, 1995.

Pratt, Fletcher. *Fleet against Japan.* New York: Harper & Row, 1943.

Pratt & Whitney Aircraft Division, United Aircraft Corporation. *The Pratt & Whitney Aircraft Story.* Hartford, Conn.: United Aircraft Corporation, 1950.

Rabl, S. S. *Practical Principles of Naval Architecture.* New York: Cornell Maritime Press, 1942.

Reynolds, Clark G. *The Fast Carriers: The Forging of an Air Navy.* New York: McGraw-Hill, 1968; reprint, Annapolis, Naval Institute Press, 1992.

———. *Admiral John H. Towers: The Struggle for Naval Air Supremacy.* Annapolis: Naval Institute Press, 1991.

Richardson, James O., Admiral (Ret.). *On the Treadmill to Pearl Harbor: The Memoirs of Admiral James O. Richardson.* Washington, D.C.: Naval History Division, Navy Department, 1973.

Robinson, Douglas H., and Charles L. Keller. *Up Ship: U.S. Navy Airships, 1919–1935.* Annapolis: Naval Institute Press, 1982.

Roskill, Stephen. *Naval Policy between the Wars.* Vol. 1 New York: Walker, 1968. Vol. 2: Annapolis: Naval Institute Press, 1976.

Rowland, Buford, and William B. Boyd. *U.S. Navy Bureau of Ordnance in World War II.* Washington, D.C.: GPO, 1954.

Ruhe, William J. *Slow Dance to Pearl Harbor: A Tin Can Ensign in Prewar America.* Washington, D.C.: Brassey's, 1995.

Schmidt, Hans. *Maverick Marine: General Smedley D. Butler and the Contradictions of American Military History.* Lexington: University Press of Kentucky, 1987.

Sherrod, Robert. *History of Marine Corps Aviation in World War II.* Baltimore: Nautical and Aviation Publishing, 1987.

Simpson, B. Mitchell, III. *Admiral Harold R. Stark.* Columbia: University of South Carolina Press, 1989.

Simpson, Edward, Rear Admiral, USN (Ret.). *Yarnlets: The Human Side of the Navy.* New York: Putnam's, 1934.

Smith, Richard K. *The Airships* Akron *and* Macon*: Flying Aircraft Carriers of the United States Navy.* Annapolis: Naval Institute Press, 1965.

Society of Naval Architects and Marine Engineers. *Historical Transactions, 1893–1943.* New York: Society of Naval Architects and Marine Engineers, 1945.

Spector, Ronald. *Professors of War: The Naval War College and the Development of the Naval Profession.* Newport, R.I.: Naval War College Press, 1977.

———. *At War, At Sea.* New York: Viking, 2001.

Sprout, Harold, and Margaret Sprout. *Toward a New Order of Sea Power.* Princeton: Princeton University Press, 1940.

Sterling, Yates, Rear Admiral *Sea Duty: The Memoirs of a Fighting Admiral.* New York: Putnam's, 1939.

Stillwell, Paul. *Battleship* Arizona. Annapolis: Naval Institute Press, 1991.

Swanborough, Gordon, and Peter M. Bowers. *United States Navy Aircraft since 1911.* 2nd ed. Annapolis: Naval Institute Press, 1976.

Sweetman, Jack. *American Naval History: An Illustrated Chronology of the U.S. Navy and Marine Corps, 1775–Present.* Annapolis: Naval Institute Press, 1984.

Thomason, John W., Jr., Captain *Fix Bayonets! and Other Stories.* Washington, D.C.: Marine Corps Association by arrangement with Charles Scribner's and Sons, 1973.

Tolley, Kemp, Rear Admiral (Ret.). *Yangtze Patrol.* Annapolis: Naval Institute Press, 1971.

Trimble, William F. *Wings for the Navy: A History of the Naval Aircraft Factory, 1917–1956.* Annapolis: Naval Institute Press, 1990.

———. *Admiral William A. Moffett.* Washington, D.C.: Smithsonian Institution Press, 1994.

United States Naval Academy. *Naval Aviation.* Annapolis: United States Naval Institute, 1933.

United States Naval Institute. *Naval Leadership*. 3rd ed. Annapolis: U.S. Naval Institute, 1929.

———. *The Bluejacket's Manual*. Annapolis: United States Naval Institute, 1940.

United States Navy. *Ship and Gunnery Drills*. Washington, D.C.: GPO, 1927.

Utley, Jonathan G. *An American Battleship at Peace and War: The USS Tennessee*. Lawrence: University Press of Kansas, 1991.

Vlahos, Michael. *The Blue Sword: The Naval War College and the American Mission, 1919–1941*. Newport, R.I.: Naval War College Press, 1980.

Weir, Gary E. *Building American Submarines, 1914–1940*. Washington, D.C.: Naval Historical Center, 1991.

Wildenberg, Thomas. *Gray Steel and Black Oil*. Annapolis: Naval Institute Press, 1996.

———. *Destined for Glory: Dive Bombing, Midway, and the Evolution of Carrier Airpower*. Annapolis: Naval Institute Press, 1998.

———. *All the Factors of Victory: Admiral Joseph Mason Reeves and the Origins of Carrier Airpower*. Washington, D.C.: Brassey's, 2003.

Williams, Robert H., Brigader General, USMC (Ret.). *The Old Corps: A Portrait of the U.S. Marine Corps between the Wars*. Annapolis: Naval Institute Press, 1982.

Willson, Russell, Captain *Watch Officer's Guide, United States Navy*. Annapolis: United States Naval Institute, 1941.

Wilson, Eugene E. *Slipstream*. New York: McGraw-Hill, 1950.

Winston, Robert A. *Dive Bomber*. New York: Holiday House, 1939; reprint, Annapolis: Naval Institute Press, 1991.

Woods, David L. *Signaling and Communicating at Sea*. Vol. 2. New York: Arno Press, 1980.

Wooldridge, E. T., ed. *The Golden Age Remembered: U.S. Naval Aviation, 1919–1941*. Annapolis: Naval Institute Press, 1998.

Yerxa, Donald A. *Admirals and Empire: The United States Navy and the Caribbean, 1898–1945*. Columbia: University of South Carolina Press, 1991.

Articles

Bibliography: Articles

Alden, John D., Commander, USN (Ret.). "Edward Ellsberg—A Naval Engineer before His Time." *Naval Engineers Journal* (July 1998): 105–10.

Allen, Charles D., Jr., Captain "Forecasting Future Forces." *U.S. Naval Institute Proceedings* (Nov. 1982): 74–80.

Allen, Keith E. "Separate Superheat Boilers in *Hornet* (CV-8)." *Warship International* 34, no. 2 (1997): 197–202.

Andrade, Ernest, Jr. "The Ship That Never Was." *Military Affairs* 32, no. 3 (Dec. 1968): 132–40.

———. "Submarine Policy in the United States Navy, 1919–1941." *Military Affairs* (April 1971): 50–56.

Andrews, Hal. "BF2C-1." *Naval Aviation News* (Jan.–Feb. 1986): 16–17.

———. "SBD Dauntless." *Naval Aviation News* (July–Aug. 1991): 24–25.

———. "F8C/O2C Helldiver." *Naval Aviation News* (Nov.–Dec. 1992): 18–19.

Armstrong, W. J. "William A. Moffett and the Development of Naval Aviation." In *Aviation's Golden Age*, edited by W. M. Leary, 60–73 (Iowa City: University of Iowa Press, 1989).

Aviation Training Division, Office of the Chief of Naval Operations. "Introduction to Naval Aviation." OPNAV 33-NY-85 (1946).

Baker, A. D., III. "Battle Fleets and Diplomacy: Naval Disarmament between the Two World Wars." *Warship International* 26, no. 3 (1989): 217–55.

Beigel, Harvey M. "The Battle Fleet's Home Port: 1919–1940." A supplement to *U.S. Naval Institute Proceedings* (1985): 54–63.

Belcher, Michael F., Midshipman, USN. "The Flying Sergeants." *U.S. Naval Institute Proceedings* (Feb. 1982): 73–76.

Braisted, William R. "The Evolution of the United States Navy's Strategic Assessments in the Pacific, 1919–31." *Diplomacy and Statecraft* 4, no. 3 (Nov. 1993): 102–23.

Broadbent, E. W. "The Fleet and the Marines." *U.S. Naval Institute Proceedings* 57, no. 3 (March 1931): 369–72.

Bywater, H. C. "Naval Construction in 1931." Reprinted in *Naval Engineers Journal* (Feb. 1982): 79–82.

———. "Naval Construction in 1933—United States." Reprinted in *Naval Engineers Journal* (July 1983): 173.

Cole, Eli K., Major General "Joint Overseas Operations." *U.S. Naval Institute Proceedings* 55, no. 11 (Nov. 1929): 927–37.

Costello, John D., Vice Admiral, USCG, and Lieutenant Commander D. N. Wood, USCG. "Guarding the Coast." *U.S. Naval Institute Proceedings* (Aug. 1985): 66–71.

Craven, F. S., Commander, USN. "The Britten Bill." *U.S. Naval Institute Proceedings* (Aug. 1932): 1127–37.

Dater, Henry M. "Tactical Use of Air Power in World War II: The Navy Experience." *Military Affairs* 14, no. 4 (Dec. 1950): 192–200.

Dodge, R. A. "Massacre in Haiti." *U.S. Naval Institute Proceedings* (Nov. 1994): 60–64.

Duncan, Donald B., and H. M. Dater. "Administrative History of U.S. Naval Aviation." *Air Affairs* 1, no. 4: 526–39.

Durand, George H., Lieutenant, USN. "Silent Communications of the Old Carrier Navy." *The Hook* (winter 1992): 28–33.

Dyer, George C., Vice Admiral, USN (Ret.). "Naval Amphibious Landmarks." *U.S. Naval Institute Proceedings* (Aug. 1966): 50–60.

Eaton, George B., Major, U.S. Army. "General Walter Krueger and Joint War Planning, 1922–1938." *Naval War College Review* 48, no. 2 (spring 1995): 91–113.

Elliot, John M. "Aviation Ordnance, 1939–1941." *Naval Aviation News* (July–Aug. 1991): 26–31.

Epstein, Marc. "The Historians and the Geneva Naval Conference." In *Arms Limitation and Disarmament*, edited by B. J. C. McKercher (Westport, Conn.: Praeger, 1992), 129–48.

Fee, Jerome J., Captain, USN. "Evolution of the Engineering Duty Officer in the United States Navy." *Naval Engineers Journal* (March 1985): 58–63.

Foster, W. F., Captain, USN. "Navy Drones as Combat Weapons." *The Hook* (fall 1990): 14–24.

Frank, Willard C., Jr. "Multinational Naval Cooperation in the Spanish Civil War, 1936." *Naval War College Review* (spring 1994): 72–101.

Freeman, Ross E., Captain, USN (Ret.). "The *Maryland* Junior Officers' Mess in 1935." *Shipmate* (March 1986).

Fulton, Garland, Commander, USN. "Some Features of a Modern Airship—USS *Akron*." *Transactions of the Society of Naval Architects and Marine Engineers* 39 (1931): 135–54.

Harralson, Richard, Commander, USN (Ret.). "Asian Cruise of USS *Augusta*." *Sea Classics* 31, no. 3 (March 1998): 20–27, 52–53.

Hayes, John D., Rear Admiral, USN (Ret.). "Admiral Joseph Mason Reeves, USN." *Naval War College Review* 23, no. 3 (Nov. 1970): 48–57.

———. "Admiral Joseph Mason Reeves, Part II." *Naval War College Review* 24, no. 5 (Jan. 1972): 50–64.

Hone, Thomas. "The Effectiveness of the 'Washington Treaty Navy.'" *Naval War College Review* (Nov.–Dec. 1979): 35–59.

———. "Spending Patterns of the U.S. Navy, 1921–1941." *Armed Forces and Society* (spring 1982): 443–62.

———. "Navy Air Leadership: RADM W. A. Moffett as Chief of the Bureau of Aeronautics." In *Air Leadership*, edited by Wayne Thompson, 83–117 (Washington, D.C.: Office of Air Force History, GPO, 1986).

———. "Naval Reconstitution, Surge, and Mobilization: Once and Future." *Naval War College Review* 47, no. 3 (June 1994): 67–85.

Hone, Thomas, and Norman Friedman. "Innovation and Administration in the Navy Department: The Case of the *Nevada* Design." *Military Affairs* (April 1981): 57–62.

Hone, Thomas, and Mark Mandeles. "Managerial Style in the Interwar Navy: A Reappraisal." *Naval War College Review* 32, no. 5 (Sept.–Oct. 1980): 88–101.

———"Interwar Innovation in Three Navies: USN, RN, IJN." *Naval War College Review* 40, no. 2 (spring 1987): 63–83.

Hone, Trent. "The Evolution of Fleet Tactical Doctrine in the U.S. Navy, 1922–1941." *Journal of Military History* 67 (Oct. 2003): 1107–48.

Jones, Howard G., Captain, USAF. "A New Rival: The Rise of the American Air Force." *Air Power History* 38, no. 4 (winter 1991): 18–29.

Jurens, W. J. "The Evolution of Battleship Gunnery in the U.S. Navy, 1920–1945." *Warship International* 28, no. 3 (1991): 240–71.

Lejeune, John A., Major General, Commandant. "The United States Marine Corps." *U.S. Naval Institute Proceedings* 51, no. 10 (Oct. 1925): 1858–70.

———. "The U.S. Marine Corps, Present *and* Future." *U.S. Naval Institute Proceedings* 54, no. 10 (Oct. 1928): 859–61.

"The U.S. Navy." Editors of *Life* magazine, a special issue, Oct. 28, 1940.

MacDonald, Scot. "*Langley, Lex,* and *Sara.*" *Naval Aviation News* (May 1962): 16–21.

———. "Carriers from the Keel." *Naval Aviation News* (June 1962): 32–37.

———. "Flattops in the War Games." *Naval Aviation News* (Aug. 1962): 28–33.

———. "Last of the Fleet Problems." *Naval Aviation News* (Sept. 1962): 34–38.

Mackey, D. M. "Mechanical Handling of Airships." Reprinted in *Naval Engineers Journal* (Nov. 1984): 81–84.

Mahnken, Thomas G. "Gazing at the Sun: The Office of Naval Intelligence and Japanese Naval Innovation, 1918–1941." *Intelligence and National Security* 11, no. 3 (July 1966): 424–41.

Nastri, Anthony D., Lieutenant Colonel, USMC. "For Whom the Bell Tolls." *U.S. Naval Institute Proceedings* (Nov. 1983): 133–37.

O'Leary, Michael. "Roll Out the Barrels." *Air Classics* 32, no. 3 (March 1996): 30–43.

Palmer, Carlton D. "Early Encounters." *Naval Aviation News* (Aug. 1980): 37–38.

Perry, Emil. B., Lieutenant, USN. "Notes from the Submarine Divisions Asiatic." *U.S. Naval Institute Proceedings* (Dec. 1929): 1031–38.

Pratt, W. V., Admiral, USN. "Our Naval Policy." *U.S. Naval Institute Proceedings* (July 1932): 953–70.

Rock, George H., Rear Admiral, USN. "The 10,000-Ton Treaty Cruisers, with Particular Reference to the *Salt Lake City* and *Pensacola.*" *Transactions of the Society of Naval Architects and Marine Engineers* 38 (1930): 219–28.

Scarborough, W. E., Captain, USN. "Fighting Two—The Flying Chiefs." *The Hook* (summer 1991): 16–35.

Shiner, John F., Lieutenant Colonel, USAF. "The Air Corps, the Navy, and Coast Defense, 1919–1941." *Military Affairs* 45, no. 3 (Oct. 1981): 113–20.

Strean, B. M., Vice Admiral, USN. "Lessons Learned Are Forever." *Naval Aviation News* (Jan.–Feb. 1986): 26.

Talbott, J. E. "Weapons Development, War Planning, and Policy: The U.S. Navy and the Submarine, 1917–1941." *Naval War College Review* (May–June 1984): 53–71.

Vlahos, Michael. "Wargaming: An Enforcer of Strategic Realism, 1919–1942." *Naval War College Review* (March–April 1986): 7–22.

Weller, Oree C., Lieutenant Commander, USNR (Ret.). "*Arizona* Survivor." *Naval History* (winter 1991): 28–33.

Whitlock, Duane L., Captain, USN (Ret.). "The Silent War against the Japanese Navy." *Naval War College Review* 48, no. 4 (autumn 1995): 43–52.

Zimm, Alan D. "The U.S.N.'s Flight Deck Cruiser." *Warship International* 16, no. 3 (1979): 216–45.1

INDEX

Admirals, number of positions for, 131–132
Advance phase of battle, 70
Aerial superiority, 71–72, 74–76
Aeronautics, Bureau of, 92–93, 100, 127, 171, 183
Aggressive action, as doctrine, 82–83, 88
Air Commerce Act (1926), 134
Air Corps Act (1926), 137, 139
Aircraft, 74, 77, 86–87, 176. *See also* Aviation
  naval aviation and, 90–109
  procurement of, 136–141
  as scouts, 71–72, 74, 86, 102
  spotting from, 81
  in war at sea, 172
Aircraft carriers. *See* Carriers
Aircraft industry, 136–137
"Aircraft Tactical Instructions," 99
Air force, separate, 91, 174
Air groups, tactics of, 102
Air Mail Act (1925), 134
Airships, 12, 95–97, 106, 115
Akron (airship), 12, 95–97, 106, 115
Alden, John D., 115
Allen, Charles D., 178
Amphibious command ship, 152
Amphibious tractors, 150, 154
Amphibious warfare, 17–18, 145–156
Analog computers, 116
Anchoring process, 40–41
Annapolis. *See* Naval Academy
Antisubmarine campaign, 3
Approach phase, 70, 73, 74, 75
Argonaut (submarine), 8, 115
Arizona, 40
Armor, 23–24
Armor-piercing shells, 69, 151–152
Arms restrictions, 2
Army, 5, 161
Asiatic Fleet, 160, 161, 163
Atlanta class cruisers, 16
Augusta, 55–56, 164–165
Auxiliary force, 18, 152, 174–175

Aviation, 3, 4, 10, 131, 136, 152–153, 172
  See also Aerial superiority; Aircraft
Aviation Cadet Program, 66

Badders, William, 123–124
Baer, George, 17
"Balanced" fleet, 8–9, 17, 173
Barracuda, 114–115
Base Force, 129, 133
Bass, 114
Bath Iron Works, 134, 140
Batteries, for submarines, 117
Battle(s). *See also* specific battles
  common vocabulary for, 69–70
  function of ship and, 44
  objective in, 77
  phases of, 70
  ship coordination in, 69
  single engagement, 68, 87
Battle cruisers, conversion of, 7
Battle Fleet, 128
Battle Force, 129, 131, 133
Battle formation, 76–77, 78
Battle line, 10, 17, 73, 74
Battleship memorials, 175
Battleships, 1, 5, 10, 173
  in battle formation, 76
  construction of, 15
  engine types in, 22
  guns on, 74
  ordnance from, 97–98
  rates of fire by, 152
BB designation, 74
Beach, Edward L., Jr., 179
Beach, Edward L., Sr., 67
Beaver, Floyd, 46
Belknap, George E., 183
Bethlehem Steel, 139, 140
Biplanes, 98
Black Fleet. *See* Fleet Problems
Blakely, Charles A., 99
Blandy, W. H. P., 27

ABOUT THE AUTHORS

Dr. Thomas C. Hone is an executive in the Office of the Secretary of Defense. He received his Ph.D. from the University of Wisconsin and has taught at the Naval War College in Newport, Rhode Island, and at the National Defense University in Washington, D.C. The U.S. Navy has awarded him the Meritorious Civilian Service Medal, and the U.S. Air Force has presented him with the Exceptional Civilian Service Award.

A graduate of Carleton College in Northfield, Minnesota, **Trent Hone** is currently an engineering manager at Trimble Mobile Solutions, Inc. He has written and published several articles on the U.S. Navy's tactical development before and during World War II.